Realizing the Civil Rights Dream

Realizing the Civil Rights Dream

DIAGNOSING AND TREATING AMERICAN RACISM

Kenneth B. Bedell

Foreword by Rev. Jesse L. Jackson, Sr.

 PRAEGER™

An Imprint of ABC-CLIO, LLC

Santa Barbara, California • Denver, Colorado

Library of Congress Cataloging-in-Publication Data

Names: Bedell, Kenneth B., author.
Title: Realizing the civil rights dream : diagnosing and treating American
    racism / Kenneth B. Bedell.
Other titles: Diagnosing and treating American racism
Description: Santa Barbara, California : Praeger, an imprint of ABC-CLIO,
    LLC, [2017] | Includes bibliographical references and index.
Identifiers: LCCN 2017010660 | ISBN 9781440853753 (hardcopy : alk. paper) |
    ISBN 9781440853760 (eBook)
Subjects: LCSH: United States—Race relations. | Anti-racism—United States.
    | Racism—United States. | Civil rights movements—United States.
Classification: LCC E184.A1 B335 2017 | DDC 305.800973—dc23
LC record available at https://lccn.loc.gov/2017010660

ISBN: 978-1-4408-5375-3
EISBN: 978-1-4408-5376-0

21 20 19 18 17   1 2 3 4 5

This book is also available as an eBook.

Praeger
An Imprint of ABC-CLIO, LLC

ABC-CLIO, LLC
130 Cremona Drive, P.O. Box 1911
Santa Barbara, California 93116-1911
www.abc-clio.com

This book is printed on acid-free paper (∞)

Manufactured in the United States of America

Contents

List of Tables and Figures

Foreword

Rev. Jesse L. Jackson, Sr.

Ken Bedell's book, *Realizing the Civil Rights Dream: Diagnosing and Treating American Racism*, comes at a time when it is impossible to ignore the stereotyping and institutional racism that survived both the American Civil War of the 1860s and the civil rights movement of the 1960s. As Bedell describes in the closing chapter, racist political strategies are not limited to one political party. At the national level neither Republicans nor Democrats have provided leadership to address racism. I ran for president as a Democrat, but even in 1984 and 1988 one of my real goals was to promote full democratic participation by all Americans in the political life of our nation. Bedell's book is an important contribution to the discussions we all, regardless of racial identity, need to participate in.

Bedell shows how racism defined as "a disease that infects cultures" has had various manifestations since British colonists invented skin color racism. The manifestation of American racism in every epoch shares a common characteristic: "one group of people claims superiority over another group that is deemed inferior by the privileged group."

Bedell uses examples from his own experiences and insights about racism identified by sociologists and social psychologists since the 1960s, as well as proposals by theologians. The approach results in a framework that describes the vehicles that preserve racism in the 21st century. These include stereotypes, racist institutional practices, and disciplinary institutions.

As he explains, disciplinary institutions like the medical, criminal justice, and educational systems play a special role in legitimizing and preserving racism today. The Civil War was required to defeat the disciplinary institution

of slavery. The civil rights movement of the 1960s made great strides in ending the disciplinary institution of legalized segregation. Bedell argues that
intentional strategies are needed to address the use of stereotypes, racist
institutional practices, and 21st-century disciplinary institutions.

Ending slavery and ending segregation were national and civil rights goals
of the past. Bedell proposes that America's civil rights goal for the 21st century should be that America "will be a nation where every race, ethnicity,
and identity group has full participation in the political, economic, and cultural life of the nation so that the barriers to fulfilling individual aspirations
are no greater for one person than another." This goal provides a way to
evaluate various strategies.

While Bedell recognizes that every individual and group must find its own
way to address racism, he provides examples of individuals and organizations that illustrate approaches to ending racism. Neither in his analysis nor
in his proposals for action does Bedell promote simplistic approaches. For
example, he demonstrates that economic inequality among the races will
not just disappear. And he proposes that white and nonwhite Americans
need to enter into discussions, and take actions, in ways where restitution
can be made for the unfair benefits that have come from having white skin.

He calls on individuals to develop a "sense of racism" so racist practices can be identified and rooted out of everyday activity and institutions.
Rooting out the racism in disciplinary institutions requires collective and
political action. Bedell argues that the civil rights dream cannot be achieved
until these institutions are changed so that they support full participation
in American society rather than perpetuate racism. His suggestion is that
special attention should be given to the transformation of the educational
and criminal justice systems.

To the priorities of transforming the education and criminal justice systems I would add a third critical priority: voter participation and the establishment of a constitutional amendment that guarantees all citizens a right to
vote. Currently voting is a state right not an individual citizenship right. The
Constitution's 15th Amendment only bars discrimination in voting on the
basis of race. It does not provide an explicit individual right to vote. A constitutional amendment is critical because ultimately only a balance of political and economic power will enable equality and justice between the races.

Since my initial days in the civil rights movement I have regularly supported voter registration drives and voter education programs. During my
1984 and 1988 presidential campaigns, approximately 3 million new African American voters were added to the voter rolls resulting in hundreds of
new elected officials at every level of government. This work is important,
but the U.S. Constitution does not currently guarantee full participation in
the political life of America. The 13th Amendment abolished slavery. The
14th Amendment provided equal protection and due process under the law.
And the 15th Amendment outlawed discrimination in voting on the basis of

race. But since its ratification in 1870 racist and undemocratic forces have creatively devised different nonracial ways of effectively barring African Americans and other people of color from voting.

Currently voting eligibility is not standardized across all 50 states. As Bedell points out there are well-documented attempts by politicians to use voter eligibility requirements to make it more difficult for nonwhite voters to vote. A constitutional amendment is necessary to give Congress the authority and responsibility for creating a uniform national voting system with certain common sense minimum standards.

Bedell's book looks at racism largely from the perspective of social structures and our participation in them. But racism is experienced and perceived personally and differently by every individual American. As a result, discussions of race and racism are often made more difficult and clouded because of different understandings of what racism is. Therefore, conversations are often conducted on different planes. We each have a view and understanding of what we mean by racism; we have a lens that defines racism for us. So definitions are important to our understanding. Over the years I have come to define racism in six different ways:

1. Racism as a system of thought: A philosophy or theory—philosophical, theological, or scientific—that argues one group is inherently superior and another group is inherently inferior (e.g., Charles Murray or Richard Spencer, curse of Ham, cephalic index).

2. Racism as prejudice: Judging an individual on the basis of a group stereotype (e.g., all Asians are smart, all African Americans are good athletes and can dance, all whites have money).

3. Racism as behavior: Actions taken on the basis of racial hatred (e.g., burning a cross on an African American lawn, painting a swastika on a synagogue).

4. Racism as political (e.g., politicians using race or racial code words to get elected or achieve a political end, such as "law and order," "welfare queen," "young buck," and "Food Stamp president").

5. Racism as cultural: People are as good as they know how to be, but are limited by knowledge, experience or exposure to another race or culture (e.g., older white people who still might refer to African Americans as "colored" or "Negroes" because some older Black people do the same).

6. Racism as institutional: This is the most deeply engrained manifestation of racism in American society. Its foundation is in our innermost private thoughts, but its concrete expression is in our most cherished institutions and structures—for example, business, employment, government, politics, media (news and entertainment), education, health, housing, religion, and recreation to name a few. Its most nuanced forms are almost always difficult to see or measure and it is definitely the most difficult to root out; for example, Americans and the world were outraged by the killing of four young girls in the Birmingham church bombing, but little concern was expressed that the infant mortality rate of African American babies was many times that of white infants.

Imagine a situation where white parents teach a third grade child a stereotype: that African Americans are poor students. The white student bullies an African American fellow student during class by applying the stereotype in a loud remark. The African American student feels frustrated and devalued. The white teacher sees a problem of class discipline because the white student is disrupting class. In this example, if the white family reflected on the situation they would view it through the lens of racial prejudice. The African American student experienced the institution of school as a place where he is attacked. The teacher views the racist act as poor behavior on the part of the white student.

In this simple example we see how race might be viewed from three different perspectives. An important step in overcoming American racism is recognizing our own perspectives and definitions of race and racism. Appreciating that other Americans have different definitions of racism makes it possible to come together to dialogue.

Before you turn the page and begin reading this book, I encourage you to take a moment and think about the way you view race and racism. When you finish reading the book, come back again and reflect on how you want to view race in America. You will find that this book gives you a framework for making sense of the racism that surrounds you. More importantly it will help you develop your own strategy for participating in America's movement toward fulfilling the civil rights dream of justice and equality for all.

Section 1

Defining the Dream

Chapter 1

Introduction

My first encounter with racism was when I was six years old. I was born in the same town in northwest Iowa as my father, grandmother, and great-grandmother. There wasn't very much diversity in Spirit Lake. In 1953, my family went on a camping trip to the Black Hills in South Dakota with our friends the Cornell family. We stopped near Winner, South Dakota, to visit a friend of the Cornells, a rancher. It was a nice afternoon, so Carolyn Cornell and I went outside to play. We happened to meet two Native American children who were about our age. After playing happily and enjoying each other's company for a while, we needed to use the bathroom, so we walked up to the kitchen door of the ranch house to go in to use the toilet. Our knocks were answered by the rancher's wife, who shouted with intense anger at the two Native American children that they had no business knocking on the door and certainly could not come in the house or use the bathroom. It was like she had completely lost control. I was confused. I had never seen anything like this before. When she shifted her gaze to Carolyn and me, her demeanor completely changed. She pushed the Indian children aside and welcomed Carolyn and me into her house.

As we drove off from the visit and I was alone in the car with my parents, I told them what had happened. They had been in another part of the house and had not heard anything. My parents explained to me that there are some people who don't treat everyone the same, but that is not the way our family is. For a six-year-old child, this was a satisfactory answer. There are some bad people and some good people. We were the good people.

Today I know that American life is much more complicated. It is not simply a matter of good and bad people. Even people who want very much to not participate in racism find themselves caught up in racist institutions.

American racism is embedded in our individual self-identity, our institutions, and our national culture. Today I also know that we were not "the good people." We were, and I continue to be, part of racist institutions. My white skin makes me the heir of a terrible and violent past that I benefit from every day. I continue to struggle to overcome racist attitudes and assumptions. And the rancher's wife was not a "bad person." Rather, the way she treated Native American children was a bad behavior based on a mistaken belief in white superiority.

Many things have changed since 1953, but what troubles me today is that racism has not disappeared. I am now in my late 60s, and I ask myself, "Why did my generation fail to make civil rights universal?" My simple answer is that everyone, whites and people of color, completely underestimated what is involved in eliminating racism. While certain advances were made in changing the legal system of segregation, we didn't have the political will to equalize the playing field. More importantly, we completely underestimated the complexities of the social customs, cultural supports, and institutionalization of racism.

Racism is not the only civil rights struggle that Americans have faced. Abolition of slavery, women's suffrage, LGBTQ rights, and other civil rights struggles are part of our national story. There are, however, two important changes since 1953 that make it both imperative and possible for Americans to address racism now more than ever before: demographic changes and advancements in social science.

Addressing racism is imperative because of demographic changes. In the very near future it will be impossible to talk about "minorities" as non-whites. No group will represent a majority of the population, so everyone will be part of a minority. Therefore, it is essential that we develop economic and political systems with full and equal participation of all citizens.

Addressing racism is possible because since 1953 social scientists have developed a better understanding of racism. Today we know much more about how individuals and institutions interact to support racism. These recent advances in social science will be discussed in the second section of this book, and I will propose a framework to use to develop and evaluate antiracist strategies. Advances in social science make it possible for us to address racism and civil rights with strategies that go beyond the measures that for the past 60 years have failed to realize the civil rights dream.

If you are looking for a quick fix for racism, you will not find it in these pages. As the title of this book suggests, racism is a chronic disease that infects our culture. It has gone undiagnosed, wrongly diagnosed, and inadequately treated for centuries. Just as a disease manifests differently in different people, racism manifests differently in different historical periods. Just as different therapies are effective for treating different individuals with the same disease, so are there multiple approaches that can treat the disease of racism. There is no simple cure.

Racism has been at the center of social life for all of American history. One of the most important lessons of that history is that racism will not just wither away. Racism must be accurately diagnosed and then intentionally treated. Our history is full of missed opportunities to recognize racism, address it, and develop strategies to overcome it. The good news, and the premise of this book, is that we can learn from our history, apply new knowledge, and break the cycle of disease. We can—and must—confront racism today to realize the civil rights dream.

DEFINING AMERICAN RACISM

Racism is a disease that infects cultures. The defining characteristic of racism is that one group of people claims to be superior to another group that is deemed inferior by the privileged group. For most of American history, the privileged group was Anglo-Saxon Protestant men. Today, any American who is white and native-born is part of the privileged group.

American racism today is usually skin-deep. White skin defines the privileged group. The distinction, however, is applied without precision, particularly in relation to Muslims and Hispanics. Arabs and other Muslims are usually lumped into the nonwhite category. This even includes Muslims with very light skin. Hispanics are also often grouped in the nonwhite category, regardless of their skin color.

White supremacy, the belief that people with white skin are better than others, has been the basis of racism since America's founding. The same is true today, but today it has two forms. This book is not primarily about the first form: Americans who are members of the Ku Klux Klan, Aryan Nations, or the American Nazi Party. These organization and others represent the most extreme form of racism. Whites with these views make a lot of noise on social media and capture the attention of the mainstream media, but they are small in number and do not represent the mainstream of American society. Most Americans believe white supremacy that transforms itself into hate is morally repugnant.

The second form of white supremacy manifests in much subtler ways than white supremacy extremism. American racism has become a natural part of our culture and often goes unnoticed or ignored. This book addresses the culture of racism that has emerged since the 1960s, when Americans were confronted with the immorality of racism and responded with civil rights laws and judicial activism. One lesson we can learn from this period of our history is this: knowing that racism exists, recognizing that it is morally repugnant, and waiting for it to disappear is a failed approach.

I do not mean to claim that Americans have just been sitting back, waiting for racism to disappear. Beginning with the Supreme Court's decision in *Brown v. Board of Education* in 1954, the courts and Congress have taken strong action to address civil rights. This opened many doors that had previously been opened only for whites. Jim Crow laws, which promoted unfair race relations before the 1960s, are now part of history. They have been replaced by more equitable laws that are intended to eliminate discrimination in public accommodation, housing, education, employment, banking, and other areas of our economy. Nevertheless, racism has not been eradicated.

Part of the reason that racism has not been eradicated is that it has mutated. The treatments that we thought would eliminate the disease have not been enough. American racism now manifests with different signs and symptoms than it did 50 years ago.

Housing segregation is one symptom of racism today. Whites are isolated in their own neighborhoods and think that everything is equitable. Many whites see very polite and friendly nonwhites only in service roles, as baristas or restaurant staff. They don't see that Hispanic Americans are only half as likely to graduate from college as white Americans.[1] White teenagers may say that they don't understand what all the fuss is about racism. They have nonwhite friends and everyone gets along. What these white teenagers don't see is that, when they buy illegal drugs, they are unlikely to end up with a police record or spend any time in jail. Young African American men, however, are not so lucky. In many large cities, more than half of the young black men are incarcerated or under the control of the criminal justice system or have a criminal record.[2]

Another symptom of American racism today is the differential income among racial groups. Despite civil rights advances for women, Catholics, Irish, Italians, Poles, LGBTQ people, and other groups over the last century, it has been the whites within each of these categories who have gained greater privileges than their brothers and sisters of color. For example, between 2000 and 2014, white women increased their constant dollar amount income and narrowed the gap between themselves and white men by more than 10 percent. Over the same period, black women only saw a very small increase in their annual income and narrowed their income gap by only slightly more than 1 percent.[3]

Whites justify their privilege with beliefs and denial, most commonly with a belief in their group's superiority. In 1961, John Howard Griffin published a book about his experiences as a white man who turned his skin black and traveled through the South. Griffin's arguments were recently updated and republished by Robert Bonazzi and Studs Terkel in an essay titled "Prison of Culture." They explain a prison of culture where one group of people sees itself as intrinsically different from another group: "profoundly different: different in his aspirations, needs, responses to stimuli. This is one of the most difficult problems involved in racism. We tend to think that the victim group somehow likes it that way; that its members respond to frustrations, for example, in a manner totally different from us."[4]

According to Bonazzi and Terkel, whites see others as different, inferior, and in need of help. In a perverse way, a symptom of racism is that some whites show an altruistic interest in helping others who they consider inferior.

Denial is the other way that whites justify their privilege. In *Two Nations: Black and White, Separate, Hostile, Unequal*, Andrew Hacker points out that whites of all political persuasions know that nonwhites have suffered because of what whites have done and continue to do. Whites deal with this knowledge in a variety of ways, but everyday life requires denial. As Hacker explains, "White people who disavow responsibility deny an everyday reality: that to be black is to be consigned to the margins of American life. . . . All white Americans realize that their skin comprises an inestimable asset."[5]

White privilege has many manifestations, but by far the most important privilege is the ability to define who is privileged. This is the foundation of all racist strategies. Shelby Steele is a senior fellow at the Hoover Institution at Stanford University who has thought and written extensively about race and racism. Steele points out, "The whole point of racism (and sexism, anti-Semitism, etc.) is to seize authority illicitly at the expense of another race."[6] In this sense, racism is recursive. The people who have power are able to define who is in the privileged group. The result is that this privileged group claims benefits not extended to others. The use of these benefits makes it possible to continue to define the nature of the privileged group. This self-perpetuating nature of racism is one of the reasons that Americans have been unable to realize the civil rights dream. Because racism is about establishing a privileged position in society, the justification can easily shift from one rationale to another. And strategies of the privileged group can quickly change and adapt.

Since the time that Griffin used his white eyes to see what being black in America was like, sociologists have learned a lot about how the prison of culture works. They have studied everyday experiences and how we create and sustain racist culture. They have discovered some mechanisms that are hidden within our language, habits, and institutions. These hidden processes of preserving racism can be rooted out only with great intentionality. The insights of sociologists show us the way to address these hidden processes, but mostly social scientists have uncovered mechanisms of cultural transmission that we can see when we look for them. Racism is embedded in our everyday lives. Just as lifestyle factors contribute to chronic disease in the body, our lifestyle also contributes to and perpetuates racism in our country.

By clarifying what American racism really is and recognizing some of its subtle signs, symptoms, and manifestations, we prepare ourselves to intentionally address the issue. The prison of culture can feel comfortable, so in order to break out, we need to honestly and continually confront our past and look for the meaning in retelling our story. We need to identify those things that keep us in prison. We need to take small steps with the big picture of where we want to be always in mind. And most importantly, we need to stay aware of the insidious signs of this chronic cultural disease.

DEFINING *RACISM, RACIST,* AND *ANTIRACIST*

Before we proceed, I would like to define how I will use the terms *racism*, *racist*, and *antiracist* throughout the rest of this book. *Racism* is a noun that refers to a social system of oppression that results in advantages for white people. This book focuses on the racism found in the United States of America in the early 21st century. *Racist* is an adjective that can be used to describe specific actions, social structures, beliefs, or strategies. I will talk about racist activity, racist beliefs, and racist strategies when describing individual or group actions. I will also discuss racist institutions and racist social structures that play a role in supporting racism.

In this book, you will not see the term *racist* used as a noun that refers to a person. All Americans are like fish swimming in an ocean of racism. It is impossible to be an American and not interact with institutions that support racism. This is true for all Americans regardless of how they identify themselves. To call an individual a racist is an act of prejudice. It is participating in a culture that supports racism by labeling other people. Racism imposes identity. In a racist society, value is assigned to various identities. It is essential, therefore, that in discussing American racism we demonstrate a commitment to developing an environment where identities are formed without social prejudices.

The term *antiracist*, like *racist*, is an adjective that describes activities. It is not a noun that refers to a person. Some Americans are intentionally working to overcome racism in their own lives and in American institutions. These people are involved in antiracist activities. People of all races are capable of performing antiracist activities. Sometimes the word *ally* is used when describing people with privilege who adopt antiracist behaviors. As Paul Kivel, the white author of *Uprooting Racism*, points out, "Acting as an ally to people of color is one of the most important things that white people can do. Ally is not an identity, it is a practice."[7]

MORE ABOUT WORDS

The words we use are extremely important. They carry culture as well as meaning. Words have been used to give racial cues and to communicate hidden meaning when talking about the civil rights dream and racism. Words also have histories. It was common in the 1960s to refer to blacks as *Negroes*. This is now out of fashion. Words that apply to groups can be slurs that are intended to communicate disrespect or—even worse—that the group is not fully human. Academics and editorial writers have presented pro and con arguments for every word that can be used to describe a racial or ethnic group. This book does not try to sort out the current language discussion. While some people prefer the word *Hispanic* and others like *Latinos/as*, I have used both interchangeably. In this case, either word covers a complex assortment of people. A Mexican American may have very little in common with an Argentinian American, yet I have used *Latinos* and *Latinas* without making the important distinctions. This is also true for *Asian*; an Indonesian American comes from a different culture than a Japanese American, but I call them both Asian at times. One antiracist strategy is to always let people self-identify. If someone identifies as Native American, then we should not call that person an Indian. Where I know that a particular person has a preferred self-identity, I use the word that person chose.

Because American racism is based on the myth that white skin is better, I have chosen to often make a distinction between whites and nonwhites. I completely agree with those who say that using the term *people of color* is a more affirming synonym for *nonwhite*. In this book, *people of color* and *nonwhites* describe the same people. *Nonwhite* is often used because it helps clarify that race in America is about the mistaken idea of white supremacy.

A premise of this book is that the academic disciplines of sociology and social psychology offer insights that make it possible for us to diagnose racism and then develop strategies to treat it. This presents another language challenge. People who have made a profession of learning about social systems use specialized language. This jargon describes what we all experience in everyday life. Since we don't always have everyday words to describe all of our everyday experiences, the language of social science can be very useful. Jargon used by social scientists sometimes has a definition that takes several sentences to express. Terms like *habitus* and *structuration* are examples. In those cases, I use the technical term.

In some cases, I have replaced jargon with other words. For example, sociologists Ferdinand Tönnies and Max Weber introduced the concepts of *Gemeinschaft* and *Gesellschaft* into sociological literature. These concepts have generated a great deal of discussion and many doctoral dissertations. In chapter 8 the concepts are discussed, but I use the words *community* and *institution*.

Jargon is a particular problem because every reader will have a different level of familiarity with the jargon of social science. I have chosen to err on the side of providing definitions in the text when I use a word that scholars give special meaning to. Like the man who wears both a belt and suspenders, I have also included a glossary.

WOMEN'S WAYS OF KNOWING

Throughout the book, I use stories from my own and others' experience. This is not because my experience is of special importance. Everyone who reads this book will have their own experiences of racism. The experiences illustrate social theory mostly developed since 1960. Social theories are validated or refuted by our experiences and stories. I use the full names of people who have given me permission or are public figures. I use first names when requested to do so. In some cases, people requested anonymity or I could not obtain permission. When a fictitious name is used, I made up a first name.

Many of the sources I used were written in the abstract style of academic sociologists in which it seems the author is a supernatural observer who knows everything. Not all social scientists use this style today. There is not only new theory since the 1960s; there is also a new method and style. The new method was developed by female sociologists who recognized the dishonesty in theorizing about society as if we are not personally involved in it. The stories we tell each other are important in the process of making meaning for ourselves and collectively. We are all sociologists.

One of the women pioneering the use of this method is Lynn Schofield Clark, now a professor at Denver University where she chairs the Department of Media, Film, and Journalism Studies. I have known Schofield Clark since she was first a student and then administrator at United Theological Seminary when I taught there in the 1980s. Shortly after her book *The Parent App: Understanding Families in the Digital Age* was published in 2013, we met for coffee in Golden, Colorado. We talked about this relational style, and I decided that if I ever wrote a book about social theory, I would do my best to emulate the methodology that is sometimes called "women's ways of knowing."[8]

A ROADMAP

This book offers a roadmap—a way to understand racism. To accomplish this, I move through a series of steps. Each step builds on the previous one. The final step is the challenge to use the tools of the sciences of sociology and social psychology to realize the civil rights dream. The steps are as follows:

1. The civil rights dream and American racism are made in America.
2. The civil rights dream in the 21st century is for both individuals and groups.
3. White-dominated America cannot be sustained.
4. Sociology and social psychology have developed new tools since the mid-20th century.
5. There are already people advancing the dream.
6. Working together, we can end racism and fulfill the dream.

THE CIVIL RIGHTS DREAM AND AMERICAN RACISM ARE MADE IN AMERICA

Every nation has its own challenges regarding civil rights. Germany, South Africa, and the United States each have histories that make the current struggles for civil rights unique. The American civil rights struggles have produced heroes who stood against racism: men and women like Governor James Oglethorpe, Thomas Paine, Frederick Douglass, Sojourner Truth, George Washington Cable, W. E. B. Du Bois, Ida B. Wells, Dr. Martin Luther King Jr., and countless others. Today we have inherited a civil rights struggle from them that is uniquely American. Chapter 2 describes the expression of racism that denied civil rights in five different periods. It also tells the stories of some of the heroes who addressed racism in their time.

THE CIVIL RIGHTS DREAM IN THE 21ST CENTURY IS FOR BOTH INDIVIDUALS AND GROUPS

In the 21st century, the civil rights dream has two interconnected expressions. The first is sometimes called the American dream. It is the dream that America is the land where people can pursue individual aspirations. Today we know that it is not enough to be able to pursue dreams. There are two additional conditions: (1) one's situation at birth must not limit possibilities, and (2) no one should have extra barriers that are not experienced by everyone. The American dream for everyone is described in chapter 3.

The second expression of the civil rights dream is a vision for an America where members of all races, ethnicities, identity groups, and associations have full participation in the cultural, political, and economic life of America. This is the dream for a pluralistic America. Pluralism is also an essential strategy in creating an America without racism. It is not enough that individuals do not experience discrimination. Hispanic Americans, African Americans, Native Americans, Muslim Americans, Hindu Americans, and all other identity groups must have equal access to cultural and political power. This dream for a pluralistic America is described in chapter 4.

These two expressions of the civil rights dream result in a single vision for the future of America. Following the language used by Jesse Jackson in his speech at the 1988 Democratic convention, the goal is to have a nation where every identity group has full participation in American life. The civil rights dream for the 21st century is that *America will be a nation where every race, ethnicity, and identity group has full participation in the political, economic, and cultural life of the nation so that the barriers to fulfilling individual aspirations are no greater for one person than another.*

A WHITE-DOMINATED AMERICA CANNOT BE SUSTAINED

Chapter 5 looks at two reasons that current race relations and the existing dominance of whites in the culture, politics, and economy cannot be sustained. Either of the reasons is sufficient for us as individuals and as a nation to change. Since a poll conducted in 2016 indicated that a majority of whites do not see racism as a major issue,[9] this chapter is extremely important for the thesis presented in this book.

Statistics are presented that demonstrate the depth of racial inequality. They show that at the current rate of change it will be centuries before equity is achieved. These statistics demonstrate that the civil rights dream will be realized for all Americans only if we seriously address racism with new strategies.

Second, statistics are reported that project the demographic changes that are rapidly reducing the majority status of whites. These demographic changes require us to take actions that make America a nation with full cultural, political, and economic participation of all groups.

When these statistics are viewed through the lens of the historical development of the civil rights struggle in America, it becomes clear that changes like the abolition movement or the end of Jim Crow racism required a commitment of the nation. To realize the civil rights dream in the 21st century, it will be necessary to involve the whole nation in a political and cultural movement, just as it was when the civil rights agenda was advanced in the past.

SOCIOLOGY AND SOCIAL PSYCHOLOGY SINCE THE MID-20TH CENTURY PROVIDE NEW TOOLS

Social psychology is a field of study that emerged in the last half of the 20th century. Scholars developed theoretical understandings of how our everyday life connects us with each other, provides us with a framework to understand what happens around us, makes each of us a contributor to a collective understanding, and supports cultural and institutional structures. Unlike academic theoretical systems like nuclear physics, sociology and social psychology are about what happens to us in our everyday lives. Since each of us lives in a social context, our own experience demonstrates or questions the theories. More importantly, by thinking about how the theories apply in our own lives, we can develop personal strategies to address the racism that surrounds us.

Chapter 6 reviews the importance of paradigms that provide a structure for us to collectively view reality. Theories related to stereotypes and microaggressions are described in chapter 7. Chapters 8 and 9 look at recent theories about institutions and how they support racism with our participation and support. Finally, in chapter 10 all of these theoretical insights are combined to create a framework of how racism prevents us from realizing the civil rights dream. This framework can be used by each of us individually and collectively to develop strategies that address racism.

THERE ARE ALREADY PEOPLE ADVANCING THE DREAM

Chapters 12 and 13 provide examples of individuals and groups who are committed to an antiracist lifestyle. The stories illustrate theories of racism as well as a variety of ways that Americans are implementing antiracist strategies. These examples exist in the midst of a society that is still dominated by racism. They are important because they give us hope, provide us with ideas, and encourage each of us to live lives filled with antiracist behaviors. But the people and organizations described here are not themselves the solution to racism. Each of us has a role to play in participating in antiracist activities.

WORKING TOGETHER, WE CAN END RACISM AND FULFILL THE DREAM

Chapters 11 and 14 are based on the observation that if overcoming racism and fulfilling the civil rights dream were easy, we would have done it in the last half of the 20th century. We now know from the work of social scientists that the solution lies in taking seriously the importance of identity formation and institutional change. In fact, these two projects cannot be separated. Stereotyping is at the intersection of structural pressures and individual identity formation. So the civil rights project requires that we all work on overcoming stereotyping, including the stereotyping that places white culture in a privileged position. Also, the civil rights vision for America is one in which the participation of cultures, races, and religions is seen as an asset. The full participation of all groups will be evidence that the civil rights dream is a reality.

The final chapter points to three examples from the 2016 presidential campaign that illustrate concepts of racism presented in this book. These examples not only demonstrate the presence and power of racism in 21st century American, they also show that if we understand racism we can realize the civil rights dream.

Chapter 2

Whose Idea Was This?

In 2008, my friend Edward Reyes came to visit me in Nashville, where I lived at the time. Edward's family has roots in Mexico, but most of his family has lived in Texas for generations. On Saturday night, we headed to the Green Hills Mall to find dinner. This mall was extremely popular, so after driving around for a while looking for a parking place, we decided to investigate the parking at the Carrabba's Italian Grill, where we saw a valet. We pulled up and Edward rolled down his window to talk to the young white man. Edward asked, "How much is it?" The valet answered, "It's minimum wage, but the tips are good."

Why does a young white man assume a Hispanic man is coming to a restaurant looking for a job rather than a meal? We can be quite certain that if I, a white man, had been in the passenger seat and the one the valet saw, he would not have misunderstood the question. Exchanges like this are common in America today. It is 21st-century racism, which is not the same as racism in America in the first half of the 20th century. Nor is the role of racism today the same as it was when slavery was legal.

One reason that racism is so difficult to eliminate is that it has become part of our way of thinking. It seems natural to look at each other and see the difference in skin color. Yet what currently seems natural and obvious would have seemed strange to people in the past, and as we will see in this chapter, racism as it manifested in the past seems strange to us now. This is good news because by looking at history, we can gain insights into ways to overcome racism today. It is also good news because there were people in the past who recognized the importance of civil rights and the role of racism. They are an inspiration. Finally, it is good news because by looking at the past, we see that those things that seem natural are not so natural. When we analyze racism in the past, we can begin to recognize its current form and address it with serious intention.

American history is filled with examples of lost opportunities to create an equitable society with civil rights for all. However, there are five distinct periods that were particularly critical in shaping American racism. In each of these periods, civil rights and racism were on the national agenda. The 21st century is not the first time that we have had the opportunity as a nation to discuss how to address civil rights. As we will see, each of the following historical periods shaped racism and left a legacy that haunts us:

British settlement, 1607–1740s

United States becomes a nation, 1775–1812

The abolition movement, 1830–1865

Ascent of segregation and Jim Crow, 1877–1944

Birth of a national civil rights identity, 1954–1968

BRITISH SETTLEMENT

The original British settlers were all white Europeans. They did not bring African slaves or have a plan in mind to build a society based on agriculture and slave labor. They were looking for gold. The first attempt by the British to settle North America was made by Sir Walter Raleigh in the 1580s. When that failed, another attempt was made in 1607. This time only men were sent. They could not find gold, so they turned to agriculture out of necessity. They needed food and quickly learned that there was money to be made by growing tobacco and selling it in Europe.

Raising a successful tobacco crop required a large amount of labor, so the wealthy settlers turned to the use of indentured servants. Poor Europeans agreed to sell themselves for a period of usually three to seven years to a master, who provided them with food and clothing and owned their labor. There were also some Natives willing to sell other Natives as slaves to the early settlers. Indentured servants and Native slaves worked under similar conditions for a master. The difference was that the white indentured servants had a term of service after which they were set free.

The origins of American racism can be seen in the relationships that developed between the first settlers and the Indians. While some settlers married Indians and adopted Indian culture, the British gentry maintained a clear cultural separation that was based on the assumption of superiority of Christianity and European culture. We know very little from the perspective of the Indians. Even from the one-sided reports of the British, however, it appears that both the Indians and the British had difficulty making sense of the customs and actions of the other. Reports that have come down to us suggest that there were lost opportunities in the early decades of the Virginia colony to establish an arrangement where British settlers and Indians could share the land. One reason this did not happen is that, from the beginning, the British did not recognize that they shared a common humanity with the Indians. This is illustrated in the well-documented relationship between Pocahontas and two of the first settlers, John Smith and John Rolfe.

John Smith, one of the original colonial leaders, reports first meeting Pocahontas when he was captured by her father, Powhatan. Smith claims that Pocahontas saved him from being killed. We know that when Powhatan realized that he could not scare the British away, he proposed that they establish a village near his own village. He probably did not fully comprehend the British concept of monarchy, but he clearly was not interested in adopting a strange religion and becoming a subject to a king across the ocean. Powhatan's alternative proposal was that the British would be a tribe and join the confederation of tribes he had assembled. Even though Powhatan did not demand that they give up their religion or customs, the British had no interest in this arrangement.

The first years of the British settlement included raids by colonists against Native people and villages, raids by Natives against the British, trade between the groups so the colonists could obtain food, and cooperative arrangements between settlers and Natives so the settlers could obtain furs and Native slaves. There were acts of terror and revenge committed by both sides.

After the missed original opportunity for a pluralistic experiment between the British and the Indians, Pocahontas was the center of a second missed opportunity. The relationship between Pocahontas and John Rolfe neither started nor ended as a fairy tale. When she was 14 years old, Pocahontas was taken as a prisoner by the British and held for ransom. After being held captive by the British for four years, she professed Christianity and married Rolfe.

Powhatan saw his daughter's marriage as a step toward developing a cooperative future, with the Indians and British living together as equal "tribes." After the marriage, he ceased his efforts to drive the British out of Virginia. For a brief period, the settlers had a reprieve from the hostility of the Indians.

The settlers saw that they might benefit by their relationship with Pocahontas, not because of her marriage but rather by converting her to Christianity. The settlers hoped to secure financial support from Britain by showing that they were converting Indians to Christianity. Pocahontas was their only example of a Christian Indian, so in 1616, Rolfe took his wife to England to raise money to support the struggling colony. While she was in England, Pocahontas met Smith. The strange and conflicting reports about their encounter suggest the possibility that while in England she understood that the British had no interest in her father's hope that the Indians and British would find a way to live together in peace. Pocahontas was in England for less than a year before she died of uncertain causes at the age of about 21. After her death, her conversion was remembered and she became a symbol of the claimed superiority of European religion and culture. The truth is that the Jamestown settlers raped and enslaved far more Indians than they converted to Christianity.[1]

In the first years of the Virginia settlement, the British looked down on the Indians not because of their skin color but because they were not Christian. In 1619, the first Africans arrived in the British colony. These Africans had been captured by English pirates from a Spanish slave ship. The settlers had not yet established the criteria of distinguishing between people based on skin color, and since the Africans had been baptized as Christians, the British treated them as indentured servants rather than slaves. These Africans worked for a master for a number of years and were then set free like other indentured servants.

In 1676, the unresolved issues regarding the rights of various groups came to a head. An armed conflict broke out between the British gentry and a coalition of others. This conflict is called Bacon's rebellion after a British settler named Nathaniel Bacon. Bacon claimed that he was attempting to preserve the interests of the king against the corrupt British gentry. The reality is that he was disgruntled because he was blocked from being part of the colonial leadership. Those who joined the rebellion had a variety of complaints. Indian and African slaves wanted freedom from a lifetime of enslavement. White indentured servants wanted more rights to protect them from their masters. British settlers who weren't part of the gentry wanted the British government to do more to remove or exterminate Indians from Virginia. In an ironic twist, free Indians joined with enslaved Indians in the rebellion because they did not like the way they were treated by the British government. At their peak, the rebels captured Jamestown and burned it. The rebellion was put down and the gentry gained control of the colony, but the conflicting interests of people living in Virginia were not resolved.

The first response of the British gentry was to rethink how they would define their relationships with the various groups. The profitability of raising tobacco drove the colonists to desire land and labor. They wanted both to be as cheap as possible. The rebellion demonstrated how expensive and disruptive it was to control access to cheap labor. Over the next few years, they established a legal system that defined the rights of the Europeans, Indians, and Africans. The elite colonists settled on a strategy to use categories that would later be based on skin color. As an historian of Bacon's rebellion, James Rice, points out, "Simply put, ordinary planters agreed to accept the rule of their elite superiors, while the gentry agreed to treat common planters and white servants more respectfully. And together, both sorts agreed to share the benefits of white supremacy."[2] Laws were passed that protected a master from being charged for murdering a slave, while other laws were passed that protected white indentured servants from abuse.

Making it more difficult to use whites for cheap labor left Indians and Africans to do the work. Some Indians were enslaved and could provide cheap labor, but the free Indians complicated the desire for cheap land because they also claimed the use of land. In a move calculated to gain the support of the common planters who had participated in Bacon's rebellion, the gentry agreed to a policy of removing or exterminating the Indians. With increased availability of land and decreased availability of Indian slaves, the way was opened for increased African slave trade. In 1705, the racial foundation of American society was firmly established. "An act concerning Servants and Slaves" in Virginia completed a process that had been evolving since Bacon's rebellion. African, Mulatto, and Indian slaves and their children became property without any civil rights. Although the law referred to Indians and Africans as people coming from non-Christian lands, the foundation for skin-color racism was established as American racism. Other southern colonies eventually followed Virginia's lead.

All the colonies, from Massachusetts to Georgia, developed the same approach toward the Native Americans. During the 18th century, the colonists supported either their removal or extermination. In his autobiography, Benjamin Franklin describes his experience with drunken Indians and then proposes that rum may be the best way to completely destroy the Native population. He points out without regret, "It [rum] has already annihilated all the tribes who formerly inhabited the sea-coast."[3] Franklin was not entirely correct. Rum may have played a part in the removal of Natives from the coast, but violence was also a major contributor.

During the 18th century, white superiority was sometimes questioned, but this did not necessarily lead to questioning segregation in the North. Again, Franklin is a good example of this. In a 1763 letter to John Waring, he describes visiting a "Negro School." Franklin reports, "I was on the whole much pleas'd, and from what I then saw, have conceiv'd a higher Opinion of the natural Capacities of the black Race, than I had ever before entertained."[4] Franklin's recognition of the intellectual equality of whites and blacks does not, however, lead him to question segregation along color lines. This is interesting in view of the fact that he specifically proposed the integration of the English and Germans. Ten years before his visit to the "Negro School," he wrote about the Germans, "Yet I am not for refusing entirely to admit them into our Colonies: all that seems to be necessary is, to distribute them more equally, mix them with the English, establish English Schools where they are now too thick settled."[5] Franklin never made a similar proposal for integration regarding blacks, even though he did become active in the abolition movement after the American Revolution.

Pennsylvania illustrates what happened across the northern colonies where slavery did not have the economic benefits that it had in the tobacco-growing South. The North developed social and legal separation of blacks and whites. Although the social customs and laws varied from colony to colony, segregation was born in the northern colonies. In Pennsylvania, for example, the customs became law in 1829 with the passage of "An Act for the better Regulation of Negroes." Among other things, it made marriage between blacks and whites illegal. Pennsylvania had previously established separate courts for blacks. The law against cross-racial marriage gave additional support to this segregation. With slavery, whites and blacks needed to live and work in close proximity. Segregation was only practical and, therefore, only developed in the North before the Civil War.

Across the colonies, what started as a commitment to the superiority of European culture and Christianity transformed into superiority based on skin color by the 17th and early 18th century. Christian religious leaders participated in this transformation. After spending time in Georgia as a missionary in the early 18th century, John Wesley, the founder of the Methodist movement, returned to England, where he explained in a sermon,

> As gross and palpable are the works of the devil among many (if not all) the modern heathens. The natural religion of the Creeks, Cherokees, Chickasaws, and all other Indians bordering on our southern settlements (not of a few single men, but of entire nations), is to torture all their prisoners from morning till night, till at length they roast them to death; and upon the slightest undesigned provocation, to come behind and shoot any of their own countrymen! Yea, it is a common thing among them, for the son, if he thinks his father lives too long, to knock out his brains; and for mother, if she is tired of her children, to fasten stones about their necks, and throw three or four of them into the river, one after another![6]

Wesley's evidence of the presence of the devil in European society is far less harsh. He claims the English are "common swearers, drunkards, whoremongers, adulterers, thieves, robbers, sodomites, murderers."[7] As the colonists dehumanized those who were not white, white superiority became entrenched.

Yet during the 18th century, there were some voices that questioned the morality of slavery. James Oglethorpe was the founder of the colony of Georgia. Oglethorpe forbade slavery in Georgia and obtained the support of the British government in this. While most of the argument in Parliament was about the economics of slavery and the possible danger that the Spanish might instigate a slave uprising, Oglethorpe argued that it was immoral.[8] But the British settlers in Georgia did not always comply with the prohibition of slavery, and soon slaves were as common in Georgia as in other southern colonies.

UNITED STATES BECOMES A NATION

The next important period in shaping American racism was the independence movement in the 1770s and the formation of the American government. The decision by the colonists in 1776 to declare independence from Britain was a bold step to break with a long European tradition of royal government. Royalty across Europe in both Protestant and Catholic nations relied on the argument that the legitimacy of their royal powers came from God and was based on inherited privilege. Political philosophers and essayists like John Locke had established a philosophical argument for a government without a king, but the main models for the colonists came from ancient Greece and Rome. Thomas Paine explained to his colonial readers of *Common Sense*, "But there is another and greater distinction for which no truly natural or religious reason can be assigned, and that is, the distinction of men into KINGS and SUBJECTS."[9]

Thomas Jefferson also made his argument for independence by claiming that "nature's God" legitimized the rebellion. In the Declaration of Independence, he referred to "the creator" as the one who made "all men equal." And the creator gave them rights. After listing grievances, he appealed in his closing paragraph to the "Supreme Judge." This judge is not the source of authority for independence; that authority comes from "the good People of these Colonies." The phrase "We hold these truths to be self-evident" was not in Jefferson's original draft. He first proposed "We hold these truths to be sacred and undeniable." It was Benjamin Franklin who proposed the final wording.[10] The founders established their argument on philosophical rather than theological grounds. They acknowledged a "supreme being," but they were not driven by a religious conviction. They appealed not to God but to what Paine called common sense.

By the 1770s, color-based racism was firmly embedded in the common sense of the white settlers who rebelled. And strange as it may seem today, it was common sense to them that "all men are created equal" only applied to white men. More specifically, it applied to the wealthy white gentry. Nevertheless, the words they used completely changed the trajectory of race relations. They claimed independence from Britain based on a civil rights argument using the language of equality for all. Since the signing of the Declaration of Independence, the recurring question for all Americans has been, What does it mean to be a nation founded on the civil rights principle that everyone is created equal?

The founders were not completely unaware of the difficulty in resolving the contradictions between what they said and what they did. They knew that the civil rights basis of their rebellion raised the issue of relations between blacks and whites, but the decision was made to not disrupt the system of slavery in the South or segregation in the North. James Madison was a Virginia planter who owned slaves. He represents what became the dominant white perspective. Madison believed that everyone in the young nation should be represented in the government, but representation did not require equal participation. He believed that slaves should be represented, but they did not need to vote or have other civil rights. Madison accepted that there would be both white and black men who could not vote. He did not even raise a question about women.

Madison was probably aware that in 1777 a petition was presented in Massachusetts to the General Court by slaves who pointed out "that they have in Common with all other men a Natural and Unalienable Right to that freedom which the Great Parent of the Universe hath Bestowed equally on all mankind." The petition was written by Prince Hall, a leader in the black community in Boston and the founder of the African Masonic Lodge of Boston. The petition requested that all blacks "may be Restored to the Enjoyments of that which is the Natural Right of all men." It was rejected, but it raised the question of what it really meant that all people are created equal.[11]

Others joined the Massachusetts slaves. Benjamin Rush, one of the signers of the Declaration of Independence, was a consistent voice against slavery. He wrote a pamphlet entitled *The plant of Liberty is so tender that it cannot thrive long in the neighbourhood of slavery.*[12] Yet these antislavery voices were unsuccessful in influencing the writing of the Constitution.

The founders from the South—Washington, Jefferson, Madison, and others—clearly recognized the dilemma posed by the ideals of natural law and slavery. There was a missed opportunity as these Southern elites were not able to bring themselves to end slavery. Washington is probably the most disappointing of the group because he was a Southern slave owner with the political capital to lead the country through an emancipation process. Yet it was not until his will was read that the world knew that he was freeing all of his slaves. Jefferson is also disappointing on this account. He originally proposed antislavery language in the Declaration of Independence and then did not hold out for an antislavery position as a justification for independence. At his death, his will freed some of his slaves, who may have been his own children. The rest were sold to cover his accumulated debts.

Shortly after independence, the white Americans encountered Mexicans. During James Monroe's presidency, in 1821, Mexico gained its independence. Americans were invited by Mexico to settle in Texas. The new settlers joined a small number of Americans who had been encouraged by Spain. The Spanish wanted to protect their interests against the French, who were developing a colony in Louisiana. At first the Americans recognized that they were living under the authority of the Mexican government, but a growing faction of Americans wanted to separate Texas from Mexico. In 1836, the Americans declared their independence. Fighting between the white American settlers and the Mexicans continued for several decades, but the English-speaking settlers retained control. Racism was an issue from the beginning. Mirabeau B. Lamar was president of the Lone Star Republic (Texas) from December of 1838 to December of 1841, and his vision for Texas was to exterminate the Native Americans and expand the Lone Star Republic to the Pacific Ocean.

Sam Houston was a Texas war hero and also served as president of the Lone Star Republic. He wanted Texas to become part of the United States. In 1830, Houston married a Cherokee woman, Tiana Rodgers, and before moving to Texas, he served as a representative of the Cherokee Nation to the American government.

The United States Congress agreed to annex Texas under Houston's leadership in 1845, and Texas became the 28th state by the end of the year. The state constitution allowed both slave holding and slave trading. The annexation and statehood were widely seen in the slaveholding states as important steps in preserving slavery. Offended by American imperialism, Mexico initiated the Mexican-American War. It didn't turn out well for Mexico. In 1848, the Treaty of Guadalupe Hidalgo ended hostilities, ceded almost half of Mexico to the United States, and added a population of about 100,000 Mexicans to the United States.[13] Mexicans were treated like Native Americans and blacks. White Americans claimed superiority over all nonwhites and denied citizenship to Mexicans in Texas.[14]

This was the beginning of an ongoing pattern where most Latinos/as living in America arrived because of imperialistic expansion into Mexico, Cuba, Puerto Rico, and Central America. It was a pattern of white superiority ideology applied to any nonwhite group living in the United States. The same ideology of color-based racism was subsequently applied to people from Asia who came looking for economic opportunity.

THE ABOLITION MOVEMENT

The contradiction between the claim that all are created equal and the institution of slavery could not be ignored. One reason was a changing religious climate. In 1830, Charles Finney kicked off a religious revival in Rochester, New York, that spread across the nation and was particularly influential in New England. Commonly called the Great Awakening, the religious landscape moved in a new direction. Much of American commitment to equality came from the "natural law" tradition of the founders. Until the 1830s, the dominant religion in America was the Calvinist teaching that the Puritans brought to New England. This was the same theology proclaimed by Franklin's friend George Whitefield, who evangelized in every colony before and after the American Revolution. The Calvinism of the period claimed that God is all-powerful and decides who will be given salvation and eternal life in heaven.

Charles Finney and other evangelists who spread the Great Awakening preached from the Arminian tradition of Christianity that claimed that God wants everyone to go to heaven. The way to get there is to accept an offer that God has made that past unrighteousness will be forgiven because of Christ. Christ accepted the punishment for each individual's past sins so true believers could move forward living righteous lives. This religion required taking personal responsibility by becoming a true believer. It also demanded moral responsibility, making slavery more problematic. The claim that "all are equal" was not just common sense; it was also true religion. But even the religious revival could not dissuade whites from their attachment to white superiority.

In a book about his visit to America in 1842, the English novelist Charles Dickens tells about attending a sermon by Rev. William Ellery Channing in Boston. Dickens, an abolitionist, was delighted that Channing spoke out against slavery.[15] This was near the end of Channing's life, and he supported immediate emancipation of the slaves. Like many Northern abolitionists, Channing fell short of accepting the equality of blacks. Although he abhorred slavery, he believed that Africans were naturally lazy and would need to be supervised by their white masters even after emancipation.

White supremacy was even a part of the political career of Abraham Lincoln—a renowned leader in the abolition movement. In his debates with Stephen Douglas in a Senate race, Lincoln said, "There is a physical difference between the white and black races which I believe will forever forbid the two races living together on terms of social and political equality."[16] This was consistent with the views of most of the whites in the North, including advocates for the abolition of slavery.

For many in the northern states, a commitment to the abolition cause did not require questioning the racism that sustained the institution. But there were other voices. The runaway slave Frederick Douglass joined the abolition cause and became a central figure in the movement. In his autobiography, he describes his experience after he was invited by the Massachusetts Anti-Slavery Society to join their efforts. The invitation came, he says, because he gave a heartfelt, but not very articulate, description of his experience as a slave at a meeting where the white abolitionist William Lloyd Garrison spoke eloquently. Douglass says that "much interest was awakened—large meetings assembled. Many came, no doubt from curiosity to hear what a negro could say in his own cause. I was generally introduced as a 'chattel'—a 'thing'—a piece of southern property." Douglass soon became frustrated because the leaders of the movement only wanted him to describe his experience, not offer his insights into the reasons for abolition. The white organizers "always wished to pin me down to a simple narrative. 'Give us the facts,' said Collins, 'we will take care of the philosophy.'"[17]

Douglass eventually gained self-confidence and began to express his moral indignation as well as or better than the white speakers at abolition events. He was counseled by Garrison and others that "people won't believe you ever were a slave, Frederick, if you keep on this way." In time, Garrison's prediction came true; Douglass did not fit with the prejudice of audiences that were committed to white superiority. He says, "They said I did not talk like a slave, look like a slave, or act like a slave, and that they believed I had never been south of Mason and Dixon's line. 'He don't tell us where he came from, what his master's name was, or how he got away; besides, he is educated, and is in this a contradiction of all the facts we have concerning the ignorance of the slaves.' Thus I was in a pretty fair way to be denounced as an impostor."[18]

The abolitionists were not stirred by a desire to create a society where African Americans would be equal. They were merely motivated by their abhorrence of the inhumanity of slavery and by their sense of moral superiority over white slave owners.

The main thrust of the abolition movement did not question racism or call for complete civil rights for blacks in either the North or the South, yet there were voices that protested racism. Sojourner Truth is one example. Born a slave in New York State, she escaped to Boston, where she became part of the abolition and women's suffrage movements. As she said, "I think that 'twixt the negroes of the South and the women at the North, all talking about rights, the white men will be in a fix pretty soon."[19]

Although the Civil War was not primarily fought as a battle to end racism, it did take on the focus of ending slavery. Lincoln's second inaugural address on March 4, 1865, makes this clear. He points out that four years before,

> one-eighth of the whole population were colored slaves, not distributed generally over the Union, but localized in the southern part of it. These slaves constituted a peculiar and powerful interest. All knew that this interest was somehow the cause of the war. To strengthen, perpetuate, and extend this interest was the object for which the insurgents would rend the Union even by war, while the Government claimed no right to do more than to restrict the territorial enlargement of it.[20]

Had Lincoln stopped here, it might seem that he believed the Civil War was fought simply to preserve the union, but he continues, "It may seem strange that any men should dare to ask a just God's assistance in wringing their bread from the sweat of other men's faces, but let us judge not, that we be not judged." He goes on to struggle with the question of why a just God would allow such a terrible war to go on so long. He concludes that it is God's time to end American slavery and explains that God "gives to both North and South this terrible war as the woe due to those by whom the offense came."[21]

Slavery presented such a challenge that the issue of equality of all people was largely put aside by whites. Abolitionists like Lincoln looked for a way to gain the necessary political and social resources to end it. For example, one proposal that Lincoln made on March 6, 1862, was to use federal funds "to compensate for the inconveniences public and private" that would result from a state adopting a "gradual abolishment of slavery." On April

16, 1862, Congress passed a law proposed by Lincoln that emancipated all slaves in the District of Columbia and provided funds to compensate slave owners. The legislation also provided up to $100 for any former slave who desired to emigrate. On July 12, 1862, Lincoln met with representatives from the border states. He proposed that they make a commitment to gradually emancipate their slaves. He argued that, since the war would end all slavery, this solution would provide them with something rather than nothing. He also suggested that land could be purchased in South America, and the former slaves could be encouraged to go there. The offer was not accepted, and Lincoln moved forward with his idea of emancipating the slaves in the rebellious states by signing the Emancipation Proclamation.[22]

In June of 1864, Lincoln announced support for a constitutional amendment to end slavery. He saw the 13th Amendment as a way to unite the Republicans behind the war. It had the benefit of avoiding the complex issue of rights for former slaves. He also wanted to end the question of emancipation before the Union had a complete military victory. Lincoln's reelection was seen by many as a referendum on the 13th Amendment. His success was celebrated by abolitionists.[23]

While there were voices like Douglass and Truth who pointed to the connections between slavery, racism, and civil rights, an opportunity was missed when the white supremacy views of the white leadership in the northern states did not recognize racism as the fundamental social problem of America. The result was that they succeeded in ending the institution of American slavery, but they left racism and the ideology of white superiority completely intact.

ASCENT OF SEGREGATION AND JIM CROW

Following the Civil War, there was a period of reorganizing race relations in the South. At first the former states of the Confederacy were occupied by federal troops. Some schools were integrated, and the Freedmen Society supported schools to educate former slaves. Mississippi established a land grant university to train former slaves. Unlike in the North, where segregation kept the races separate, slavery had required a certain amount of contact between the races, so blacks and whites in the South were accustomed to each other. This is not to say that the racism that sustained slavery disappeared with emancipation. But the first response in the South was not segregation.

Historian of Jim Crow racism C. Vann Woodward reports that Northerners and Southern white radicals were surprised and disturbed to find that "the two races now eat together at the same table, sit together in the same room, work together, visit and hold debating societies together."[24] This was not typical or very common, but it is important to note that it happened at all and was particularly troubling to Northern white visitors, who were accustomed to segregation. While social mixing may not have been universal, federal troops enforced many civil rights for former slaves, including serving on juries, voting, and running for public office.

In 1868, Horatio Seymour from New York ran as the Democrat for president. His campaign slogan was "This Is a White Man's Country."[25] He got 47 percent of the popular vote. He carried New York and New Jersey; the border states of Delaware, Kentucky, and Maryland; the southern states of Georgia and Louisiana; and the western state of Oregon. General Ulysses Grant won that election, but politicians could see that the public was not ready to support full civil rights for black. The abolitionists had achieved their aim. The leaders of the Republican Party believed that the 15th Amendment, which gave blacks the right to vote, assured the Republican Party a majority in Congress. With blacks in the South supporting Republicans, elections of Republican presidents for years to come was also assured. In 1877, federal troops left the South to determine its own future.

The removal of federal troops did not immediately result in Southern segregation. Left on their own, Southern whites debated and experimented with different approaches to race relations before settling on segregation and white supremacy. The approach that won the day put whites firmly back in control of the politics and economy of the South. It was led by whites who believed that blacks were inferior but who did not want to return to the days of robbing blacks of all human dignity. These conservatives told blacks that they had their best interest in mind when they discouraged blacks from asking for full civil rights. They were paternalistic and believed that they deserved to control social, political, and economic activity. As they gained political power, they adopted the segregation strategies that were already well developed in the North.

A pivotal year for American racism came in 1895. In February 1895, Frederick Douglass died. His strong black voice for equity was gone. In September of the same year, another former slave, Booker T. Washington, gained prominence by giving a speech that has been called the Atlanta compromise. In the speech, Washington provided a justification for white supremacy strategies in both the South and North. Washington was convinced by his experience at Hampton Normal and Agricultural Institute in Virginia (now Hampton University) that blacks were best suited for manual labor and subservience. In 1895, he was the principal of Tuskegee Normal Institute for Industrial Education in Tuskegee, Alabama. In this position, he was a leading black voice in education.

Washington delivered his 1895 speech to an audience at the Atlanta World Exposition, distributed it widely, and even made a sound recording of a portion of it, quickly becoming the black voice for white superiority. He argued that "blacks were best fitted for manual jobs like carpentry, cooking, brick masonry, house keeping, and blacksmithing." Washington gave comfort to white supremacists by arguing against equality. He said, "The wisest among my race understand that the agitation of questions of social equality is the extremist folly, and that progress in the enjoyment of all the privileges that will come to us must be the result of severe and constant struggle rather than of artificial forcing." He proposed that blacks should recognize that "it is at the bottom of life we must begin, and not at the top."[26]

Washington formed an alliance with a white sociologist named Robert Ezra Park. Together they worked with philanthropists who were interested in promoting Washington's proposals that blacks are primitive. Park used his experience working at Tuskegee to gain a position in the sociology department at the University of Chicago. There, through teaching, writing, and organizing, he provided academic credibility for white supremacy.

There were alternative voices. Most prominent among them was the African American W. E. B. Du Bois. When Park went to the University of Chicago, Du Bois had academic credentials as impressive as Park's. Both had degrees from Harvard, and both had studied sociology with the leading scholars in Europe. What Park lacked and Du Bois possessed was a record of quality research on blacks and race relations. Du Bois had published two books about his research that had made him a world-famous sociologist: *The Philadelphia Negro* and *The Souls of Black Folk*. His scientific study completely debunked the theories of white sociologists who claimed the inferiority of blacks. But the white establishment, both academic and philanthropic, either ignored Du Bois or actively worked to suppress his work. As Aldon Morris summarized in his book *The Scholar Denied: W. E. B. Du Bois and the Birth of Modern Sociology*, "at Atlanta, Du Bois was trapped in poverty and a degraded status while Park became a professor at Chicago, a bastion of white privilege and academic prestige."[27]

In summarizing the years between the end of the Civil War and 1900, Woodward says,

> Things have not always been the same in the South. . . . The race policies accepted and pursued in the South were sometimes milder than they became later. The policies of proscription, segregation, and disfranchisement that are often described as the immutable "folkways" of the South, impervious alike to legislative reform and armed intervention, are of a more recent origin. The effort to justify them as a consequence of Reconstruction and a necessity of the times is embarrassed by the fact that they did not originate in those times. And the belief that they are immutable and unchangeable is not supported by history.[28]

As the end of the 19th century approached, blacks had been let down by the withdrawal of federal protection, diminished interest and support from Northern liberals and radicals, and increased violence by whites. A new system of race relations was established in the South, called Jim Crow. Woodward explains, "In the early years of the twentieth century, it was becoming clear that the Negro would be effectively disfranchised throughout the South, that he would be firmly relegated to the lower rungs of the economic ladder, and that neither equality nor aspirations for equality in any department of life were for him."[29] Both laws and customs enforced a strict system of segregation where African Americans were restricted from participating with whites in churches and schools. African Americans were also kept separate from whites on public transportation, public swimming pools, sporting events, hospitals, prisons, funeral homes, and even cemeteries. Employers had separate bathroom facilities for blacks and whites. The extremes of this enforced segregation are symbolized by the public drinking fountain with a sign above it reading, "Whites Only."

Whites in both the North and South moved toward more extreme views on white superiority and supported segregation. A symptom of these shifts was the Supreme Court's unwillingness to support the civil rights of blacks as the 19th century came to an end. In the *Plessy v. Ferguson* case of 1896, the court legalized segregation with the "separate but equal" rule. Then in 1898, in the *Williams v. Mississippi* case, the court put an end to federal protection of civil rights by approving a plan in Mississippi to deny blacks the right to vote.

Jim Crow segregation was enforced formally by both laws and customs. Police and the court system were controlled by whites, who denied equal protection of the law to African Americans. In addition, there was extralegal violence that ensured the compliance of African Americans. Most notorious is the Ku Klux Klan, a secret society of white men who intimidated and murdered African Americans. Lynchings were another form of violence used to frighten African Americans into accepting life without civil rights. Lynchings were not limited to the South, but they played a particularly important role in defining race relations there.

The methods of enforcing segregation in the southern states via laws, citizen violence, and control of education and economic institutions were applied across the country. In 2005, James Loewen reported on his research into "sundown towns" that existed between 1890 and 1968. He identified thousands of towns outside of the South that were "Whites Only" after dark. This practice was widespread. Loewen discovered that of the 621 incorporated places in Illinois with a population of more than 1,000 people, 472 had a history of being sundown towns. The practice was also popular outside of the Midwest, and it was not limited to excluding African Americans. Loewen reported,

> Whites in many communities indulged in little race riots that until now have been lost to history. Whites in Liberty, Oregon, for example, now part of Salem, ordered blacks to leave in 1893. Pana, Illinois, drove out its African Americans in 1899, killing five in the process. Anna, Illinois, followed suit in 1909, Pinckneyville probably in 1928. Harrison, Arkansas, took two riots by Whites before the job was done—in 1905 and 1909. Decatur, Indiana, expelled

its black population in 1902. White workers in Austin, Minnesota, repeatedly drove out African Americans in the 1920s and 1930s. Other towns that violently drove out their black populations include Myakka City, Florida; Spruce Pine, North Carolina; Wehrum, Pennsylvania; Ravenna, Kentucky; Greensburg, Indiana; St. Genevieve, Missouri; North Platte, Nebraska; Oregon City, Oregon; and many others. Some of these mini-riots in turn spurred Whites in nearby smaller towns to have their own, thus provoking little waves of expulsions. White residents of Vienna, Illinois, set fire to the homes in its black neighborhood as late as 1954![30]

The ideology of white superiority was applied to all groups that were nonwhite. Asians were treated like African Americans, with added restrictions and attempts to keep them out of the United States. Because the Philippines was a colony of the United States, Filipinos presented a complication and were treated as a special case. There was a great deal of confusion about what whites wanted to do with nonwhites living in places that the United States colonized. World War II brought additional suffering to people of Japanese ancestry. In 1942, President Franklin Roosevelt ordered the internment in concentration camps of all people of Japanese ancestry living in the United States. The majority were American citizens.

By the beginning of World War II in 1939, white Americans were secure in their belief in white superiority. They had captured the political and economic systems. Racism without shame defined race relations. The period that began with emancipation ended with a white-controlled nation. The abolition movement was stimulated by a religious revival, but almost every Christian church was segregated by the 1930s. Racism was the norm.

BIRTH OF A NATIONAL CIVIL RIGHTS IDENTITY

It is difficult to know when the tide started to turn against Jim Crow and racial segregation. Mary McLeod Bethune was the founding president of the National Council of Negro Women in 1935. She worked tirelessly for education reform and women's rights and established a foundation for the civil rights movement. In 1957, Dorothy Irene Height became the president of the National Council of Negro Women. She was at the center of the developing civil rights movement and continued to provide leadership until her death in 2010.

In the early 1940s, a Swedish economist, Gunnar Myrdal, visited the United States. In *An American Dilemma: The Negro Problem and Modern Democracy*,[31] Myrdal argued that the contradiction between the American ideal of freedom and equality and the practice of racism was immoral. As an economist, he also made an argument that the treatment of African Americans was against the economic and foreign policy interests of the United States. The book was widely read and discussed.

The rise of a global communist movement also worried whites. Might nonwhites join this international movement for economic equality? Also in the early 1940s, an interracial organization, Congress of Racial Equality (CORE), was founded. This group promoted the nonviolent tactics of Mahatma Gandhi and established the foundation of civil disobedience in the civil rights struggle.

Before the end of World War II, the Supreme Court signaled that it was ready to become active in addressing racism. The court ruled in 1944 in *Smith v. Allright* that the Democratic Party could not hold all-white primaries in Texas. Texas law allowed political parties to establish rules for who could vote in their primaries. Thurgood Marshall, representing the National Association for the Advancement of Colored People (NAACP), argued successfully that since the Democratic Party had a majority in the general election, the disenfranchisement of black voters in the primary was the same as disenfranchising them in the general election. This was the beginning of a string of civil rights Supreme Court rulings supported by the NAACP. Winning legal cases weakened Jim Crow laws, and the NAACP provided a voice for racial justice, but the victories resulted in a white backlash and little integration.

World War II started a chain reaction. Nonwhite soldiers returned from the war in 1945 with a sense of accomplishment and a belief that they were fully American. The war effort required that everyone, regardless of race, share in a common goal. The destruction of Japanese and European manufacturing and economic infrastructure left America with a strong, expanding economy. More importantly, the war propaganda claimed that America was in a battle against the immorality of Nazi Germany and the Japanese. How could Americans of all races go to war in Asia and Europe to defeat racism but refuse to face American racism?

The 1960s brought a grassroots movement that developed rapidly with dramatic impact. Many young black leaders emerged to lead the thousands of people ready to demand an end to Jim Crow laws. Some of them were killed because of their leadership, including Medgar Evers, a NAACP leader, and Dr. Martin Luther King Jr., the president of the Southern Christian Leadership Conference (SCLC). Others were murdered because they were white supporters, and still others were killed simply to spread terror. Between 1961 and 1963, thousands of protesters were arrested across the South. Others suffered beatings from police and white mobs.

The Student Nonviolent Coordinating Committee (SNCC) quickly grew out of a meeting at Shaw University in Raleigh, North Carolina, in 1960. Marion Barry, who later became mayor of Washington, D.C., was the first chairman. John Lewis, who later became a leader in Congress, was an original organizer and served as chairman. Stokely Carmichael became chairman in 1966. Carmichael coined the phrase *black power* and later worked with the Black Panthers organization. SNCC organized thousands of grassroots people to engage in voter registration, protests, and civil disobedience. By 1970, civil rights laws had been passed and the leadership moved on to other activities.

Other oppressed groups raised their voices in the 1960s. Hispanic consciousness was raised by Cesar Chavez, who founded the National Farm Workers Association in 1962 along with Dolores Huerta. Then Dennis Banks, Clyde Bellecourt, Eddie Benton Banai, and George Mitchell founded the American Indian Movement (AIM) in 1968. Richard Aoki, a Japanese American, was a leader in the Black Panthers. He supported civil rights activities in several organizations, although his reputation was tainted because of revelations that he was an informant for the FBI. Mary Yuriko Nakahara was a Japanese American civil rights and antiwar activist. She worked with Malcolm X and was present when he was assassinated.

In 1968–1969, the Third World Liberation Front (TWLF) organized a strike at San Francisco State College. The strike was a united effort organized by African American, Asian American, Latin American, and Native American student groups. As the name implies, the TWLF brought attention to the connection between the American civil rights struggle and the struggle of people around the world against colonialism. Students across America lobbied and often succeeded in forcing colleges and universities to add cultural studies to the curriculum.

Television began to bring greater awareness to the civil rights movement. The presidential debates of 1960, between Richard Nixon and John Kennedy, were televised for the first time. People across the nation saw police dogs and fire hoses turned on nonviolent protesters. In August of 1963, the Great March on Washington was held in Washington, D.C. Thousands of people stood on the Washington Mall to hear King give his "I Have a Dream" speech. Millions more saw him on television. Then in September of 1963, Americans saw images from the bombing of a church in Birmingham, Alabama, where four black children were killed.

There was also strong white antiracist national leadership. President Kennedy supported change and, in June of 1963, promised that he would submit civil rights legislation to Congress. President Lyndon Johnson continued to provide national leadership after Kennedy's assassination by pushing civil rights legislation through Congress and by enforcing civil rights laws.

There are two important legacies from the commitment and sacrifices of people in the 1960s: the national consensus that racism is morally wrong and a system of federal civil rights laws. First, the message that racism is morally wrong came from the black leaders of the movement in the South, many of whom were Christian clergy. Malcolm X was a Muslim voice for civil rights. There were also white clergy like James Reeb, a white Unitarian minister, who died after being attacked by a group of white supremacists in Selma, Alabama. Rabbi Abraham Heschel not only joined King and others in marching from Selma to Montgomery but also wrote about the connection between Jewish prophetic teaching and civil rights. President Kennedy repeatedly used language that referred to racism as "morally wrong." In his 1963 civil rights speech, he said, "We are confronted primarily with a moral issue. It is as old as the Scriptures and is as clear as the American Constitution."[32] The belief that racism is immoral continues to dominate the American consciousness, with the exception of a small minority of citizens.

The second legacy of the 1960s—a system of federal civil rights laws—is exemplified by the Civil Rights Act of 1964. Its long title was "An act to enforce the constitutional right to vote, to confer jurisdiction upon the district courts of the United States of America to provide injunctive relief against discrimination in public accommodations, to authorize the Attorney General to institute suits to protect constitutional rights in public facilities and public education, to extend the Commission on Civil Rights, to prevent discrimination in federally assisted programs, to establish a Commission on Equal Employment Opportunity, and for other purposes."[33]

The Voting Rights Act followed in 1965 and the Fair Housing Act in 1968. These laws established a clear federal authority to promote civil rights. The expectation that the federal government is responsible for protecting the civil rights of all citizens is an important legacy of the 1960s movement.

What the civil rights movement did not produce is an America with equal opportunity for all. It did not end the use of racism to preserve a privileged position for whites. We now find ourselves in the 21st century, in a new period of race relations in America. This period shares with all previous periods the fact that it carries with it the legacy of past racisms. Just as each period has its own expression of civil rights goals, the 21st century requires a restatement of the civil rights dream. The desire that America be a land of opportunity is still with us. It is part of our civil rights dream. Importantly, the 21st century will see the end of a white majority and therefore require a transition to a truly pluralistic nation. Chapters 3 and 4 propose a civil rights dream for the 21st century.

Chapter 3

Tearing Down Barriers

Like many white children growing up in the 1950s, I was told that America is the place where anyone can fulfill his dreams. My father never seemed to tire of telling people that his grandmother had a saying, "You can do almost anything within reason if you will only put your mind to it."[1] He saw himself as someone who rose from being poor to becoming a successful businessperson. America as a nation also could do "almost anything." Defeating the Germans and Japanese proved that we were the moral leaders of the world. Our small town adopted a German family made homeless by the war. This demonstrated that we could love our enemies. We were good people living in a good country.

Most people in the small town of Spirit Lake in northwest Iowa knew that my grandmother struggled to raise my father and his brother when their father was in jail. I only knew that my grandfather was impossible not to love. People in town had a special respect for him. It was not until his funeral, however, that I understood that some of that respect came from their observations of his struggle with alcoholism. For me, my grandfather became another example of what it means to live in America, where perseverance and overcoming difficulties, both personal and national, are simply a matter of fortitude and willpower. I don't remember thinking about it as an American dream; it was just the way that America was presented to me.

This image of America—as the place where anyone can succeed with the proper effort—was shattered when I was in high school. I discovered the book *The Other America*. In the first chapter, Michael Harrington described the extent of poverty in the United States in the late 1950s. He presented figures from the federal government that showed around one-quarter of Americans lived in poverty. This was troubling because the number was so high, but I already knew that some Americans lived in poverty. I had friends whose families could not afford indoor plumbing. A few of the people on my newspaper route did not always have the dollar a month to pay for the Sunday paper. I would see them hiding behind the curtain when I went to their door to collect.

But what was completely new and shocking to me was Harrington's claim that "the first step toward the new poverty was taken when millions of people proved immune to progress. When that happened, the failure was not individual and personal, but a social product. But once the historic accident takes place, it begins to become a personal fate."[2] This was my introduction to the idea that social structures can make it very difficult for some individuals to "do almost anything." Life in America was not as simple as I had been led to believe. As Harrington explained, "There are mighty historical and economic forces that keep the poor down; and there are human beings who help out in this *grim business*, many of them unwittingly" (italics added).[3]

After graduating from high school I left Iowa and went off to Cornell University, where I was introduced to economics by Professor Douglas Dowd. I remember a lecture where he explained how the federal government sometimes takes action to increase unemployment if there appears to be a threat of inflation. This can happen if the Federal Reserve raises interest rates to slow down inflation and the economy slows down, creating more unemployment. Here was an example of the "grim business" that Harrington had talked about. It was action by the government that resulted in making it impossible for some people to get a job even if they were eager to find work. I knew that my childhood understanding needed to be revised. I was looking for a vision of what is possible. I, like many others at the time, wanted a dream.

DR. KING PROVIDED LANGUAGE FOR A CIVIL RIGHTS AMERICAN DREAM

Rev. Dr. Martin Luther King Jr. connected all the dots for me and millions of other Americans. King made it impossible to ignore the failure of America at mid-20th century to provide every citizen with the possibility of "doing almost anything." For King, civil rights for all citizens was a national moral responsibility. He famously addressed this civil rights dream in a speech from the steps of the Lincoln Memorial in the nation's capital in August of 1963.[4] King told us his dream that one day his children would be "judged not by the color of their skin, but by the quality of their character." This phrase is so rich that it provides a language to articulate the value of individualism that is an essential part of the American dream.

The promise of the dream that King hoped for his children was personal and individual. He described the dream in terms of relationships. King talked about a time when the children of former slaves and the children of former slave owners would live in fellowship. This was based on his vision of common humanity. His point was clear. He saw the relationship between our common humanity and equity. A civil rights dream with the intention of making it possible for every American to follow an individual dream is only possible when collectively we pursue creating a nation based on shared humanity. King claimed that we needed to return to the fundamentals of what we wanted the nation to look like. Put another way, there cannot be both a white dream and a black dream.

The "I Have a Dream" speech was part of the Great March on Washington led by a coalition that included the Southern Christian Leadership Conference (SCLC) that King led. This speech was a powerful call for equality for blacks, but it was in the context of a movement to bring economic justice for all Americans. King made it clear that although the final goal of his dream was to make it possible for individuals like his children to have equality of opportunity, the dream was for a changed America—an America that would address all the forces that resulted in different outcomes for people of color and whites.

For the nation, the speech marked a turning point. There was no way to ignore the description of America with its inequity and racism. Equally important, the speech offered language for a civil rights dream. The speech signaled that the country could not ignore the call for action on civil rights. King made this last point in the speech itself. He said there would not be tranquility until all people were granted full citizenship rights. Even longtime civil rights advocates like Bayard Rustin were encouraged by the speech. Rustin was an African American Quaker and pacifist who helped organize civil rights activists in the early 1940s. He also helped King organize SCLC. After the "I Have a Dream" speech, Rustin explained, "I am against the present economic and social structure in this country. . . . What I want people to do is accept fundamental ideals of American society, democracy and equality, and try to work out an economic and social system which fits them."[5] King, Rustin, and other civil rights leaders in the 1960s connected the political, economic, and social systems. They clarified that the American dream is the civil rights dream where the social systems make it possible for all Americans to pursue their own happiness. When the civil rights dream was articulated by King and others, they always talked about both fellowship and individual opportunities along with the need for systemic changes, including political action.

The dream that King presented was specific to the context, but it was also based on his description of the foundation of American values. King began with the founders' civil rights commitment. He said that the Constitution and Declaration of Independence made a promise. He pointed out that the language of these documents was for all people, which included nonwhites. Then he said that the obligation to nonwhites had not been fulfilled. His challenge to Americans was to take responsibility for fulfilling the promise and in so doing fulfill the promises of democracy.

King was not the only voice competing for the hearts and minds of Americans in the 1960s. He was in the nation's capital with a clear intent of forcing President Kennedy and Congress to fulfill his dream. He argued that he was proclaiming a way forward that built on the intent of those who had written the Constitution. He wanted the government to use its power to protect voting rights, integrate schools, ensure equal economic participation of all citizens, and more. He claimed to be asking for the fulfilment of what the founders promised. In this, King took a middle ground on the question of the role of government.

In the 1960s there were others who saw the intent of the founders very differently from King. There were some who thought that the American system had failed the American people because capitalism is an economic system designed to generate inequity: the left. Others thought that the problem was that capitalism was not being given full rein: the right.

In this chapter I will first consider the political context of the 1960s that shaped King's description of the civil rights dream. The roots of American individualism are then described. The American founders are particularly important because King claimed that the justification for the civil rights agenda is the unfulfilled promise of the founders of American democracy. This is followed by a consideration of the way the civil rights dream has evolved and has been described by recent presidents. The chapter ends with a proposal for the wording of the portion of the civil rights dream that addresses opportunity and individual aspirations that is needed in the 21st century.

CIVIL RIGHTS FROM THE RIGHT IN THE 1960s AND BEYOND

The intellectual leader of the movement to keep the government out of the civil rights business was a playwright, novelist, and essayist, Ayn Rand. Born in Russia in 1905, Rand and her family experienced persecution by the Communists. She moved to the United States in 1925 looking to pursue her interest in becoming a writer. Her breakthrough as a novelist came in 1957 with the publication of *Atlas Shrugged*.[6] The novel described the dangers of a government that interferes with the economy in any way. She wanted the government to encourage every citizen to pursue self-interest.

Rand shared with King an abhorrence of Jim Crow racism. In 1963, Rand wrote, "The policy of Southern states toward Negroes was and is a shameful contradiction of this country's basic principles. Racial discrimination, imposed and enforced by law, is so blatantly inexcusable an infringement of individual rights that the racist statutes of the South should have been declared unconstitutional long ago." As much as she disliked the racism of the 1960s, she was equally opposed to the federal government passing civil rights laws. She argued that "so long as the Negro leaders were fighting against government enforced discrimination—right, justice and morality were on their side. But that is not what they are fighting any longer."[7] Rand correctly observed that civil rights leaders were asking the government to protect nonwhites from discrimination across the economy. She believed that "it is proper to forbid all discrimination in government owned facilities and establishments; the government has no right to discriminate against any citizen. And by the very same principle, the government has no right to discriminate *for* some citizens at the expense of others. It has no right to violate the right of private property by forbidding discrimination in privately owned establishments" (italics in original).[8]

In the 1950s, Rand envisioned an economy where everyone pursued self-interest and the government left the economy alone. In her imagination, the result of unregulated self-interest is prosperity for all. In her 1963 book titled *Virtues of Selfishness*, she contributed to the national debate as Americans struggled to redefine the civil rights dream that looked beyond Jim Crow racism. She was critical of states' rights advocates who were against federal civil rights legislation because they wanted to preserve racist policies at the state level. Her view of government was that "the only proper, *moral* purpose of a government is to protect man's rights, which means: to protect him from physical violence—to protect his right to his own life, to his own liberty, to his own *property* and to the pursuit of his own happiness. Without property rights, no other rights are possible" (italics in original).[9]

As Rand's ideas moved out of the 1960s, they have taken on slightly modified forms. Unfettered capitalism and very limited government intervention in the economy was central to the economic theories of Chicago University professor Milton Friedman. He summarized his economic philosophy in a newspaper article in 2003, where he says, "I have long said, 'I never met a tax cut I didn't like.' . . . I believe that government is too large and intrusive, that we do not get our money's worth for the roughly 40 percent of our income that is spent by government supposedly on our behalf."[10] This is the philosophy embraced by President Ronald Reagan in his first inaugural address in 1981: "We are a united people pledged to maintaining a political system which guarantees individual liberty to a greater degree than any other. . . . In this present crisis, government is not the solution to our problem; government is the problem."[11]

Some on the right have picked up on Rand's antigovernment views opposing government interventions to support civil rights without the antiracist commitment she had. Sadly, however, the language of limited government has been adopted by hate groups and is used to justify racism. The Southern Poverty Law Center monitors militia groups that train members in military tactics out of an antigovernment perspective. They also monitor other patriot groups that oppose the government. In 2015, they identified antigovernment (patriot) groups in all 50 states. Altogether there were almost 1,000, with many promoting racist propaganda.[12] As Morris Dees, the founder of the Southern Poverty Law Center, says, "This mixture of armed groups and those who hate is a recipe for disaster."[13] These groups illustrate the importance of finding a balance between individualism and collective responsibility.

CIVIL RIGHTS FROM THE LEFT

In the 1906 presidential election, Eugene Debs garnered 6 percent of the popular vote as the candidate of the Socialist Party. The political philosophy of the party was based on Marxism. According to the Marxist ideology, a government-managed economy would bring equality until the values of equality were so well established that the government would wither away. The Russian Revolution of 1917 established the Union of Soviet Socialist Republics (USSR). This created a global power with the moral authority of an ideology of equality. Leading up to the 1960s, some prominent civil rights leaders were attracted to this philosophy. A number participated in or supported the Socialist or Communist Parties at one point or another in their careers. This included academic W. E. B. Du Bois, activist Bayard Rustin, actor Paul Robeson, and others. While some Americans were attracted to this revolutionary dream as a route to defeat racism, by the 1960s, anti-Soviet sentiment had taken over. The Cold War between the United States and the USSR made advocating for a socialist solution impossible for leaders like King to embrace, primarily due to two factors. First, particularly under the totalitarian leadership of Joseph Stalin, communism was disgraced by its complete disregard for civil rights. Second, in the 1950s, Wisconsin senator Joseph McCarthy used Senate hearings to badger people he suspected were Communists and to frighten people from freely discussing Marxism.

There were still small pockets of people who supported various forms of Marxist approaches to establishing civil rights goals through Socialism. For example, in the 1960s a movement calling itself Students for a Democratic Society briefly flourished on several college campuses. The primary influence of the Socialist movement on civil rights leaders in the 1960s is that they were careful to distance themselves from even the appearance of sympathizing with anything that could be called Socialist or Communist.

By claiming that the civil rights movement of the 1960s was based on the values of the founders of the nation, King was able to ignore the paranoia regarding Socialism and the noise from the far right. In affirming each individual's right to pursue aspirations and the government's responsibility to protect us from each other, King was doing what Americans had done with varying degrees of success for almost 200 years: finding a middle ground. As the 20th century came to an end, the issues of individualism and collective responsibility were studied by a team of sociologists led by Robert Bellah. They published the results of their study in 1996 in a book titled *Habits of the Heart: Individualism and Commitment in American Life.*[14] Their main point is that throughout America's history, there has always been a struggle to find a balance between two values: individualism and collective responsibility. While we have sometimes emphasized one or the other, throughout our history we have looked for a middle ground. The competition between these values has played itself out at the state and national levels of government.

A HERITAGE OF INDIVIDUALISM

In the 19th century, debate about liberty focused on what an individual does rather than what the government does. Ralph Waldo Emerson (born in 1803) wrote essays that argued for individualism. In his 1841 essay *Self-Reliance*, he wrote, "Nothing is at last sacred but the integrity of your own mind." For Emerson, following one's own mind made one great. "What I must do is all that concerns me, not what the people think. This rule, equally arduous in actual and in intellectual life, may serve for the whole distinction between greatness and meanness." This individualism did not grow out of a selfish motive to be able to do whatever you want. Emerson believed that by connecting with your mind, you are connecting with a deeper level of shared humanity. For him, "God is here within."[15]

A friend of Emerson, Louisa May Alcott, wrote novels that encouraged young people to adopt a self-reliant attitude. She wrote a scene in which young people are discussing their dreams for the future. Laurie is talking about his grandfather and says,

> "I've got to do just as he did, unless I break away and please myself, as my father did." . . .
> Laurie spoke excitedly, and looked ready to carry his threat into execution on the slightest provocation; for he was growing up very fast, and, in spite of his indolent ways, had a young man's hatred of subjection, a young man's restless longing to try the world for himself.
> "I advise you to sail away in one of your ships, and never come home again till you have tried your own way," said Jo, whose imagination was fired by the thought of such a daring exploit.[16]

Alcott may have done more than Emerson to spread the idea that people should follow their own dreams. Henry David Thoreau was mentored by Emerson. Thoreau's understanding of individualism was that it is individual. He wrote,

> I would not have any one adopt my mode of living on any account; for, beside that before he has fairly learned it I may have found out another for myself, I

desire that there may be as many different persons in the world as possible; but I would have each one be very careful to find out and pursue his own way, and not his father's or his mother's or his neighbor's instead. The youth may build or plant or sail, only let him not be hindered from doing that which he tells me he would like to do.[17]

For Thoreau, individualism was not just a matter of making sure that the government protected liberty. Part of his simple lifestyle was motivated by the desire to be free to not pay taxes. He believed that slavery and war are immoral. His response was what he called civil disobedience, refusing to pay taxes to a government that would not prohibit slavery and that made war.

Emerson, Alcott, and Thoreau were born after the American government was established, and they believed that the individual is not bound to support the government if what the government does is not consistent with their conscience. The founders had the luxury of figuring out the social contract. These second-generation Americans wanted to be able to make their own social contract. Their writings influenced Mahatma Gandhi, King, and other civil rights advocates in the 1960s and before. Civil disobedience thus became a political strategy for collective action.

THE FOUNDERS AND CIVIL RIGHTS

We turn now to the founders and the legacy we have from them. What exactly are the promises of democracy? As King stated, there are *promises*, not a single promise. And as King said, they are promises "to which every American was to fall heir."[18] This result is the paradox of the American experiment. How can we have a society where each person has a right to pursue happiness and at the same time each person is denied the right to pursue happiness that denies another person the right to pursue happiness?

When the colonists declared their independence from Britain in 1776, they said what they wanted to do: they wanted to govern themselves without Britain. They already had democratic traditions to varying degrees in each colony, but they did not have a consensus on how they would cooperate or what a democratic government would look like. The first step was to expel the British military.

Because the founders were addressing questions of the role of government with a relatively blank slate, their debates and opinions are particularly helpful for us today. The persistence of racism makes it necessary for us to look again with fresh eyes at what our government should be doing.

The founders were not all of one mind. Yet in their words and actions we can see two underlying driving forces. We might even call them obsessions. First, they did not want royalty to control the government. Second, they didn't want the government to tell them what to do. These obsessions grew out of their experience with Britain and King George. They were also influenced by John Locke and an emerging philosophy of government and human rights. In some ways, their anger at King George clouded their vision so that they were particularly focused on liberty and almost blind to a hope for equality and participation by all.

The founders who gathered in Philadelphia to write the Constitution were thoughtful men. Many of them were college educated. Even participants like George Washington, who presided at the meetings and had not gone to college, were well read. They were all familiar with the writings of Thomas Hobbes and his theory of a social contract. In *Leviathan*, published in 1651, Hobbes argues that individuals enter into a social contract where they agree to give up some of their freedoms to a government that is responsible to use that power to preserve order. In his 1689 book, *Two Treatises of Government*, Locke added to this political theory by arguing that the people should determine how much freedom they will give up when they form their own government. This left the founders with the question of how much liberty should be given up by each individual in this social contract. Here Thomas Paine, Benjamin Franklin, John Adams, and Alexander Hamilton illustrate the range of opinions. All four of these founders developed their idea in response to what they understood human nature to be.

Paine presented the argument that government should be as limited as possible. He wanted people to be able to pursue happiness without the government getting in the way. But he saw a problem. He feared that Americans' fellow citizens were imperfect and so needed to be protected from each other. He claimed that the purpose of government is to provide security, including security from the evil nature of others: "WHEREFORE, security being the true design and end of government, it unanswerably follows that whatever FORM thereof appears most likely to ensure it to us, with the least expense and greatest benefit, is preferable to all others." The role of providing security was not just from foreign enemies. Paine also recognized that Americans needed security from each other: "For were the impulses of conscience clear, uniform, and irresistibly obeyed, man would need no other lawgiver; but that not being the case, he finds it necessary to surrender up a part of his property to furnish means for the protection of the rest." For Paine, government structures and paying taxes meant giving up liberty and limiting the right to pursue happiness. Yet he proposed paying taxes and giving up liberty because "this he is induced to do by the same prudence which in every other case advises him out of two evils to choose the least."[19] He saw a national government as a necessary evil.

Franklin used an economic argument as the basis for how the government should be organized. We might say that Franklin feared people's selfishness. His observations of the British government convinced him that wealthy people corrupt government and society. Therefore, he supported a single legislature based on population. He thought that a popularly elected legislature would protect the interests of society from the self-interest of the wealthy. We can see his influence in an early draft of the Pennsylvania constitution where Franklin presided over the convention. It included a warning about wealth: "That an enormous Proportion of Property vested in a few Individuals is dangerous to the Rights, and destructive of the Common Happiness of Mankind; and therefore, every free State hath a Right by its Laws to discourage the Possession of such property."[20]

John Adams was the scholar of the founders. He read widely and carefully. He also wrote extensively. In 1776, he published his *Thoughts on Government*.[21] Adams did not attend the Constitutional Convention, but his *Thoughts* were very influential. He outlined an organization of government that is very similar to what was eventually adopted. As he grew older, he became concerned about the lack of sophistication of members of Congress and the American people in general. As George Washington's vice-president, he presided over the Senate and gave senators lectures about proper decorum. He thought that preserving order required a strong executive. As the second president, he engaged in an undeclared war with France. He also signed the Alien and Sedition Acts. These laws greatly expanded the powers of the president. Among other things, they allowed the president to imprison and deport noncitizens who were deemed dangerous. The president could also send noncitizens back to their home country if that nation was hostile to the United States. From a civil rights perspective, one of the most onerous laws criminalized making false statements that were critical of the federal government. Although at the time Adams was sometimes accused of wanting to establish a monarchy, a better way to characterize his vision for the government was that an elite would protect the country from a democracy controlled by an uninformed public. He believed this was the only way to ensure the stability necessary for people to pursue happiness.

Alexander Hamilton had a more positive attitude about the ability of the people to govern themselves. He also expected that there would be some people who govern and some people who are governed. In *Federalist 35*, Hamilton addresses the question of how the interests of various classes will be represented in the House of Representatives. He first dismisses the idea that each class will be represented by a person from the class. "The idea of an actual representation of all classes of the people, by persons of each class, is altogether visionary. Unless it were expressly provided in the Constitution, that each different occupation should send one or more members, the thing would never take place in practice." He explains, "Mechanics and manufacturers will always be inclined, with few exceptions, to give their votes to merchants, in preference to persons of their own professions or trades." The reason for this is, according to Hamilton, "that the influence and weight, and superior acquirements of the merchants render them more equal to a contest with any spirit which might happen to infuse itself into the public councils, unfriendly to the manufacturing and trading interests."[22] In other words, the merchants are more capable of ruling than the manufacturers. But more importantly for our consideration, Hamilton presented an argument to his contemporaries that it is the quality of the men who will serve under the proposed Constitution that will give it legitimacy. They will look out for the interests of others.

Different as the perspectives of the founders were, they were able to work out a plan to organize the government. From their perspectives, we can extract several concepts that are helpful today in addressing civil rights:

- Keep an eye on government overreaching (Thomas Paine).
- Make sure the poor are protected (Benjamin Franklin).
- Sometimes use the power of government to lead the people (John Adams).
- Expect those who govern to protect the interests of all (Alexander Hamilton).

The founders debated possibilities and finally came up with a very limited government. Hamilton, Washington's secretary of the treasury, established the relationship between the economy and the government. Specifically, the government supported infrastructure projects that benefited the economy, tariffs were a means of managing international trade, and a national bank managed monetary policy. The founders thought they were establishing a system where all white men could pursue their happiness.

King was correct in saying that the founders got something started. They established a government structure that has allowed Americans to continue to work on the question of how to ensure equality and give up as little liberty as possible. The founders, however, left many civil rights issues for future generations.

POST-COLD WAR CIVIL RIGHTS

Before the fall of the Soviet Union in 1991, Americans saw the tyranny of Communist-inspired nations. The Communists used a rhetoric that they adopted from sociologist and activist Karl Marx, which envisioned a future with equality for all. For many Americans, the reality of Communist tyranny made it impossible to consider expanding the role of government to create equality. FBI director J. Edgar Hoover tried to subvert civil rights activities of the 1960s in part because of his belief that they were Communist inspired.[23] Today the threat of global Communist tyranny has disappeared. We can reclaim a balance in our understanding of the civil rights dream and the way we pursue it. The issues of government support for equality can be discussed using our reason rather than our emotional fear of tyrannical Communism.

Ronald Reagan was the last president to serve his entire presidential term during the Cold War, when Americans still felt threatened by the Soviet

Union's Communist government, with its history of tyranny and its propaganda of equality. During George H. W. Bush's presidency, the Soviet Union fell. President Bill Clinton was still living under the shadow of the Cold War. George W. Bush was the first president to open the discussion of a civil rights agenda that was post Cold War. His administration did not always fight for greater equality, but he helped us find words to describe our future that Reagan would not have used.

President Reagan's antigovernment rhetoric was politically expedient because Americans wanted to hear that their country was different and better than the Soviet Union. There may be examples where government is a problem, but the larger lesson of history is that the government needs to play a role for rights to advance. As we redefine the civil rights dream for the 21st century, politicians, and particularly presidents and presidential candidates, are important in helping us find the words that describe our dream.

The public discussion of civil rights in the 21st century has shifted significantly. The focus is now on the things that prevent people of color from achieving their personal aspirations. White privilege is not only used to protect benefits for whites; it is used in subtle ways to prevent people of color from following their personal dreams. Since the 1960s, white privilege has shifted its strategy to setting up barriers for people of color.

President G. W. Bush used the word *story* to convey the connection between the American heritage of civil rights and the civil rights dream today. In his first inaugural address in January of 2001, Bush talked about the "American story: A story of flawed and fallible people, united across the generations by grand and enduring ideals. The grandest of these ideals is an unfolding American promise that everyone belongs, that everyone deserves a chance, that no insignificant person was ever born."[24] The civil rights dream that Bush articulated is a 21st-century dream built on the principles established by our nation's founders, but it is also bolder than their dream. Bush used the word *everyone*. The founders said that "all are created equal." A civil rights dream for today demands that we take the words *all* and *everyone* seriously. They really do mean *all people*.

The civil rights dream is a dream because it is based on a recognition that some Americans face barriers to fulfill their aspirations because of their race. As Bush said in his first inaugural address, the dream is based on a promise: "Americans are called upon to enact this promise in our lives and in our laws." Bush went on to remind the nation that "though our nation has sometimes halted, and sometimes delayed, we must follow no other course."[25] Bush's words are an echo of W. E. B. Du Bois, who wrote in *The Souls of Black Folk* in 1903, "I insist it was the duty of someone to see that these [African American] workingmen were not left alone and unguided, without capital, without land, without skill, without economic organization, without even the bald protection of law, order, and decency."[26]

Bush called us to a civil rights agenda, but during his administration little progress was made. In contrast, President Barack Obama followed on Bush's heels and made great strides because he was surrounded by people who worked hard to advance opportunities for people of color. Progress was made in health care, education, public housing, and other areas. In January 2011, Obama stood before a joint session of Congress to deliver his State of the Union address. He had just suffered a humiliating defeat in the midterm election. Republicans picked up 6 seats in the Senate and 63 seats in the House of Representatives. This gave Republicans a majority in the House. With the Senate controlled by Democrats and the House by Republicans, the president needed to find common ground where both parties shared commitment. He chose to challenge them to begin with their shared vision of the American dream. He looked back to find a point of shared commitment. "We are the first nation to be founded for the sake of an idea—the idea that each of us deserves the chance to shape our own destiny."[27]

Obama referred to the American dream by reminding the American people and members of Congress that "sustaining the American Dream has never been about standing pat. It has required each generation to sacrifice, and struggle, and meet the demands of a new age."[28] The president wanted the members of Congress to see the dream as a starting point for their collective nonpartisan action.

Later in his speech, Obama returned to the American dream and defined it more clearly. "We may have different opinions, but we believe in the same promise that says this is a place where you can make it if you try. We may have different backgrounds, but we believe in the same dream that says this is a country where anything is possible. No matter who you are. No matter where you come from."[29] In the *Audacity of Hope*, then-senator Obama describes what he understood to be the American dream. It is not a college-educated married couple living in an unattached house on a small lot in the suburbs with two or three children, a dog, two cars, and enough money for annual trips to Disney World. He considers what is necessary to support the American dream:

> Politics will need to reflect our lives as they are actually lived. It won't be pre-packaged, ready to pull off the shelf. It will have to be constructed from the best of our traditions and will have to account for the darker aspects of our past. We will need to understand just how we got to this place, this land of warring factions and tribal hatreds. And we will need to remind ourselves, despite all our differences, just how much we share: common hopes, common dreams, a bond that will not break.[30]

His approach was to describe the dream as it related to specific people. He showed that the American dream is not an abstract concept; it is something that is expressed in the lives of individual Americans. In his 2016 State of the Union address, he used these examples:

- the dreams of a little girl in Tucson
- the dream of turning a good idea into a thriving enterprise
- the dream of Kathy Proctor, who at 55 years old earned a degree in biotechnology and inspired her children to pursue their dreams
- the dreams of a working-class kid from Scranton (Republican House Speaker John Boehner) who became Speaker of the House in the greatest nation on Earth[31]

For Obama, the best way to describe the civil rights dream is to show what it means in the lives of real people. Obama's words echo Bush's second inaugural address. In 2005, Bush was coming off a strong personal showing in the election and an increase in the Republican majorities in both the Senate and House of Representatives. His speech was his opportunity to set the agenda that would determine his legacy as president. He challenged Congress to make the dream of individual opportunity a reality. Bush said, "By making every citizen an agent of his or her own destiny, we will give our fellow Americans greater freedom from want and fear, and make our society more prosperous and just and equal." The 21st-century articulation of this civil rights dream includes what Bush called "the idea that each of us deserves the chance to shape our own destiny."[32] Bush was talking to members of his own political party and calling on them to use the federal government to make the United States a land where all people, including nonwhites, could pursue their dreams.

WE HAVE A DREAM FOR ALL AMERICANS

The language Bush and Obama used to describe the dream for the 21st century takes us back to the admonition of my great-grandmother: "You can do almost anything within reason if you will only put your mind to it." The condition of "almost anything within reason" is important because our dream is that there are no greater barriers for one person than another. While we encourage our children and each other to reach for the stars, there is much more to it than "just putting your mind to it."

Take the example of a child who is inspired by a doctor and decides that her aspiration is to help people become and stay healthy. The way to become a doctor is to go to medical school. There are many barriers to getting into and graduating from medical school. One of them is that each year the medical schools accept only a certain number of students. To be accepted one needs to complete a college degree. There are barriers to obtaining a college degree, including needing to pay for it. Even with a college degree, the medical schools establish additional criteria for who is admitted. Usually medical schools require a passing grade in college chemistry. These barriers prevent some people who put their mind to it from becoming doctors. In the end, becoming a doctor requires overcoming many obstacles. Our civil rights challenge is to address the barriers that are added for people of color.

The individual civil rights dream for the 21st century is that the government at all levels, businesses and institutions, organizations, and the public will do what is necessary to ensure that every American can pursue an individual dream without being hindered because of race, gender, disability, sexual orientation, limited family wealth, or any other personal characteristics. Another way to say this is that *barriers to fulfilling individual aspirations will be no greater for one person than another*. This is the dream for every American. The following chapter looks at the civil rights dream for the United States as a nation.

Chapter 4

The Dream of Full Participation

My own vision of what America can become was awakened in 1988. While the Democratic convention met in Atlanta, I visited my in-laws in Portland, Connecticut. On July 19, the convention was running behind schedule, so the rest of the family gave up watching and went upstairs to bed. I sat alone in the TV room, waiting for Jesse Jackson to speak. I was eager to hear what he would say to those of us who had supported his bid to be president of the United States.

Jackson arrived at the convention with 1,219 delegates supporting him—29 percent of the required number to win the nomination. Michael Dukakis brought 2,877 delegates or 70 percent of the total. It might seem that with Jackson's proven ability to rally voters to his vision for the future of America, he would be in a very strong position to determine what happened at the convention, but it turned out that the best he could negotiate was the opportunity to address the delegates and the nation on prime-time television. Then the convention was running late, so he came on after 11:00 p.m. on the east coast.

Jackson spoke as if he had won the nomination:

There are differences of religion, region, and race; differences in experiences and perspectives. But the genius of America is that out of the many we become one. . . . With so many guided missiles, and so much misguided leadership, the stakes are exceedingly high. Our choice? *Full participation* [italics added] in a democratic government, or more abandonment and neglect. And so this night, we choose not a false sense of independence, not our capacity to survive and endure. Tonight we choose interdependency, and our capacity to act and unite for the greater good.[1]

He was giving a concession speech, but it did not concede defeat for the values he had promoted during his campaign. He went on to develop the theme "out of the many we become one":

> America is not a blanket woven from one thread, one color, one cloth. When I was a child growing up in Greenville, South Carolina, and grandmamma could not afford a blanket, she didn't complain and we did not freeze. Instead she took pieces of old cloth—patches, wool, silk, gabardine, crockersack—only patches, barely good enough to wipe off your shoes with. But they didn't stay that way very long. With sturdy hands and a strong cord, she sewed them together into a quilt, a thing of beauty and power and culture. Now, Democrats, we must build such a quilt. . . . But don't despair. Be as wise as my grandmamma. Pull the patches and the pieces together, bound by a common thread. When we form a great quilt of unity and common ground, we'll have the power to bring about health care and housing and jobs and education and hope to our Nation.[2]

Jackson presented a civil rights dream for America that complements the civil rights dream for each American. Achieving either will be impossible without achieving both. In the speech, Jackson called for "full participation in the democratic process." This is a centerpiece of the civil rights dream for the 21st century. Full participation in the political process is part of full participation in all of the institutions and organizations that make up American society. This is a dream *where every race, ethnicity, and identity group has full participation in the political, economic, and cultural life of the nation.* This dream complements the dream for each American that *barriers to fulfilling individual aspirations are no greater for one person than another.*

Jackson's bold proposal offered a new way to see the civil rights challenge. First, it was a new paradigm that challenged the white paradigm established by the founders. Second, it has roots in the commitment that the founders had to religious tolerance. Third, it goes beyond political theories proposed for a melting pot, races and ethnic groups as competing interests, and a society based on a blanket of justice defined by white values. Fourth, it is a moral, not a pragmatic, proposal. And, fifth, full participation goes beyond tolerance and everyday pluralism. Immediately after the speech there was pushback—pushback that continues to this day.

Jackson proposed what sociologists call a paradigm shift. A paradigm is a way that people view the world around them. The history of American racism described in chapter 2 produced a paradigm based on white racism: the foundational belief that white skin has value and that people who are nonwhite are of less value. (Paradigms are discussed more fully in chapter 6.) Jackson proposed a different paradigm for America, a patchwork quilt paradigm, where every group has full participation. When compared to the founders' civil rights proposal, we can see the creativity of Jackson's paradigm.

PATCHWORK NATION IS NOT WHAT THE FOUNDERS HAD IN MIND

Jackson talked about those who had gone before. He made a direct connection between his message and the 1963 "I Have a Dream" speech by Dr. Martin Luther King Jr. Jackson said, referring to King, "Tonight he must feel good as he looks down upon us. We sit here together, a rainbow, a coalition—the sons and daughters of slavemasters and the sons and daughters of slaves, sitting together around a common table, to decide the direction of our party and our country. His heart would be full tonight."[3] But Jackson does not look back farther to establish a foundation for his dream of a patchwork quilt nation. It is difficult to draw a straight line from the actions of the founders to the dream Jackson described. The founders have a somewhat mixed record, but mostly they left us with a heritage of intolerance that is with us into the 21st century. Chapter 2 outlines the development of racism during the revolutionary period, but a closer look at the wording of the Declaration helps us see why Jackson was presenting a new vision for America. Examining the founders' perspectives clarifies how Jackson's vision is a paradigm shift for Americans. Jackson's dream was not the dream of the founders; it was a new dream based on the principles of the civil rights movement.

Even though the founders used the words "all men" in the opening paragraphs of the Declaration of Independence, they did not have a plan or an intention to create a patchwork quilt nation. They listed 27 "facts" (which are better called complaints) to justify their independence, all of which showed that racial concerns were central to their motivations. Robert Parkinson, an assistant professor of history at Binghamton University, makes a convincing argument that the Declaration of Independence was as much "if not more, about racial fear and exclusion as it was about inalienable rights."[4]

The first five complaints in the Declaration of Independence are about the process King George III used to govern the colonies. The sixth describes a consequence of his inattention, poor judgment, and mismanagement. The founders claimed that Indians were ready to invade the colonies and that slaves had been encouraged to rebel. One thing the members of the Second Continental Congress could agree on was that slaves and Indians posed a threat. They needed independence so that they would have the power of law and government to deal directly with the racial situation.

The seventh complaint was that the king was not allowing whites from Britain and other European nations to become citizens of the colonies. Increasing the number of whites was part of a racial strategy. This complaint clarified to people living in the colonies that the Second Continental Congress intended to establish a white nation.

The last complaint was the most unambiguous regarding their racial intentions. It read, "He has excited domestic insurrections amongst us, and has endeavoured to bring on the inhabitants of our frontiers, the merciless Indian Savages, whose known rule of warfare, is an undistinguished destruction of all ages, sexes and conditions." The "domestic insurrections" referred to slave rebellions. There was a widely circulated report that the British were recruiting Indians to join them in putting down the colonists' rebellion.

The primary audiences for their declaration were the international community and British living in the colonies. They needed the support of European countries, particularly France, to succeed in establishing a new nation. They also needed the farmers and merchants to join an army to expel the British. Jefferson's first draft included the complaint that the king was forcing slavery on them. In the debate and compromising, this was lost. In its place was a pandering to the racial anxieties of the colonists. It was not enough to say that the king provided bad government. They needed to convince the white colonists that the American gentry would provide better government. One way that independence would be better is that they would deal with protecting people from slave rebellion and Indian attacks.

The people in villages across the colonies got the message: The gentry wanted to ease their racial anxiety and get rid of the king. In Huntington, New York, on Long Island, the citizens made an effigy of King George. Before they burned him, they blackened his face. And according to a New York City newspaper, they then stuck feathers in his wooden crown "like savages." Finally, they wrapped his body in the Union Jack before burning it.

Parkinson also describes a report in a Philadelphia newspaper where a white woman was upset because a black man refused to make way for her on the sidewalk. The man is reported to have said, "Stay, you damned white bitch, till Lord Dunmore and his black regiment come and then we will see who is to take the wall."[5] Lord Dunmore was the British appointed governor of Virginia. He had raised anxiety by offering to emancipate any slave who volunteered to fight to support British control over the colonies. Reports like this were widely distributed to stir up support for the war.

Even though the American Revolution and the establishment of constitutional government have racism as the foundation, the issues they dealt with and the approaches they took can help us clarify what a patchwork nation would look like and some of the issues it would face. Washington and Jefferson provide examples of the concerns of the founders for religious tolerance. The founders had both racial and religious diversity to contend with as they established the government of the new nation. Their approach to religious diversity established government structures that have made it possible for later generations to consider racial diversity within the framework of the Constitution.

WASHINGTON AND INTERFAITH TOLERANCE

In 1790, a delegation from the federal government, including George Washington and Thomas Jefferson, visited Rhode Island. Washington had just been elected president the year before. They were greeted in Rhode Island by leaders with religious diversity.

The religious diversity at their reception should not surprise us. Rhode Island was established in 1636 when Roger Williams, banished from the Massachusetts Bay Colony for his religious views, settled at the tip of Narragansett Bay on land purchased from the Narragansett tribe. He called the site "Providence Plantation" and declared it a place of religious freedom. Then in 1663, King Charles II granted a charter that provided for religious freedom. It stipulated that "no person should be in any way molested on account of religion."[6] Roger Williams became the pastor of the first church established in the colony. This Baptist congregation was soon followed by Quaker, Congregational, Presbyterian, and Episcopalian congregations. Religious freedom, however, did not include freedom for Catholics to worship during William's lifetime. This was granted only in 1780 because of the positive impression that French soldiers made during the Revolutionary War. Very few Catholics lived in Rhode Island until after the Revolutionary War.

Jews arrived in Rhode Island as early as 1658. They built a synagogue in 1763 that is still in use today. Moses Seixas, a leader of the Jewish synagogue Yeshuat Israel, was part of the local community welcoming Washington and his delegation in 1790. In his speech, Seixas said, "Deprived as we heretofore have been of the invaluable rights of free Citizens, we now (with a deep sense of gratitude to the Almighty disposer of all events) behold a Government, erected by the Majesty of the People—a Government, which to bigotry gives no sanction, to persecution no assistance—but generously affording to All liberty of conscience, and immunities of Citizenship: deeming every one, of whatever Nation, tongue, or language, equal parts of the great governmental Machine."[7]

This view that the Jews in the United States have "All liberty of conscience, and immunities of Citizenship" was shared by Washington. Following his visit to Rhode Island, Washington wrote to the Jewish congregation. The letter established the language for a pluralistic America, not limited to Christians. He wrote,

> The citizens of the United States of America have a right to applaud themselves having given to mankind examples of an enlarged and liberal policy—a policy worthy of imitation. All possess alike liberty of conscience and immunities of citizenship. It is now no more that toleration is spoken of as if it were the indulgence of one class of people that another enjoyed the exercise of their inherent natural rights, for, happily, the Government of the United States, which gives to bigotry no sanction, to persecution no assistance, requires only that they who live under its protection should demean themselves as good citizens in giving it on all occasions their effectual support.[8]

After thanking the Jewish community for its support of his administration, he continues, "May the children of the stock of Abraham who dwell in this land continue to merit and enjoy the good will of the other inhabitants— while every one shall sit in safety under his own vine and fig tree and there shall be none to make him afraid."[9] Washington's letter was widely distributed at the time. This exchange between the white gentry controlling the young government and a small Jewish community established a tradition of tolerating and protecting minorities. The Jews were not invited by Washington to be part of the new government beyond "giving it on all occasions their effectual support."

This desire for unity was the theme of Washington's Farewell Address:

> The unity of government which constitutes you one people is also now dear to you. It is justly so; for it is a main pillar in the edifice of your real independence, the support of your tranquility at home, your peace abroad, of your safety, of your prosperity, of that very liberty which you so highly prize. . . . Let me now take a more comprehensive view and warn you in the most solemn manner against the baneful effects of the spirit of party, generally. This spirit, unfortunately, is inseparable from our nature, having its root in the strongest passions of the human mind. It exists under different shapes in all governments, more or less stifled, controlled, or repressed; but in those of the popular form it is seen in its greatest rankness and is truly their worst enemy. . . . Sooner or later the chief of some prevailing faction, more able or more fortunate than his competitors, turns this disposition to the purposes of his own elevation on the ruins of public liberty.[10]

Washington's commitment to religious freedom provided a starting point for Americans to embrace diversity. Yet, as his Farewell Address shows, Washington was primarily concerned about unity. He was willing to have people worship as they wanted, but he did not want diversity to disrupt the unity of everyone accepting the government run by the wealthy gentry like himself.

JEFFERSON AND RELIGIOUS FREEDOM

From an early age, Jefferson connected his distaste for the British government with the Anglican Church. His biographer, Fawn Brodie, suspects that some of this may have come from his experience as a 14- and 15-year-old student of an Anglican clergyman, James Maury, immediately following the death of his father, Peter Jefferson. The elder Jefferson believed in religious freedom; Maury had the opposite view. One time Maury characterized a speech by a non-Anglican as "the frantick [sic] ravings of fanaticism, or artful fictions of imposture."[11]

Jefferson believed that one of his life's greatest accomplishments was authoring Virginia's Statute for Religious Freedom, which passed the Virginia General Assembly on January 16, 1786. The statute has the spirit and language of the 1st Amendment of the Constitution but was passed two years before the Constitution was ratified by the states. He obviously viewed it as an important accomplishment because he asked that it be engraved on his tombstone along with the fact that he authored the Declaration of Independence and founded the University of Virginia. The fact that he served as the third president of the United States didn't make it to his tombstone.

In his *Notes on the State of Virginia*, Jefferson wrote in 1790 that he proposed doing completely away with laws against apostasy and heresy.[12] He explained his reasoning for complete religious liberty,

> The rights of conscience we never submitted, we could not submit. We are answerable for them to our God. The legitimate powers of government extend to such acts only as are injurious to others. But it does me no injury for my neighbour to say there are twenty gods, or no god. It neither picks my pocket nor breaks my leg. If it be said, his testimony in a court of justice cannot be relied on, reject it then, and be the stigma on him. Constraint may make him worse by making him a hypocrite, but it will never make him a truer man. It may fix him obstinately in his errors, but will not cure them. Reason and free enquiry are the only effectual agents against error.[13]

Religious liberty continued to be an issue for Jefferson when he retired from public life and devoted himself to the establishment of the University of Virginia. His commitment to this work was largely motivated by a desire to educate gentlemen prepared for public service in his own image rather than that of the northern schools of Harvard and Yale. One criticism he had of the northern colleges was the role of religion. In his 2012 biography, Jon Meacham explains Jefferson's perspective this way: "As a politician and a devotee of republicanism, Jefferson hoped that subjecting religious sensibilities to free inquiry would transform faith from a source of contention into a force for good, for he knew that religion in one form or another was a perpetual factor in the world. The wisest course, then, was not to rail against it but to encourage the application of reason to questions of faith."[14]

In 1822, Anglicans, Baptists, Methodists, and others were putting pressure on Jefferson to make the teaching of Christianity a part of the curriculum by hiring a professor of divinity. Jefferson responded by offering them more than they asked for. He proposed that they could each build and fund their own school on the grounds of the university. "The library would be open to all, and officials would allow students the ability to attend classes of a sectarian nature as well as ordinary university courses—but always understanding," Jefferson wrote, "that these schools shall be independent of the University and of each other."[15] The various faith groups did not have the energy or resources to take Jefferson up on his offer, but this offer may be the first American example of an attempt to create a religious pluralistic community.

LOCKE AND RELIGION

The commitment on the part of the founders to enshrine the separation of church and state in the Constitution set the United States apart from the governments then current in Europe. Several of the colonies had experimented with various forms of religious tolerance. Even after the Constitution and Bill of Rights were adopted, however, a number of states continued to have official religions that were supported by the state governments. The Constitution did not forbid states from supporting religion. These states included Massachusetts, Connecticut, New Hampshire, South Carolina, and Georgia.

The decision to separate the roles of government and religion was a bold experiment. The founders, however, did not invent the idea. John Locke is probably responsible for first proposing this idea. Locke was a British philosopher and writer who was born in 1632. Between 1669 and 1675, he served in a capacity that today we would call a consultant to the colonists of Carolina. This included advising them on the Fundamental Constitution of Carolina: the document that established the government of the colony. The constitution makes provisions for Indians and people of other faiths, but it also establishes the Church of England as the responsibility of the government. The language is very clear: "It shall belong to the parliament to take care for the building of churches, and the public maintenance of divines, to be employed in the exercise of religion, according to the Church of England; which being the only true and orthodox and the national religion of all the King's dominions, is so also of Carolina; and, therefore, it alone shall be allowed to receive public maintenance, by grant of parliament."[16]

By 1689, Locke had changed his mind. In a pamphlet titled *A Letter Concerning Toleration*, he wrote, "I esteem it above all things necessary to distinguish exactly the business of civil government from that of religion and to settle the just bounds that lie between the one and the other." The sole purpose of government, he claims, is "for the procuring, preserving, and advancing" of civil interests. He explains, "Civil interests I call Life, Liberty, Health, and Indolency of Body; and the Possession of outward things, such as Money, Lands, Houses, Furniture, and the like."[17] Here we not only see the source of the Declaration of Independence's phrase "life, liberty, and the pursuit of happiness" but also the basis for the government not being responsible for ensuring correct religion.

It would be difficult to overstate the influence that Locke had on the thinking of the founders. He expanded his ideas on the role of government in a two-volume work titled *Two Treatises on Government*, also published in 1689. There he goes further and explains that if a king does not fulfill his responsibilities to provide good government by serving the civil interests, then the people have a right to rebel against the king.[18]

A FRENCH PERSPECTIVE

In the 1830s, Alexis de Tocqueville published his two volumes of *Democracy in America*. Tocqueville, a pioneer in the study of sociology, visited the United States specifically to learn about the social systems. He was particularly interested in how different groups related to the government. He picked up the discussion that Washington began:

> Parties are a necessary evil in free governments; but they have not at all times the same character and the same propensities. . . . Minor parties, on the other hand, are generally deficient in political good faith. As they are not sustained or dignified by lofty purposes, they ostensibly display the selfishness of their character in their actions. They glow with a factitious zeal; their language is vehement, but their conduct is timid and irresolute. The means which they employ are as wretched as the end at which they aim.[19]

The desire to establish a unity without "minor parties" was partly because political philosophers did not think of an alternative. Politicians could only think in terms of the blanket of white dominance that Jackson described. As the number of nonwhites who vote has increased, their role has been to support that unity by getting behind one white party or another. This was the plan of the Northern Republicans after emancipation for the black vote in the South. Later the white Democrats in the South argued that they had the interests of blacks at heart. Jackson called for something very different with his proposal for a patchwork paradigm, where there would be full participation by all races in the political process.

PROPOSALS FOR NONWHITE PARTICIPATION SINCE THE 1960s

New ideas for ways to establish American unity controlled by whites continue to surface as political philosophers struggle with the question of what it means to be an American. One example is John Rawls's proposal for Americans to adopt his theory of justice. Another is the melting pot proposal. A third proposal is that interest groups work out compromises that result in unity.

Rawls published his massive *A Theory of Justice* in 1971 and then revised it several times. Like most of the founders, he starts with the theory of a social contract where we all give up some of our liberty to establish a government. But he proposes a slightly different goal for our participation in this social contract. He rejects the idea of self-interest and giving up our liberties to ensure personal protection that the founders had proposed. "Rather, the guiding idea is that the principles of justice for the basic structure of society are the object of the original agreement."[20] If our goal is justice in forming a government, then we are still left with the question of how to do it. Rawls proposes that there are two principles. The first is that everyone has equality in basic rights and duties. The second principle is that decisions that result in unequal distributions of wealth and authority are made by determining "if they result in compensating benefits for everyone, and particularly for the least advantaged members of society."[21]

Rawls tries to solve the problem of creating unity by defining a moral criterion. He proposed fairness. Fairness then becomes a blanket that defines how decisions are made. Kennan Ferguson criticizes this proposal because it attempts to establish rules that everyone must follow. The resulting unity demands that every cultural expression would come to exactly the same understanding of what is fair. Yet fairness is a moral category defined differently by different groups.[22] This illustrates the problem of trying to design a vision for America's future based on rules. The patchwork paradigm proposes that participation, not rules, is the starting point. Then policies and practices grow out of the full participation of all groups.

Another stream of political philosophy comes under the category of "melting pot." This is not at all what Jackson had in mind. In its most sophisticated form, the melting pot proposal is that various ethnic and racial groups bring their cultures to North America where they get stirred into the American experience and both the new group and America become changed into a new America that is better than before. A variation on the melting pot proposal was suggested by Arthur Schlesinger Jr., an historian who served as advisor to President Kennedy. Schlesinger worried, "*What is it that holds a nation together?*" (italics in original).[23] He believed that America will shatter with a plurality of ethnicities. He claims that the history of America is that people from various cultures have created a uniquely American culture with a "unifying vision of individuals from all nations melted into a new race."[24] Schlesinger does not ask that people completely give up cultural identities. Rather, he wants us to be Americans first and any other identity after that. This proposal has one of the same difficulties as Rawls's proposal: if everyone is required to have the same values to be an American, then there is a blanket that smothers nonwhite perspectives. The patchwork paradigm does not begin with a search for a way to find or develop shared values. In a patchwork nation, values come from our cultural identities. Full participation, not imposed values, is the source of our national unity.

Nathan Glazer and Daniel Moynihan studied the culture and politics of New York City. They titled their 1963 study *Beyond the Melting Pot: The Negroes, Puerto Ricans, Jews, Italians, and Irish of New York City*. Their perspective is that, in New York City, the various ethnic and racial groups "are also *interest groups*" (italics in original). These interest groups are always shifting in both their membership and culture. They point out that ethnic groups "even after distinctive language, customs, and culture are lost, as they largely were in the second generation, and even more fully in the third generation, are continually recreated by new experiences in America."[25] According to Glazer and Moynihan, the result of the maintenance of ethnic and racial groups is that "all policies in the city are inevitably policies for ethnic and race relations."[26] Glazer, who grew up in New York City, continued his academic career with positions at Harvard and Berkeley, where his writings sometimes express a disappointment that there has not been more success in the integration of blacks and others into white society. He expressed this hope explicitly in 1970: "All the work of incorporating Negroes, as a group and as individuals, into a common society—economically, culturally, socially, politically—must be pushed as hard as possible."[27]

Moynihan, who only wrote one chapter and helped with the conclusion of *Beyond the Melting Pot*, went on to apply his understanding of coalitions and competing interests in a career as a politician. He was elected to represent New York in the Senate for three terms beginning in 1976. Moynihan's success in applying the philosophy of competing interest groups to politics is impressive. He successfully organized coalitions not only to win elections but also to advance legislation. There are, however, a number of problems with the competing interests model. First, it creates winners and losers. In a coalition, the losers need to receive just enough to keep them in the coalition, but the winners will always be those with power. The interests of whites will always be protected. The second problem is that it begins with self-interest. The difference between a patchwork quilt and coalition model is that the patchwork paradigm is based on offering gifts rather than compromises of self-interest. The patchwork quilt is about contributing and giving rather than getting and taking.

VALUES NOT PRAGMATISM

Jackson's 1988 speech explained that the thread that holds the patches together is not pragmatism. He challenged the delegates and all Americans to let our morals guide our politics. This is a critical distinction between the patchwork quilt and the white paradigm. Jackson starts with identity groups—patches. The groups are the source of morals that contribute to the collective determination of basic moral principles. Jackson proposed basic principles: "international law . . . human rights . . . self-determination . . . economic development."[28] The list in Jackson's speech is the starting point for a fulfilled civil rights dream: a global perspective, commitment to universal rights, respect for individual differences, and equality of economic opportunity. The patchwork paradigm is contrasted with what Jackson called *pragmatism*. The political pragmatist sees races and identity groups as special interests that need to be accommodated. According to the logic of pragmatism, some groups can be completely ignored because they are either too small to matter or they do not have a political alternative. The patchwork paradigm starts by affirming the importance of every identity group.

Recognizing that nonwhites bring gifts rather than competing interests is an idea that has its roots in the life work of William James. James is most often remembered as the father of American psychology and as a philosopher. Important as those contributions were, they pale in comparison to his insights regarding pluralism. After an experience of spending a week at Lake Chautauqua in 1896, he recognized the importance of diversity. At first, he was excited about the community because it seemed idyllic. There were learning opportunities for people of all ages, health facilities, and an orderly environment. Rather than strife and conflict, he observed "unfettered thought, humanistic concern, and brotherly fellowship."[29] But James realized after a week that there was something missing. The community didn't have the vitality and excitement that naturally comes from a diversity of perspectives.

James wasn't committed to a pluralist perspective just because he considered it more interesting. In his psychology textbook, he pointed out that each person has a particular perspective—a world. James understood that each of us has a set of beliefs. In his 1890 book on psychology, he is interested in how that plays out for us individually.[30] Before recent advances in social psychology, James saw that each person constructs a "world" that results from experiences. If we have diverse experiences, then our world is richer.

The diversity that James longed for was not simply a variety of opinions, which were missing at Lake Chautauqua. He missed relating to those who are different. Patchwork pluralism has diversity of participation, but it is not just participation—it is "full" participation. At Chautauqua, this would have involved a diverse participation in the people who attended, the people who presented from the stage, the people who planned events and invited speakers, and the people who managed the facilities and planned for the development of the grounds. James used the word *pluralism* in the same way that Jackson used *patchwork*.

TOLERANCE, PLURALISM, AND RELIGION

Princeton sociologist of religion Robert Wuthnow points out that up until the end of the 20th century, "American Christians have thought of themselves as the reigning power and the dominant cultural influence. . . . Tolerance proceeded without having to carry the burden of genuine interreligious understanding or interaction. . . . Yet in another sense the new religious diversity posed a challenge that would not so easily be met. This was the challenge of having to rethink the presumption that America itself was basically Christian (or Judeo-Christian)."[31]

This description of Christians relating to people of other religions is also true for whites relating to nonwhites. There are three possible postures that can be taken regarding others who are different. The first is intolerance or bigotry. This posture says, "I am right and others should become like me. If they can't become like me, then they are not fully human." The second posture is that of tolerance. This posture says, "I am correct and others are wrong, but I allow them the freedom to hold their opinion." The third posture is pluralism. Pluralists would say, "I have my belief that I am committed to, but I recognize that others hold different beliefs that are as valid for them as my beliefs are for me." The patchwork form of pluralism adds one more dimension. It includes the concept that in our shared institutions, others' beliefs have contributions to make to our common good. This means that, when I engage with others, I bring the conviction of my beliefs. Just as it brings me pleasure to gain new ideas and insights from the opinions of others, I am fulfilled when others find my contributions helpful.

This form of pluralism can be illustrated by religion. Religion can be divisive, but it doesn't need to be. A desire to convert others to one's point of view is present in proponents of many religions, political parties, and social movements. As long as this is not accompanied by intolerance—a rejection of the humanity of others—it is not a problem. Pope Francis would like to see everyone in the world become Roman Catholic, but this is not a problem for a patchwork nation because he does not reject the humanity of those who will not. This is illustrated by his reception of the American Jewish Committee at the Vatican, where among other things he said it is "important to find ways in which Jews and Christians can cooperate in constructing a more just and fraternal world." He called this effort "a true religious obligation."[32] From a civil rights perspective, the problem occurs when a group is unwilling to learn from others and claims superiority in a way that denies the humanity of another group.[33]

BACKLASH THEN AND NOW

As I mentioned above, Jackson's speech received immediate backlash. The Democratic convention continued. On Wednesday night, July 21, 1988, the governor of Arkansas, Bill Clinton, gave a very strange nomination speech for Michael Dukakis. R. W. Apple Jr., writing in the *New York Times*, described the speech as "the calamity that befell the man chosen to state the prime-time case for Mr. Dukakis, his friend Bill Clinton, the young Governor of Arkansas. . . . For reasons that few here could fathom, he prepared an 18-page speech, far too long, and read almost every word of it in a damp style that lost his audience within the first couple of minutes. . . . When he finally finished, his reputation as an orator was in ruins and all of the enthusiasm in the hall had been dissipated."[34]

With the passing of the possibility that a black man would capture the nomination, the white leadership lost all interest in incorporating the message that had attracted voters to Jackson. Clinton talked about himself and how both he and Dukakis had lost elections. He claimed a close friendship with Dukakis and testified to Dukakis's personal character with examples like "he mows his own lawn with a hand-powered mower."[35] Clinton was like the best man making a toast at the wedding of his fraternity brother. He talked about himself as much as he talked about Dukakis. And he talked too long. For Clinton and the white leadership, this was a time to celebrate that the threat to the "old boys' club" had been disposed of. It was back to politics as usual, controlled by whites. Clinton's speech confused the delegates. They interrupted him repeatedly, not with applause but with demonstrations. The general consensus was that the speech was an opportunity for Clinton to establish himself as a national leader and that he failed.

What kept Clinton from building on the speech that Jackson gave? Why didn't he say clearly that the patchwork quilt image is exactly what he and Dukakis hoped for America? Why didn't Clinton celebrate the role of the Jackson delegates in formulating the Democratic platform? He could have talked about a Dukakis presidency with a patchwork cabinet. I didn't see the speech on television; I only read about it in the newspaper. Reading the text now, more than 25 years later, I believe that the speech was brilliant from the perspective of political pragmatism. Clinton shifted the focus of the convention from Jackson's energetic passion for justice and full inclusion. He prepared the Democratic Party and the nation to embrace Dukakis as a man who deserved to be president because of his character, not because of his vision. In this, Clinton was doing much more than reestablishing the tone of the convention. He was clarifying the dominant role of white politics. Without making a reference to the blanket in Jackson's speech, Clinton made it clear that Jackson had not fundamentally changed the Democratic Party. Clinton affirmed the alternative blanket imagery—of everyone sleeping under a blanket of white supremacy.

ENGLISH-ONLY BACKLASH

Realizing the civil rights dream for America of a patchwork quilt nation requires celebration of language as an essential component of culture. Spanish-speaking Americans have come under attack from white supremacists, but members of the liberal establishment have also expressed concerns about America being a land of multiple languages. This was one of Schlesinger's concerns.

The English-only movement goes back at least as far as Benjamin Franklin. It proposes that the English language is part of the essential nature of being American. Sociologists who study different language communities have discovered something quite different. Put in the strongest terms, making

English the only language in an educational setting destroys the possibility of developing a pluralistic society. As Donaldo Macedo explains, "Bilingual education offers us not only a great opportunity to democratize our schools but is itself a utopian pedagogy."[36] He uses the language of Paulo Freire, who demonstrated by his work teaching people in Brazil that empowering people with their mother tongue in an educational setting provides a context for them to develop their self-identity. English-only policies deny students the full use of their mother tongue to form their self-identity. Children with a non-English mother tongue are damaged psychologically when they learn the stereotypes in English that they come from a culture that is backward, barbaric, uncivilized, and unintelligent. Macedo translated Paulo Freire's *The Politics of Education: Culture, Power and Liberation*. Freire points out that "it is not education that molds society to certain standards, but society that forms itself by its own standards and molds education to conform with those values that sustain it."[37] The English-only movement is an example of a racist desire to deny the validity of cultural expressions that are not white.

DREAM OF A PATCHWORK QUILT NATION

Jackson ended his speech with the plea, "Keep hope alive. Keep hope alive! Keep hope alive! On tomorrow night and beyond, keep hope alive!"[38] The hope that Jackson wanted to keep alive is the hope of the civil rights dream. It is a dream that has no historical precedent or contemporary example. It is a dream that goes beyond multiculturalism, where different cultures live side by side. History provides examples of nations where a variety of cultural expressions were tolerated. For example, the Ottoman Empire during some periods aspired to a multiculturalism where Christians and Jews had certain rights, but they were second-class citizens under Muslims. The Roman Republic included a rich mix of languages and cultures, but those cultures were not integrated into a unified nation. Modern nations have also failed to produce an example of Jackson's dream. The Soviet Union included a wide variety of cultures within its borders, but when leaders in Moscow lost their will to use violence to hold the union together, people chose not to try to create a multicultural nation. The possibility of a patchwork democracy that was Gandhi's dream for India was shattered by violence and the separation of Pakistan and Bangladesh from India.

As we saw in chapter 2, the expression of the civil rights dream has a history. In each period of our history, the dream has been to expand participation in our national life and to identify strategies that promote the pursuit of happiness for more people. The 21st century is no different. The civil rights dream needs to address both full participation of all groups and the elimination of barriers that individuals experience because they are nonwhite. So half of the civil rights dream is creating a nation where *barriers to fulfilling individual aspirations are no greater for one person than another.*

Replacing the white paradigm with the patchwork paradigm addresses the second issue of participation in our national life. The complete statement of the civil rights dream for the 21st century is that *America will be a nation where every race, ethnicity, and identity group has full participation in the political, economic, and cultural life of the nation so that the barriers to fulfilling individual aspirations are no greater for one person than another.* Section 2 examines how racism functions to prevent full participation and create barriers. But first, chapter 5 examines why addressing racism is an absolute necessity.

Chapter 5

White Cultural Dominance Is Not Working

A friend recently introduced me to a middle-aged white woman at a party. I'll call her Ann. When my friend mentioned that I was writing a book about racism, Ann looked tense and began, "Don't you think there is too much emphasis on race?" Before I could respond, she went on, "Racism has almost disappeared. Just look at the young people. If we will stop talking about it, it will go away completely. All this talk about race is making things worse." Obviously, she was not interested in my answer to her first question. Ann's attitude is not unusual among whites in the early 21st century.

WHITES DON'T SEE A PROBLEM

For Ann and many whites like her, there are reasons to think that race can be ignored. At the beginning of the 21st century, race relations appeared to be stable. In 2008, Barack Obama became the first African American president. Rev. Al Sharpton was promoted by the white media as the voice of African Americans. He was an early supporter and later defender of Obama. Sharpton's message on the white media was that blacks should celebrate that an African American was elected president. Sharpton called on blacks to remain peaceful and use the political system. He advocated lobbying Congress and became an advisor to Obama. The strongest opposition to the first black president came from Tea Party Republicans, but they generally used coded language to avoid making explicit racist criticisms of Obama. Other blacks were on the sports TV channels explaining basketball and football. It is easy to see why Ann thought that racism had almost disappeared.

Ann's views were held by a majority of whites in 2015. A survey by the Pew Research Center asked Americans to identify items they saw as top policy priorities. Just under half of respondents checked "addressing race relations." This put race relations below 14 other priorities. By contrast, 76 percent checked "terrorism," and 75 percent thought that the economy should be one of the top priorities for Congress and President Obama. This survey was conducted in January of 2015—shortly after the shooting of Michael Brown in Ferguson, Missouri, brought racism to the national consciousness. In similar surveys in 2013 and 2014, addressing race relations didn't even make the list of issues Americans thought should be priorities for Congress and the president.[1]

Avoiding the conversation helps preserve whites' self-image. Derald Wing Sue points out that "keeping the oppression from being acknowledged and enforcing a conspiracy of silence allows oppressors to (1) maintain their innocence (guilt-free); and (2) leave inequities from being challenged."[2] The silence is justified in part because of the belief that all barriers have been removed so that nonwhites can succeed if they want to. Any inequities are blamed on the deficiencies of nonwhites.[3]

A survey conducted in early 2016 by the Pew Research Center found that about 38 percent of whites believe that enough changes have already been made to provide equal rights for blacks. An equal number thought that America is moving in a direction that will eventually make the necessary changes needed for blacks to have equal rights. Only 11 percent expressed doubt that America will achieve equal rights for blacks and whites.[4] The study also found that 57 percent of whites with annual family incomes of $75,000 or more "report that they are very satisfied with the quality of life in their community." In contrast, only 34 percent of blacks with the same incomes are satisfied with their quality of life. In short, whites in America generally think things are just fine. They like race relations the way they are. Ann's desire not to talk about race could be called the "if it isn't broken, don't fix it" approach. That would be nice if it wasn't actually broken, but it is.

As Algernon Austin points out in *America Is Not Post-Racial: Xenophobia, Islamophobia, Racism, and the 44th President*, "The first step in solving a problem is admitting that one has a problem. The alacrity with which individuals declared that Obama's election signified that America is post-racial shows that many Americans do not wish to admit that we have a problem. In fact, they are eager to engage in denial about prejudice and discrimination in America."[5] Is racism a problem? Or are whites right and we should just ignore racism?

EVIDENCE FOR THE PROBLEM

What is broken? What do people of color know that whites are overlooking? The best way to know if all groups enjoy full participation in American society is to look at the outcomes. Are all groups treated fairly, and do they have equal opportunity? The systems of criminal justice, education, and the economy demonstrate that we have not come very far since the 1960s. The gaps in social indicators demonstrate that white cultural dominance is not working. These gaps, however, are not the problem. The gaps are only indicators—or symptoms. They are useful because we will know that we are making progress in eliminating racism as the gaps disappear.

The chronic disease of racism in society, much like a disease in the body, has symptoms. And like disease in our body, we can only know that the disease is gone from our society when the symptoms are no longer present. Taking the analogy one step farther, any given symptom must be interpreted. A pain in the arm, for example, could mean something as serious as a heart attack or as harmless as exercising too hard. Societal symptoms also have multiple possible meanings.

A sociological study, for example, might discover that Mexican Americans are more likely to enjoy spicy foods than Anglo Americans. This does not make eating spicy food a symptom of racism. Mexican Americans, however, are also less likely to complete college once they begin than white students; this *is* a symptom of racism. By measuring and observing the symptoms of racism like the rate of college graduation, we will know when racism is being addressed. Some symptoms are subtle and difficult to measure. Consider this example: a white man says to Hispanics when the elevator door opens and the elevator is half full, "I'll wait for the next elevator," then another elevator door opens and the man gets on a crowded elevator full of whites. Was the white man expressing a disdain for Hispanic Americans? Or, when the next elevator came, was it a case of being tired of waiting for an empty elevator?

The symptoms of racism are constantly changing, so care must be taken to identify meaningful symptoms. Until 1865, the most visible symptom of racism was slavery in southern states and segregation in the rest of the nation. Until the 1960s, the most visible symptom of racism was called Jim Crow, with both legal and cultural privileges reserved for people with white skin. Today the most obvious and visible symptoms of racism are white supremacist activity and schemes to make it difficult for nonwhites to vote. These are symptoms of racism that cannot be denied.

In addition to the obvious symptoms of racism, social scientists have studied the emerging symptoms of racism in three particular areas: criminal justice, education, and economic opportunity. The question is the same in all three areas: Do Americans benefit from having white skin?

CRIMINAL JUSTICE

Michelle Alexander, in her book *The New Jim Crow: Mass Incarceration in the Age of Colorblindness*, builds an iron-clad case that the criminal justice system is not working, and the root cause is racism. She starts with the inequity of the outcome. For example, it is estimated that, in the nation's capital, three out of four young black men can expect to serve time in prison. In some poor neighborhoods, that figure is almost 100 percent.[6] She then shows that the criminal justice system is not only based on racism but also supports racism across society.

The National Association for the Advancement of Colored People (NAACP) has a long history of legal advocacy for civil rights and identifies criminal justice as one of its focus areas. The NAACP website features a fact sheet that addresses the question of whether the justice system is working. Here are a few of the facts they compiled:

- African Americans now constitute nearly 1 million of the total 2.3 million incarcerated population.
- African Americans are incarcerated at nearly six times the rate of whites.
- Together, African Americans and Hispanics comprised 58 percent of all prisoners in 2008, even though African Americans and Hispanics make up approximately one-quarter of the U.S. population.
- According to Unlocking America, if African American and Hispanics were incarcerated at the same rates as whites, today's prison and jail populations would decline by approximately 50 percent.
- One in 100 African American women are in prison.
- Nationwide, African Americans represent 26 percent of juvenile arrests, 44 percent of youth who are detained, 46 percent of youth who are judicially waived to criminal court, and 58 percent of youth admitted to state prisons.
- Five times more whites than African Americans are using drugs, yet African Americans are sent to prison for drug offenses at 10 times the rate of whites.
- African Americans represent 12 percent of the total population of drug users but 38 percent of those arrested for drug offenses and 59 percent of those in state prison for a drug offense.
- Of children grades 7 to 12 who have been suspended or expelled at some point in their school careers, 35 percent are black compared to 20 percent Hispanics and 15 percent whites.[7]

Behind the statistics are the specific cases where the criminal justice system is not working. Lisa Bloom, an attorney and civil rights activist, was sent by NBC News and MSNBC to Sanford, Florida, to report on the trial of George Zimmerman. On February 26, 2012, Zimmerman shot an unarmed 17-year-old African American, Trayvon Martin. Bloom reported how the criminal justice system had failed to provide justice for the non-white community. The Zimmerman trial started with a jury selection process that resulted in a jury made up exclusively of women—some of whom had racist attitudes. One juror was completely confused by the process, and Bloom enumerates 11 additional failures of the system, including the fact that the prosecution did not seriously attempt to convict Zimmerman. The

Zimmerman case shows in detail what is happening in thousands of unreported cases where the criminal justice system is failing to provide justice for the nonwhite community.[8]

After Michael Brown Jr. was shot by police officer Darren Wilson on August 9, 2014, Missouri governor Jay Nixon established a blue-ribbon commission to conduct a "wide-ranging, in-depth study of the underlying issues brought to light by the events in Ferguson." The commission noted that "for policy and training changes to take hold, there must also be a change in law enforcement culture."[9] This is based on the evidence that the system is not working for the nonwhite population. Examples just from the town of Ferguson include the following:

- Black residents were 68 percent less likely than others to have their cases dismissed by the municipal judge.
- African Americans were at least 50 percent more likely to have their cases lead to an arrest warrant.
- Black residents accounted for 92 percent of cases in which an arrest warrant was issued.
- Black citizens accounted for
  - 95 percent of all "manner of walking" charges,
  - 94 percent of all "failure to comply" charges,
  - 92 percent of all "resisting arrest" charges,
  - 92 percent of all "peace disturbance" charges, and
  - 89 percent of all "failure to obey" charges.

About one-third of the residents in Ferguson are white, yet they hardly show up in the statistics of police activity. The pattern we have described within the criminal justice system is also endemic in the education system, which we will explore next.[10]

EDUCATION

African American Allan Golston is the president of the U.S. Program of the Bill and Melinda Gates Foundation. He wrote in an Urban League report, "My own parents raised my siblings and me to embrace the challenges and opportunities available to us through education. They taught us that education wasn't just important—it was vital. It was the path that we would travel to make a better life for ourselves, just as they had." In that report, he laments that today black students do not have the same level of achievement as white students. While the national high school graduation rate is 82 percent, only 73 percent of African Americans graduate from high school. This statistic hides a far greater problem. Research supported by the Gates

Foundation uncovered that only 12 percent of black high school graduates who decide to go to college are ready to succeed without taking remediation courses. This means that for the vast majority of black high school graduates, obtaining a college degree requires paying tuition for instruction in basic skills courses that are part of a quality high school education.[11]

Jawanza Kunjufu has spent years as a consultant working with schools that have a high number of African American students. He says, "Public schools that serve low-income communities are not all the same; however, I find the same problems over and over again in schools that are failing African American students. The usual culprits are as follows: poor school leadership, low teacher expectations, low student time on task, irrelevant curriculums, an abundance of left-brain lesson plans, an individualistic vs. communal student approach, and coed classrooms."[12] Kunjufu asks, "If America were serious about closing the achievement gap and eliminating classism, should not the students in regular, remedial, and special ed receive the best teachers, smaller student-teacher ratios, and an advanced curriculum and pedagogy?"[13]

The inequities are evident in the achievement of high school graduates. Student outcomes can be measured in many different ways. The chart below shows the difference in achievement of various subgroups when they graduate from high school. This data is from a sample of 11 states where extensive data was collected.[14]

Table 5.1 Percentage of students proficient in mathematics and reading

Percentage of students proficient in mathematics	
Race/ethnicity	%
Asian/Pacific Islander	47
White	33
Two or more races	26
American Indian/Alaskan Native	12
Hispanic	12
Black	7
Percentage of students proficient in reading	
Race/ethnicity	%
Asian/Pacific Islander	47
White	47
Two or more races	38
American Indian/Alaskan Native	26
Hispanic	23
Black	16

Source: National Center for Education Statistics, "Public School Graduates and Dropouts from the Common Core of Data: School Year 2009–10," January 22, 2013, http://nces.ed.gov/pubsearch/pubsinfo.asp?pubid=2013309rev.

These statistics are for students who reach the 12th grade and graduate. Data collected by the Department of Education shows gaps in those who achieve high school graduation.[15] Across the nation, the graduation rate for Asian/Pacific Islander students was 93.5 percent. The rates for other groups were 83 percent for white students, 71.4 percent for Hispanic students, 69.1 percent for American Indian/Alaska Native students, and 66.1 percent for black students.

The dropout rate is a strong indicator of the failure of the education system to meet the needs of all students. As Secretary of Education Arne Duncan said when he announced the results of the Civil Rights Data Collection (CRDC),

> Our deep concern for equity and closing opportunity gaps drives everything we do at the Department. From access to high-quality preschool, to turning around low-performing schools, to ensuring access to college and career-ready coursework, our work is motivated by the belief that all students, regardless of race, gender, income, disability, and English Learner status, need and deserve a world-class education. Unfortunately, the overarching conclusion of the CRDC is that the everyday educational experience for far too many students of color, students with disabilities, and English Learners falls short of meeting the American promise that if you work hard and study hard, you will have a fair shot to succeed. The CRDC shows we have come a long way yet still have a long way to go before our education system truly provides equal opportunities.[16]

It would be impossible to claim that the American system of education results in the same outcome for all groups of children. Some have argued, however, that the varying outcomes for students result from socioeconomic, class, culture, or other demographic and environmental characteristics. They claim that academic outcomes are determined by factors that are outside the control of the school. The premise of this book is that—regardless of a child's circumstance in life—it is the role of the education system in cooperation with families and communities to give every child the same opportunity for a high-quality education. The white paradigm is not working when it comes to providing a quality education for all Americans.

ECONOMY

Finally, the American economy has far from equal outcomes. There is no economic data to back up the 38 percent of whites who think we have done enough as a nation to ensure equal economic participation by everyone. Since 1975, the Urban League has issued an annual *State of Black America* report. In 2016, the report included a section that looked at changes over the previous 40 years. The statistics are clear. The report summarized economic progress:

- With every economic downturn, communities of color bore the brunt of the decline.
- Black Americans remained nearly twice as likely as whites to be unemployed.
- Since 1976, the black unemployment rate has consistently remained about twice that of the white rate across time, regardless of educational attainment.
- Black Americans are only slightly less likely to live in poverty today than they were in 1976.[17]

These statistics make it impossible to claim that things are getting better for black Americans. The story is the same for Hispanics and other non-whites. Gaps are not only in income and employment. A Pew Research Center study using 2014 data discovered that "the current gap between blacks and whites has reached its highest point since 1989, when whites had 17 times the wealth of black households. The current white-to-Hispanic wealth ratio has reached a level not seen since 2001."[18] Chuck Collins, a senior scholar at the Institute for Policy Studies, reviewed data about the wealth gap and reported, "The Great Recession deepened the longstanding racial and ethnic wealth divide in the United States. The typical white family held a net worth six times greater than the typical black family at the end of the 20th century. That gap has now doubled. The wealth gap between white and Latino households has widened as well."[19]

The economic prospects for nonwhites did not improve greatly during the last half of the 20th century and the early years of the 21st century. What are the prospects for the future? Are whites who think we are on a path to equity correct? In 2016, Collins joined Dedrick Asante-Muhammed, Josh Hoxie, and Emanuel Nieves in updating the study of the wealth gap between whites and nonwhites. They discovered that, unless something is done, the gap in wealth between whites and nonwhites will go from large to extremely large. Between 1983 and 2013, "the average wealth of white families has grown by 84 percent—1.2 times the rate of growth for the Latino population and three times the rate of growth for the Black population. If the past 30 years were to repeat, the next three decades would see the average wealth of White households increase by over $18,000 per year, while Latino and Black households would see their respective wealth increase by about $2,250 and $750 per year."[20]

Looking ahead, things are not working their way toward equality. "If the average Black family wealth continues to grow at the same pace it has over the past three decades, it would take Black families 228 years to amass the same amount of wealth White families have today." That is the wealth white families have today, not the wealth they would have in 228 years. "For the average Latino family, it would take 84 years to amass the same amount of wealth White families have today." They conclude: "In the absence of significant reforms to large-scale public policies that currently exacerbate racial and economic inequality, closing the racial wealth divide will not happen anytime soon."[21]

The statistical economic inequality between whites and nonwhites is undeniable. This leads us to a question of what would happen if we decided to do away with inequality. Do whites need to fear that they will fall to the bottom of the economy if racism were to no longer provide special privileges for their children? Is the hidden message in all the talk by politicians about equal opportunity for nonwhites really a signal that whites should look forward to accepting their fair share of the burden of poverty? Do the laws of economics create a zero-sum game where someone needs to be at the bottom?

Another way that people sometimes deny the influence of race on economic inequity is by arguing that this is the very best we can do. I heard a version of this argument from one of the black leaders at the small Full Gospel Tabernacle Church in Old Saybrook, Connecticut. To a congregation that was all black (except for me), he explained, "I praise God that my ancestors were captured by slave traders and suffered a terrible voyage and life in slavery. Because of their suffering, I live in the United States of America. I am so blessed compared to those who are still left in Africa." Another form of this argument is the very questionable claim that the poor in the United States today live better than royalty in the past. Could a credible argument be made that the current racist environment that limits the full participation of people of color actually produces the greatest good for the greatest number of people? Does the inequity produce a wealthy white class that then ensures the best possible lives for nonwhites?

Sam Pizzigati addresses these questions in his book *Greed and Good: Understanding and Overcoming the Inequality That Limits Our Lives*. He explains the general outline for the justification for inequity. There are three basic ideas: First, only if people are greedy will there be incentives to work hard and become wealthy. Second, those who become wealthy deserve their good fortune. And third, "we all benefit when some of us become far wealthier than others, when the greedy fulfill their ambitions to become rich."[22] Pizzigati looks at each of these ideas and provides evidence that each is flawed. While incentives are important in many ways, he points out that they are always in context. Since the election of Ronald Reagan in 1980, there has been a well-documented transfer of wealth to 1 percent of the American population.[23] Pizzigati shows that the context of the multimillion-dollar incomes received annually by corporate leaders have little to do with their actual performance and nothing to do with the economic context that 99 percent of Americans experience. As Pizzigati points out, would anyone really think that an executive with a possible annual income of $100 million is going to work 10 times harder than an executive who only has a shot at making $10 million a year?[24]

The idea that people who have accumulated America's wealth deserve it is also impossible to defend. Corporations have generated huge profits since 1980, but that does not mean that the top executives are deserving of an exaggerated portion of these profits. According to Henry Blodget, the editor of the popular website *Business Insider*, Walmart made a before-tax income of $22 billion in 2010, and CEO Mike Dukes was paid more than $6 million. There were 1.4 million Walmart employees in the United States during that same year, about 1 percent of the total U.S. workforce. With the average Walmart employee making about $21,000 per year, the CEO received more than 280 times an associate's salary.[25] Since 2010, things have only gotten worse. In 2015, the total pay to top executives at Walmart was more than $72 million. The new CEO, Douglas McMillon, was paid almost $20 million. This means the CEO was paid almost 1,000 times what a cashier was paid.[26]

Although it makes no sense to think that one person's contribution to an organization is 1,000 times greater than another person's, we do know something about what makes companies become great. Jim Collins spent five years studying companies and discovered that successful leaders "channel their ego needs away from themselves and into the larger goal of building a great company . . . their ambition is first and foremost for the institution, not themselves."[27] Second, Collins says that becoming a great company requires what he calls "getting the right people on the bus." He "found no systematic pattern linking executive compensation to the shift from good to great" companies.[28] Organizations are successful because of a collective effort. Everyone is important. We don't need a few very wealthy CEOs to make corporate America successful.

The closing argument is the one that really matters. Is it true that we all benefit because there are a small number of extremely wealthy people? Who would support the arts? Who would give money for cancer research? Who would support institutions of higher education? Pizzigati looked at the numbers and concluded, "The more wealth concentrates, the fewer the dollars that make their way to good causes."[29] Good causes are only half of the justification for allowing the rich to become filthy rich. Don't rich people create all the new jobs? Do poor people build factories? Pizzigati goes on to document the real costs of economic inequity. Rather than everyone benefiting, it is more accurate to say that everyone—including the rich—are losers. This includes limits on economic growth, stress on the environment, decreasing health, and more. But the most devastating impact of the concentration of wealth is that it has destroyed the middle class. With well-paying jobs disappearing in the middle, poor people have no possibility of moving up. Because the rich use their economic and political power to keep the rewards of increased productivity to themselves, the middle class does not expand and the poor are stuck in their poverty.

I have known Pizzigati since the mid-1970s when he edited a nonprofit weekly newspaper and I was the United Methodist minister in Newfield just outside of Ithaca, New York. He was, as he still is, a tireless advocate for the poor. I remember going to a Newfield town council meeting with him. He explained to the elected officials that the request from the cable company to raise the monthly rates they charged was the same as raising taxes on the low-income people who lived in a trailer park where TV antennas were not an option. In Newfield, he was always the first one to smell an injustice. So in 2013, over a lasagna dinner at his home in Silver Spring, Maryland, I asked him, "Did you know in 1976 that the concentration of wealth was going to be such a bad idea?" He pointed out that back then we focused on the injustice of poverty, but it did not occur to us that the middle class could ever be threatened. The goal was to move the poor into the middle class. After World War II, our parents set to work to build lives for themselves and their children. Income tax rates were as high as 91 percent for top earners. And investment income was taxed at the same rates as earned income. Even Pizzigati didn't see what was coming just before the election of Reagan. The idea that the middle class could be decimated was not even considered. The idea never came to mind.

Does the concentration of wealth mean that poverty is with us and it is just a matter of whether it is whites or nonwhites who are poor? Pizzigati answered that question in his 2012 book, *The Rich Don't Always Win: The Forgotten Triumph over Plutocracy That Created the American Middle Class, 1900–1970.* The important lesson is that the current system based on racism that is designed to keep nonwhites from full participation in the economy is not working. Whites who instinctually turn to racism because they fear an economic challenge from nonwhites misunderstand the danger they face. The threat to white middle-class prosperity is not nonwhites. The threat comes from the wealthy who continue to expand their wealth and power. The white paradigm that justifies unequal participation in the economic system is founded on racism. Eliminating racism, therefore, is an essential component in reestablishing a strong middle class. All races have a stake in an equitable economic system. As Pizzigati concludes, "History teaches a valuable lesson: The rich don't always win. We can create a significantly more equal society. We also know we must."[30]

WHITES CAN'T HOLD ON FOR LONG

The Pew research tells us that the majority of whites are not committed to addressing racism and the resulting inequity. But the research does not tell us exactly why they are convinced that everything is fine. In the end, it doesn't matter. The demographic data shows that white domination of American society cannot continue for long.

In 2015, the U.S. Census Bureau updated its population projections. According to their predictions, in 2044, whites will no longer be a majority of the American population. Authors Sandra Colby and Jennifer Ortman say,

The non-Hispanic White alone population is currently the "majority" group, as it is both the largest racial and ethnic group and accounts for greater than a 50 percent share of the nation's total population. By 2060, however, the share of this group is projected to be just 44 percent, as its population falls from 198 million in 2014 to 182 million in 2060. The point at which the non-Hispanic White alone population will comprise less than 50 percent of the nation's total population has been described as the point at which we become a "majority minority" nation. According to these projections, the majority minority crossover will occur in 2044.[31]

Already in 2014, Hawaii, New Mexico, and California do not have white-majority populations. Asians are the largest racial group in Hawaii. Latinas/os outnumber whites and Native Americans and Latinas/os combined make up more than half of the population in New Mexico. Latinas/os are the majority in California.[32]

Since 2014, students of color have been the majority in elementary and high schools. The U.S. Department of Education made projections through 2022. They see the number of white students decreasing slowly over that period. African American and Native American/Alaskan Natives remain about the same, and Hispanics and Asians increase their actual number of students. In 2022, the predicted student population will be as shown in the table below.[33]

In his book *The End of White Christian America*, Robert Jones documents the demographic changes that signal an end to white domination. As he points out, the demographic changes are not just from white to non-white; there are shifts in demographics within the white population as well. Until 1993, the majority of Americans identified as white Protestants, but the tide quickly turned. By 2014, only 32 percent identified as white Protestants.[34] Since British settlers arrived in North America, white Protestants have controlled the political, economic, and cultural institutions. The system of racism throughout our history has depended on the unyielding support of this demographic group. This is the group that established color-based slavery and invented Jim Crow racism.

Table 5.2 Predicted student population in 2022

White	45%
Black	15%
Hispanic	30%
Asian	6%
Native American/ Alaskan Native	1%
Mixed Race	3%

Source: Sandra L. Colby and Jennifer M. Ortman, "Projections of the Size and Composition of the U.S. Population: 2014 to 2060, Current Population Reports, P25-1143" (Washington, DC: U.S. Census Bureau, 2015), 9.

In the past, it was possible for white Protestants to hold on to a belief that their own beliefs were universal or American beliefs. However, television, the Internet, and experience have made this much more difficult for white Protestants. Jones says that "many white Americans are temporarily holding at bay a full awareness of the encroaching diversity. Within the regions where White Christian America still reigns supreme, its descendants are maintaining a kind of vitality that is reminiscent of previous generations, and in many cases still wield formidable power and influence." Then he concludes, "Over the coming years, regardless of their defense strategies, the slow tectonics of demographic and religious change will finally reach these communities."[35]

Of course, some white Protestants lent support to the abolition movement and the civil rights reforms of the 1960s. Yet 21st-century racism since the 1960s has been largely organized by white Protestants working with white Catholics, Jews, and others. The loss of influence of white Protestants, who have been the backbone of support for racism, may be as critical in making racism untenable as the loss of a white majority.

The hope that Ann expressed that racism will just disappear if we stop talking about it is clearly a false hope. The data does not support the claim that the impact of racism is disappearing, and the demographics make it clear that whites cannot expect to continue to be the dominating majority for long.

The next section examines what social scientists have learned about the social structures that support and sustain racism. While the symptoms of racism make it possible for us to recognize and diagnose the problem, an understanding of the causes and contributing factors is needed to move toward a treatment. Only by understanding the working of society can we hope to develop strategies that will successfully treat racism.

Section 2

Social Science of Racism

Chapter 6

The Power of Paradigms

As the 1970s came to a close, I was the United Methodist minister in Preston, a small town on the eastern shore of Maryland. Racism there was impossible to ignore. The public school was integrated, but everything else continued to be segregated. While I served a congregation with all white members, there was another United Methodist church on the edge of town with a completely black membership. I joined the Lions Club, which had an entirely white membership. The economy was managed by whites. For example, there was a local bank with all white directors and employees. The United Methodist churches in the state of Delaware and on the eastern shore of Maryland were organized into what was called the Peninsula Conference. A bishop presided over this conference and coordinated various activities, one of which was a series of workshops on racism for clergy.

I attended a workshop along with other black and white pastors. The leaders presented the definition of racism: power applied to prejudice. As I remember it, I was perfectly willing to explore the possibility that I had prejudice, although I wasn't sure. I thought I might be prejudiced, but it made no sense to me to say that I had power. I didn't make any decisions where I could exercise powers. I wasn't on the board of the local bank. I didn't hire anyone where I might be prejudiced in who I hired. I would certainly welcome anyone of color who wanted to attend the church I pastored. Truth is, at the time, I thought that racism was immoral and if I had the power I would put a stop to it immediately.

The definition was confusing to me, but the biggest problem with the definition is that it sounds to nonwhites as if they are only recipients of racism and completely dependent on whites to solve the problem. There was never any suggestion that blacks are prejudiced. That would have seemed silly. Even if blacks had power, which was never suggested, they wouldn't use it to support a prejudice that they didn't have. Hidden in the definition was the racist message that white is better because whites have power. As long as we attempt to understand racism by defining it in terms of prejudice against nonwhites, we will be unable to develop strategies to end racism. Racism is not based on a prejudice against nonwhite skin. It is based on practices where white skin has benefits, and barriers are erected to ensure the privileges are preserved. This is the white paradigm; white is better.

THE WHITE PARADIGM

Chapter 4 described the white paradigm as the blanket of American racism. That chapter showed how the civil rights dream for the 21st century requires that we address replacing the white paradigm. This chapter looks more closely at paradigms and how societies adopt new paradigms. Since the 1960s, social scientists have studied paradigms extensively. Their new insights provide a way for us to become a nation without racism.

"White" is the best way to describe the paradigm of race relations in America because it is based on the premise that white skin is better. White privilege is just one of the consequences of a white paradigm. Nonwhites are denied opportunities because of a preference for whites, and opportunities are reserved for whites.

The white paradigm defines the way we interact with each other across racial and cultural lines. Barack Obama has a white mother and an African father. He is an African American. Neither his mother nor he could have decided that he is white. Why do we think that a white woman can have a black baby, but a black woman can't have a white baby? The short answer to this question is that every American grows up surrounded by a culture that assumes that a black woman could never have a white baby. According to the white paradigm, white babies are more valuable, so to be a white baby one must have only white parents. This "fact" becomes part of our unquestioned understanding of reality. It is silly when we think about the logic, but it makes sense because of the white paradigm.

Examples of the benefits of white skin are all around us. In encounters with law enforcement, white skin is valuable. Educational options are greater if you have white skin. White institutions have more resources. Historically black colleges and universities cannot compete with white institutions to build endowments. Black religious denominations do not have as many resources as white denominations. The definition of academic respectability is controlled by people with white skin. Hollywood and television productions have a preference for white values. Blacks, Latinos/as, Asians, Indians, and everyone who does not have white skin experiences the same reality.

Nonwhites know "I wouldn't have been questioned by the store clerk if I were white" or "I could have rented that apartment if I were white."

Popular culture is a good example; movies and television programs are created within the white paradigm. Henry Louis Gates interviewed African Americans in Hollywood and uncovered stories about the benefits of being white. He also reported how the white paradigm is at work even related to how dark skinned an actor is. Actor Nia Long told him that "dark-complexioned black women have a harder time making it in Hollywood than light-complexioned black women do."[1]

Politics is another arena where the white paradigm is at work. Pointing to President Obama and telling a 12-year-old that in America you can succeed in politics hides the reality that there is a benefit to being white if a child wants to become a senator or governor—the most likely routes to the presidency.

While nonwhites experience the white paradigm directly, whites make every effort to hide its impact even from themselves. Andrew Hacker wrote one of the best descriptions of the way this paradigm is experienced by different people. He explains, "All white Americans, regardless of their political persuasions, are well aware of how black people have suffered due to inequities imposed upon them by white America. As has been emphasized, whites differ in how they handle that knowledge. Yet white people who disavow responsibility deny an everyday reality: that to be black is to be consigned to the margins of American life."[2]

One way some whites handle the knowledge that nonwhites experience unjust barriers is the private and public statements of white supremacists. They know that there is a benefit to being white, and they justify it by saying that nonwhites are inferior.

All whites live in the white paradigm by accepting the benefits of privilege. Because paradigms do not need to be explained, the added value of being white does not need to be explicitly given as a reason for behavior or stated beliefs. Hacker gives an example of this: "This helps to explain why white conservatives so vehemently oppose programs like affirmative action. They simply do not want to admit to themselves that the value imputed to being white has injured people who are black."[3] It is not just white conservatives who hide from themselves the benefits of being white. Another example is the white executive who looks around a boardroom and sees all whites. Rather than recognizing that there must be some advantage to being white that would result in the absence of nonwhites, all the executives in the room think that their presence was earned and, therefore, deserved. They don't want to admit that accepting benefits from being white injures people who are not.

Although Hacker was particularly interested in the black–white divide, his analysis can be applied to the way the white paradigm plays out in situations involving all people of color. The stereotyping of nonwhites is part of day-to-day activity. Everyone, whites and nonwhites, learn that the white way of doing things is normal.

DEFINING PARADIGMS

I use the word *paradigm* to describe the role of racism. Other words used to describe overlapping concepts include *ideology*, *world view*, *zeitgeist*, and *cultural climate*. Each of these words has its own history and associations, and the terms are used inconsistently throughout the literature. I have chosen to use *paradigm* only because it was the word used by Thomas Kuhn in his groundbreaking 1962 book, *The Structure of Scientific Revolutions*. While some, including Kuhn, have raised questions about how generally the paradigm concept he described can be applied to social change, it is the most commonly used word to describe a foundational belief that provides an understanding of reality.

Kuhn was a physicist who became interested in the history of science. He made the observation that most scientists live in eras in which there is "normal" science. This is a time when scientists apply and perfect a particular way of understanding reality. Kuhn's first book was *The Copernican Revolution*, which was about the historical period when normal astronomy was based on the shared understanding of reality that the earth is the center of the universe and all the heavenly bodies move around the earth. Then he described the social process that resulted in a new normal astronomy in which the shared understanding of reality is based on the sun as the center of the universe.

In the preface to *The Copernican Revolution*, Kuhn points out that the change from earth-centered to sun-centered astronomy involved changes far beyond the way astronomers made calculations about the movement of planets in the sky. "Its core was a transformation of mathematical astronomy, but it embraced conceptual changes in cosmology, physics, philosophy, and religion as well."[4] This is one of the characteristics of a paradigm. It is a characteristic of the white paradigm. The transformation of race relations from the white paradigm to the patchwork quilt paradigm will embrace conceptual changes in religions, politics, education, popular culture, and more.

In chapter 2, we saw how race relations have moved through different periods of stability. There was a normal period of slavery and segregation before the Civil War. Then Jim Crow and segregation produced a period of normal race relations. Since the 1960s, the white paradigm has been a period of stable race relations. Kuhn says that even in normal times, some people recognize that things are not quite right. In chapter 2, we also saw examples of people who were troubled by racism during each period of normal race relations. They recognized contradictions in the existing race relations and their vision for America. And we saw how at some point those prophets and social critics forced a change in race relations and an adjustment to a new normal. This is called a paradigm shift. Kuhn describes how this works in science: "When, that is, the profession can no longer evade anomalies that subvert the existing tradition of scientific practice—then begin the extraordinary investigations that lead to the profession at last to a new set of commitments, a new basis for the practice of science."[5] In the opening years of the 21st century there are anomalies in the white paradigm that cannot be ignored. These anomalies are subverting the normal times of the white paradigm in the 21st century.

SOCIAL CONSTRUCTION OF REALITY

Paradigms describe what is real. If we are going to make sense of the white paradigm and how we can move beyond it to a patchwork paradigm, we need to understand how people come to "know" what is real. In 1966, Peter Berger and Thomas Luckmann published a groundbreaking study that they subtitled *A Treatise in the Sociology of Knowledge*. It opened a new discussion on how we know what is real.

Before the 1960s, most of the discussion about reality was limited to the philosophy departments at universities, where scholars and students often started with Plato, Aristotle, and other Greek thinkers. This is an important foundation for our understanding of how we experience reality.

Plato thought that reality is the objects that we construct in our mind, which result from our senses. This led philosophers known as Neoplatonist to believe that there is a common reality that is the existence of these mind objects or ideas. A competing philosophical position called materialism argued that the only thing that exists is physical reality; material objects are real. Aristotle influenced this line of thinking. According to materialism, we can only know what is real by looking for it in the physical world that surrounds us. Karl Marx was influenced by this view and developed a philosophy of historical materialism where our social structures result from the way we have organized our material world to survive throughout history.

Berger and Luckmann looked at the question of what is real from a new perspective. They left the philosophical discussion behind and thought about everyday knowledge. They asked the questions, What is common sense? What is obviously true without needing to be described? Where does knowledge come from? First, they point out, "the most important vehicle of reality-maintenance is conversation."[6] Our everyday life goes on, and what is known as real is supported by events and confirmed by our social interactions. This is the first way that truth is dependent on social interaction. Second, Berger and Luckmann observed that people "together produce a human environment, with the totality of its socio-cultural and psychological formations."[7] They called this "the social construction of reality," the title of their book.

The theory of the social construction of reality answers the question, How do we know what is real? We know what is real because we are part of a society in which we interact with other people. We learn a language, participate in rituals, and share sensory experiences. Reality is constantly reinforced by our everyday interactions. Our ability to function on a day-to-day basis depends on paradigms. Paradigms provide a big-picture view of reality. Paradigms organize reality with a general principle so that everyday life is simplified. Interactions with others make sense because of shared, socially constructed paradigms. The theory of socially constructed reality helps us understand institutional reality and racial identity, discussed below.

INSTITUTIONAL REALITY

An institution comes into being when two or more people become a group and share common practices. Berger and Luckmann think of them as having shared habits. An institution always has a history. People remember their cooperation, and this cooperation brings a number of benefits to the group. The first is that they are able to predict the behavior of others. Second, they identify specific roles with defined behaviors. This is the source of the division of labor. It is also the source of hierarchy. Within the cooperative relationship, not all roles are given equal value. Initially, two people are conscious that they can change their relationship. For their children, however, this part of the history is quickly lost. As Berger and Luckmann point out, the change is from "There they go again" to "This is how things are done." This is the social world. Children adopt the reality of their parents into their individual habits. The institution becomes real in the same sense that objects are real. Objects have a name and could not be called anything else. Parents and other adults take the task of making sure children know the "correct" names for objects and actions. They also make sure that children know how institutions work. The rules of a grocery store are taught. Preschools are designed to teach children how to participate in institutions like schools. Institutions are real and could not be any different. Even the process of transmitting reality supports the collective establishment of reality. When parents or teachers or other adults repeat to children, "This is the way things are," which means this is real, they reinforce their own commitment to the reality.

If a child tries to breathe with her head underwater, she will quickly lift her head or an adult will save her from downing. The child may learn from repeated experiments that humans cannot breathe in water, but there may come a time when the child asks, "why?" Or to help the child understand physical reality, adults offer an explanation. Even our physical reality requires justification. The explanation gives legitimacy to what is real. In the same way, the givenness of an institution will usually be accepted without question. When a question arises about a particular institution, it is justified first by tradition: This is the way we do things. Second, by the general principle of institutionalization: the cooperation brings benefits. Institutions bring order to our lives in the modern world.[8]

Through this process, each individual comes to understand that institutions are real in the sense that they are out there in the world where everyone else sees them and knows about them. They are just as real as a chair or table because they cannot be wished away, changed, or avoided. Institutions are a product of human society when people share patterns of interaction, accept power relationships, and respect a tradition in the form of predefined patterns of conduct. This is what is meant by the phrase *the social construction of reality*.

The reality of the white paradigm is supported by two generalized characteristics of institutional reality. Both provide a rational for inequity. These are the division of labor and hierarchy. A characteristic of institutions is that various roles are played by specific people. This is called division of labor and is characteristic of all institutions. These roles are defined so that they do not depend on the person who fills them. While one person may "do a better job" as the president of a college, when one president resigns or retires, the institution hires another president who understands the role of being a college president. This is also true for the dean of students and the janitor. Sometimes an institution will adjust the definitions of specific roles and rewrite job descriptions, but the concept of having implicit or explicit job descriptions is never questioned. This legitimation of different roles supports the white paradigm because it is common knowledge that people have different roles to play. So it makes sense that white people have a different role than nonwhite people.

The second characteristic of institutions that supports the white paradigm is hierarchy. Institutions give certain roles greater respect, responsibility, and power. This is true for all institutions. It is part of the common knowledge that everyone will not be equal in an institution. If people are not equal in institutions, then why should people be equal in the larger society? This commonsense understanding that inequality is a part of institutions becomes part of the justification for racism.

The role of paradigms was missing from the way racism was explained to me in the 1980s. I was told that power is used by whites. It was not explained to me that the power comes from the paradigm that we all share. Knowledge is what we believe to be true because of a social construction of reality that includes the dominant paradigms. This makes the word *power* meaningful in a variety of situations that I as a white person participate in. The social construction of categories of racial identity is an example of the use of the white paradigm to define race relations and exercise white dominance. The white paradigm that I did not recognize in the 1980s is the mechanism of whites exercising power in everyday life.

RACIAL IDENTITY IS SOCIALLY CONSTRUCTED

The theory of the social construction of reality helps us understand racial identity. Self-identity is who we think we are. It may seem like this is a very personal activity, but it is always conducted in a social context. Berger and Luckmann point out, "To retain confidence that he is indeed who he thinks he is, the individual requires not only the implicit confirmation of this identity that even casual everyday contacts will supply, but the explicit and emotionally charged confirmation that his significant others bestow on him."[9]

Social interaction requires considering what other people are thinking and what they will think about what we say or do. We assume we are surrounded by others who know what is real, but we constantly ask ourselves the question "Do I know what is real?" Once Berger and Luckmann have established the way reality is constructed, it becomes clear as they say, "Identity is formed by social processes. Once crystallized, it is maintained, modified, or even reshaped by social relations."[10] Even the process of identity formation is determined by a social structure that has been collectively constructed.

To say that race is socially constructed means that the categories of possible identities have histories and emerged. In that sense, black, white, Hispanic, Asian, and Indian are real. These and other categories of identity continue to exist because they can be observed in the society. They become commonsense or real because anyone can look around and see that Latinos/as are different from Japanese people. Berger and Luckmann call this "pre-scientific" knowledge. One place where Americans sometimes begin a discussion about racism is to point to the commonsense or prescientific knowledge that it is possible for them to identify different races. Yet, as we saw in chapter 2, the emergence of white as an identity that distinguishes itself from nonwhites was a historical process in the early years of British settlement in North America. At that time, a decision was made to distinguish between white servants and black and Indian slaves. During the historical period that white became an identity, white indentured servants disappeared as a possible category of identity. The indentured servants became the same as the gentry. Both were white, and that made them different and better than everyone else who was nonwhite.

The categories of identity are reasonably stable as the product of social construction, but their adoption by individuals is complex. We can see how this process is at work in the assimilation of European immigrants into American society. The categories of Polish and white American identity are available to a child born to Polish immigrant parents. That child can be socialized in one of two general ways. The family and community may make a special effort to ensure the child learns to speak Polish, to enjoy and pre-pare Polish foods, to know Polish history and customs, and to have a special respect for the opinions of Polish people. Or the child could be socialized very differently. The family could be very intentional about ensuring the child learns English to the extent that they do not speak Polish at home. The family may encourage experiences beyond the Polish community and make little effort to share Polish customs.

In this case, white skin gives the child the advantage of making a choice about identity. In the first case of a family loyal to Polish identity, the child may decide to claim a strong Polish identity, but because the child has white skin, the child may decide to identify with the dominant culture defined by the white paradigm. Or a child with parents intent on moving their child into the mainstream of American culture may "discover" a Polish identity and intentionally seek out a community of Poles, learn about Polish culture, and study the Polish language.

For people of color, the question of identity involves the management of stigma that Erving Goffman identified, which is described more fully in the following chapter. The white paradigm carries with it an understanding that nonwhite is inferior. This stigma needs to be managed within the confines of what is a collective socially constructed reality. While this is a very personal activity, the categories of race have been constructed by the social process that constructed reality. In a racist society, nonwhites do not have the same options that persons born to Polish parents have. There is a process of social construction that assigns black, Hispanic, and other racial identities without the permission of the people involved.

PARADIGMS AND EMOTIONS

Once a dominant paradigm is established, any challenge to the paradigm is very disruptive to our sense of security. Since paradigm shifts involve a reorganization of our understanding of reality, we are extremely reluctant to make a leap as individuals. This is one of the reasons that racism is some-times expressed as emotion. Paula Ioanide studied the emotional politics of racism. She observed,

Emotions shape the ways that people experience their worlds and interactions. They give people's psychic realities and ideological convictions (however fictional or unfounded) their sense of realness. Emotions cinch or unravel people's sense of individual and group identity. They help motivate actions and inactions, often in unconscious or preconsciously reflexive ways. . . . Thus emotions function much like economies; they have mechanisms of circulation, accumulation, expression, and exchange that give them social currency, cultural legibility, and political power.[11]

It should not surprise us that during times of normal race relations, when the white paradigm provides the knowledge that people have about race, anyone who questions this reality is confronted by an emotional response.

Ioanide concludes, "The presumption that we can combat systemic gendered racism, nativism, and imperialism by generating more empirical facts and more reasonable arguments is severely challenged by the reality that people's emotions often prevent and inhibit genuine engagements with knowledge."[12] Our immediate response to something that threatens our knowledge about reality is fear or anxiety. Once this sets in, our ability to participate in rational discussion is diminished. There is little likelihood that we will be able to hear evidence that contradicts what we know to be true. As Ioanide points out, this commonly happens when people attempt to have cross-racial discussions about race. Whites have difficulty accepting the report of people of color about their personal experience of racism.

RACES ARE NOT BIOLOGICALLY DIFFERENT

As well as emotional reactions that support the white paradigm, some whites have looked for rational arguments that will establish racism. Like the white paradigm, the idea that whites are biologically different and superior has a history of its own. With the end of legalized slavery following the Civil War, white Americans, both in the North and South, needed a new way to think about African American citizens. The young science of sociology came to their rescue. Herbert Spencer, a popular scholar in England, was born in 1820. In 1863, just as Americans were looking for a way to understand the new environment, Spencer published *First Principles*. As a philosopher, he claimed that he had discovered the organizing principle of everything. Before Darwin published his *On the Origin of Species*, Spencer argued that everything is evolving. He saw a progression in everything from its current state to a higher level of organization. These higher levels were more perfect. According to Spencer, this included subjects studied by the "astronomer and the Geologist, as well as those which Biology, Psychology, and Sociology [study]."[13]

His ideas were those of a philosopher; they were completely speculative, but he presented them as if they were scientific even though there was no evidence for what he proposed. For example, he claimed, "The substance of every planet in passing through its stages of nebulous ring, gaseous spheroid, liquid spheroid, and spheroid externally solidified, has in essentials paralleled the changes gone through by the general mass; and every satellite has done the like."[14] The general public as well as scholars were attracted to his ideas. In sociology and psychology, Spencer's philosophy provided an explanation for why individuals and social systems differ; they are all in the process of evolving. For those of European ancestry, the best news was that European culture could now be proven to be superior without the necessity of depending on religion. The very nature of the universe proved that all other cultures and people were in the process of evolving toward what Europeans had already become. These ideas were proposed first by Spencer, but soon they were referred to as *social Darwinism*.

Spencer argued for the development of superior nations, saying, "Any one of these primitive societies, however, that evolves, becomes step by step more specific. Increasing in size, consequently ceasing to be nomadic, and restricted in its range by neighboring societies, it acquires, after prolonged border warfare, a settled territorial boundary. The distinction between the royal race and the people eventually amounts, in the popular apprehension, to a difference in nature."[15]

Just like Hitler used a naive understanding of genetics and evolutionary theory,[16] American racism has used genetics and evolution as a justification. In the early 20th century, scholars at the University of Chicago played a dominant role in establishing sociology as an academic discipline in the United States. Robert Ezra Park was one of the leaders. He studied at Harvard and the leading schools in Germany, where the discipline of sociology was being defined. Park was greatly influenced by Booker T. Washington, the African American founder of Tuskegee Normal Institute for Industrial Education. Both Washington and Park accepted the premise first put forward by Herbert Spencer that human societies evolve, so there are some cultures and groups of people who are superior to others because of their genetic development.[17]

As Robert Bonazzi argues, this idea of genetic differences between people became completely untenable once the results of the Human Genome Project were announced in 2003. It turns out that all humans share almost all the same genetic material. Each human is unique, but 99.9 percent of our genetic material is shared in common.[18]

Even though both biologists and social scientists have demonstrated that race is not a biological category, the idea persists. An introductory textbook used in college classrooms across the country says that "despite the reality of biological mixing, people are quick to classify and rank each other racially." Then race is defined in this textbook as "a category composed of people who share biologically transmitted traits that members of a society deem socially significant." This is followed by an argument that Americans are genetically mixed. College students must be confused when the text claims that "in short, whatever people may think, race is no black-and-white issue." What is the issue? Students are told that "indeed, some analysts point out that in the United States, the concept of race has less and less meaning."[19] It is true that race has less meaning as a biological category. In fact, it has no meaning as a biological concept because it is a characteristic of social systems; the categories of race are socially constructed. Another problem with this sociological introduction is that saying the concept of race has less meaning denies the everyday experience of students of color.

Another proposal to support racism is that our brains are hardwired to make distinctions between people who are like us and people who are different. Since our brains make the distinction, it is only natural for us to prefer people like ourselves. Science is also proving that this is not true. Neuroscientists recently became interested in what happens in our brains in racist situations. Studies by psychologists at the University of Illinois demonstrate the potential for this line of research. For example, the team led by Karen D. Rudolph used magnetic resonance imaging scans to study the brains of 47 adolescent girls. All of the girls had histories of peer victimization and had been exposed to social exclusion. The researchers demonstrated a relationship between symptoms of depression and social anxiety with "neural sensitivity in the social pain network" of the brain. While it seems intuitive that impacts of emotional difficulties, such as the ever-present reminder of stereotypes, will result in responses in the brain, this line of research is already showing that the impact of social rejection on people's minds is not imagined.[20]

Jennifer Kubota and Elizabeth Phelps at New York University reviewed the neurological research in 2015. They discovered that the activity of the brain varies widely from person to person when people are shown pictures of people of the same or different races. In studies that measure the activity in a part of the brain used to recognize faces, they conclude that "differences are in part a function of the underlying cultural associations and not a hardwired prepotent tendency."[21] This neurological evidence is consistent with the genetic evidence that we are all human, and races are not part of our biology.

The neurological research also supports the social psychology theory that racism and stereotypes have a conscious and unconscious component. Scientists have identified areas of the brain that become active when there is a conflict between an unconscious racial bias and a conscious egalitarian value. By observing changes in the activity of these areas, they have been able to demonstrate that intentional intervention can modify unconscious race bias. Studies suggest that positive intergroup interactions diminish unconscious race bias. Other controlled experiments directing participants' attention away from group and toward individual characteristics show reduced conflict between the unconscious and conscious responses to pictures of people who are different.[22]

With the evidence from neural science that bias can be reduced and possibly eliminated in our unconscious, it is not surprising that the first studies showed that people vary greatly in the way the brain responds to interracial encounters. And more importantly, our unconscious bias is not fixed and with us forever. Experiences modify our unconscious as well as our conscious bias.

SHARED KNOWLEDGE

In our everyday lives, we apply many knowledge systems. A man who goes off every morning to work as a chemist uses normal chemistry. As a trained chemist, he has the knowledge about how molecules and atoms function. This truth or knowledge of chemistry not only makes it possible for him to discuss chemical reactions with other chemists, but he can think creatively within the system to discover new chemical reactions and even to produce new chemical compounds. So the chemist can use his knowledge to think about how particular compounds might be combined to make tires for airplanes that must not rupture when an airplane lands. Using his knowledge, he develops an idea, possibly discusses it with other chemists, conducts an experiment to produce the new material, measures the characteristics of the material, refines his idea, and repeats the process until he makes a discovery or decides to give up on his original idea. We can say that his knowledge of reality gives him power to act within a particular system of knowledge.

For a chemist working in this normal time of modern chemistry, it makes no difference to him that in previous eras chemists had a very different understanding—reality was different. For example, the alchemists had their own chemistry system. They saw material things change; among other things, they looked for a universal solvent that would break every substance into its components. This understanding of reality provided them with the power to think about how they might convert lead into gold. Chemists today use their knowledge to give them power to make new discoveries. This example illustrates the generality that knowledge gives us the ability to take actions. We can act because we have systems of reality that give us confidence about what is true. We do not need to worry about what other people will think about us or whether we are in touch with reality. Knowledge systems also provide constraints on our actions. We can only imagine within the limits of the truth represented by the system. So in the case of the chemist, he doesn't even consider the possibility that all atoms are made up of a few substances that he can separate and find a base material like gold. He works from the truth that an atom of lead will remain an atom of lead.

Knowledge systems have a lot in common with paradigms like the white paradigm. They differ because they do not claim to provide answers to existential questions such as, "Who am I?" "Why am I here?" and "What is my purpose?" The white paradigm and the patchwork paradigm provide different starting points to answer those questions. The white paradigm asks everyone to agree that white skin is better. The white paradigm is intolerant of alternative perspectives. The patchwork paradigm begins from the position that the existential questions are discussed and answered in the context of our everyday lives. It is based on a belief that America will be enriched by a diversity of answers. A pluralistic culture is open to a variety of cultural and individual answers to existential questions. No nation has ever succeeded in establishing a society based on pluralism, so it is not surprising that there are some people who think that it is necessary to find a national paradigm that is unifying and at the same time not based on racism.

A UNIFIED PARADIGM OR A PLURALISTIC PARADIGM

In 1982, Fritjof Capra published his study of science, society, and the rising culture in a book titled *The Turning Point*. Like Thomas Kuhn, Capra is a physicist. He picked up the concept of paradigms and applied it to the shift from Newtonian physics to a new globally interconnected paradigm where "biological, psychological, social, and environmental phenomena are all interdependent." Capra called for a new paradigm that he defined as "a new vision of reality, a fundamental change in our thoughts, perceptions, and values."[23] Capra thinks in broad terms of a paradigm shift in values—"From self-assertion and competition to cooperation and social justice, from expansion to conservation, from material acquisition to inner growth."[24]

As we headed into the 21st century, white authors like Thomas Friedman engaged in grand thinking that globalization is creating a unified human culture with a common paradigm. In his 2005 book, *The World Is Flat*, he identifies 10 forces that are flattening the world. Most of them relate to technology. Friedman wants to see everyone recognize this new reality and get on board. For example, he praises Bill Cosby's call for African Americans to take responsibility and work hard to succeed.[25] Writers like Capra and Friedman follow a long line of writers who have tried to understand the forces that bring transformations in societies and who have presented their proposals from the perspectives of white culture and history. Although the new paradigm that Capra proposes is rooted in Eastern spirituality, it continues the tradition of Western scientific progress. Because they look for a unitary future that grows out of white culture, they contribute to the cultural support of the white paradigm.

INTERSECTIONALITY

Sociologists recognized the role of supporting paradigms in the early 1980s. A group of mostly black women pointed to the overlap of racism, sexism, and classism. They were particularly interested in providing analytical and theoretical tools for equity activists. To talk about this overlap, they used the word *intersectionality* because there is an intersection of a variety of social forces that create inequity in American society. Margaret L. Andersen and Patricia Hill Collins explain the importance of intersectionality in the introductory chapter of *Race, Class and Gender*: "Race, class, and gender still matter because they continue to structure society in ways that value some lives more than others. Currently, some groups have more opportunities and resources, while other groups struggle. Race, class, and gender matter because they remain the foundations for systems of power and inequity that, despite our nation's diversity, continue to be among the most significant social facts of people's lives."[26]

Stimulated first by the work of feminists, scholars have recognized that analyzing racism requires being aware that various groups will be impacted differently by racism because of the overlap of gender, economic history, education, and many other categories. This line of research has been particularly important for people working on policy development.

Policies are the articulated rules that structure institutions, including schools, hospitals, businesses, and more. Some policies are written into laws. One helpful intersectional insight related to policy is described by Mari J. Matsuda.[27] She calls it "asking the other question." So, if there is a policy that is designed to address an issue related to racism, one might ask, "How does this look from a LGBTQ perspective?" A second example of intersectionality research related to policy development looks at the source of new policies: we get better policy when it comes from the grassroots up. If the goal is to develop policy that will empower people, then begin with the question, "What would you like to see changed?" Racism impacts people, so people are the best source of information about what needs to be changed.

While this book is focused on the role of racism and what can be done to eliminate it, the insights from intersectionality remind us that individuals cannot be reduced to one dimension. Race is never the only thing that defines a person or a group. And racism is not the only strategy used to preserve privilege. As we discover truth, it falls into many overlapping categories. Some of these are supported by stereotypes like classism and sexism. Others are related to institutional structures like employment, housing, education, and the distribution of wealth.

Job Opportunities

Housing Distribution

Classism   Racism   Sexism

Education

Wealth Concentration

As the web that connects these overlapping social structures, intersectionality reminds us that we need to consider the larger picture. This is particularly true when policy decisions are being made. It is also true when individuals decide on a particular antiracist action. If addressing the racism of a landlord might result in losing one's apartment, then the calculus of how to approach the issue may be impacted.

This book is based on the thesis that the 21st century is an opportune time for Americans to pick up the civil rights struggle and adopt the patchwork paradigm. A new paradigm will not be adopted just because it can be described. It is necessary to have resources to implement it. In the case of racism, the analytic tools developed by sociologists since the 1960s are available for us. The following chapters in this section describe these tools.

Chapter 7

Everyday Racism

Secretary of Education Arne Duncan regularly invited guests to meet in a seminar-style discussion with his senior staff, which was held in the secretary's conference room. The discussions were informal, and guests were encouraged to talk freely about their research or experiences. The idea was to keep the secretary and his staff current on the best thinking about how to improve the quality of education for all American students. At one of these sessions, the topic was racial incidents at institutions of higher education. Jonathan Alger, the white president of James Madison University (JMU), a public university in Virginia, was one of the invited guests. Alger came to JMU in 2012. By then, issues of institutional racism were already being discussed. A 2009 study and resulting report pointed to issues that particularly African American students identified. In 2014, the student body was about 80 percent white with almost equal numbers of African American, Asian, and Hispanic students making up the remainder. Alger's response to racial harassment incidents had brought him national notoriety, so just two years into his presidency he was advising the secretary of education.

Another guest at this session was a junior at a prestigious university. He asked that his name not be used, so I'll call him William. At his university, about 10 percent of the students are black like he is. Racial incidents had brought national attention to the school and William's role as a student leader. William made introductory comments where he described recent racial harassment incidents and the general climate of hostility toward African Americans, but most of his presentation centered on his personal experience of being called on by the university to represent African Americans as the institution reacted to racist situations. He was asked by the university "to attend meetings, to sit on committees, to organize student response, etc." Rather than claim this as a wonderful opportunity to provide leader-ship, he complained that he went to college to get an education, not to solve the institutional problems at his university. With all the demands that were placed on him to respond to the racial harassment, he had limited time for schoolwork and socializing. William was clearly speaking from his heart.

Then it was President Alger's turn. He spoke from notes he had prepared about the racial incidents at JMU. As soon as incidents came to light, he met with students. He not only listened to them; he worked with them to develop strategies to respond. The main point of his presentation was that institutions of higher education need to follow student leadership to make changes and respond to the existence of racial harassment. Alger's prepared presentation was followed by an hour of discussion and presentations.

None of the other presentations directly addressed the central question that William asked: Is it reasonable to ask African American students to fix the racism that exists in institutions of higher education? In the questions, no one asked Alger to respond to William's rejection of student responsibil-ity to fix universities. Alger ignored William's presentation. At one point in the discussion, William presented his main point again, but it was not picked up. At the end of the time, each presenter was asked to give a closing com-ment. William repeated his argument that African American students should not be denied a college academic and social experience because they are asked to solve the problem of racism in higher education. Alger summarized his belief that colleges and universities can only solve the problem of racial harassment on campus by relying on student leadership.

This session illustrated many of the characteristics of racism in the 21st century. Even when we gather around a table and the topic is racial incidents on college campuses, the subtle and sometimes not so subtle processes of perpetuating racism are at work. Since the mid-20th century, social scientists have proposed important new theories about how society works that have greatly increased our ability to analyze and understand what happened in this meeting. These ideas were brewing and in the formative stages during the 1960s, but they were not fully developed and readily available at that time.

The study of sociology grew out of an interest in understanding how humans interact to create and sustain societies. As Nijole Benokraitis says in an introductory text for a college course in sociology, "Stated simply, sociology is the systematic study of human behavior in society."[1] The study of psychology is another matter. Psychology has to do with minds and how individuals react in social settings. For the most part, until the mid-20th cen-tury, sociologists were interested in white societies. They left older and what they sometimes called "primitive societies" to anthropologists. The critical breakthrough was made when sociologists recognized that what goes on in our minds and what goes on in our society are intimately connected.

At the same time that sociologists began to recognize the connections between the way groups function and what individuals think and do, psychologists were coming from the other direction and beginning to see that understanding social interactions is part of the study of the mind. This insight of the inseparability of traditional psychology and traditional sociology resulted in the academic discipline called social psychology. These theories of social psychology have opened many doors into our ability to understand racism. More importantly, the theories lead to an analysis of ways we can free ourselves from the bondage of racism.

The session with William and Alger illustrates how we can use four of the insights from the theories of social science to understand racism in the 21st century:

- stereotyping
- microaggressions
- structuration
- habitus

STEREOTYPING

Stereotyping is when a characteristic or characteristics are associated with a group of people. The university administrators applied a stereotype to William. Their prejudgment or prejudice was that all African Americans with demonstrated leadership abilities have improving race relations as their top priority. When William arrived at college, he was clearly a leader, and the white-dominated college administration applied the stereotype. Because of the color of his skin, he was asked to represent African American students. The pressure that William was under to adopt an identity defined by the university was intense. If William had been a white student, he would not have been sitting with the U.S. secretary of education and senior staff at the Department of Education on a panel with a university president. There were certain benefits from accepting the role defined by the stereotype, one of them being that he was recognized as a campus leader, and in this case, a national leader.

In a sociological sense, a stereotype can carry a positive, negative, or neutral value judgment. Women, for example, are stereotyped as caring, a positive characteristic; poor at math, a negative characteristic; and liking to dance, a neutral characteristic. Stereotypes have two important features. First, they are imposed, not chosen. William didn't choose to be identified as an African American leader eager to solve the issues of race relations. Second, stereotypes create boxes around people. They limit options. A white student with William's leadership abilities would have multiple options. Like many institutions of higher education, his university has over 400 student groups. A white student can choose to participate and give leadership based on interests and aspirations, while a stereotype imposed on William limited his options. Because of the expectations of the university administrators, it would have been difficult for William to join a nuclear disarmament interest group and provide his leadership skills to that movement.

Like all students, William has values that he brought with him when he entered college. He had prepared himself to enter and succeed at one of the top universities in America. Gaining admission required that he demonstrate leadership and ability to do academic work. He saw college as a place where he could obtain skills and credentials. His self-image also included being social, making friends at college, and preparing for the future. But he reported that with all the demands of dealing with the agenda set by the university administration, he didn't have time for a social life or just hanging out with friends.

Shelby Steele describes a similar experience in *White Guilt: How Blacks and Whites Together Destroyed the Promise of the Civil Rights Era*. He says,

> I got very tired of the schizophrenia. Elsewhere I have called this "race fatigue,"
> an almost existential weariness with things racial, not because you don't care,
> but because the racial identity you are pressured to squeeze into is a mask you
> wear only out of calculation. This mask is tethered from your real life so that,
> over time, it draws you into a corrupting falseness—and an inner duplicity—
> that grows more and more rigid with the years. Ultimately it affects the integrity
> of your personality. You have to start living off rationalizations and falsehoods
> that a part of you *knows* to be false. (italics in original)[2]

A stigma is a stereotype that carries with it an implication of abnormality. It is a stereotype that has a negative connotation. To understand how stigmas function in society, sociologists begin by looking at the development of self-identity: How do people understand themselves as fitting into society? Erving Goffman was part of a wave of social scientists who brought a new perspective to help us understand society and identity today. In 1963, he published *Stigma: Notes on the Management of Spoiled Identity*. Since the mid-1960s, there has been intensive study of how stigmas impact behaviors and relate to self-identity.

Goffman's starting point for the study of stigmas is the same as that for the study of everyday reality. Namely, for us to function on a day-to-day basis, we need to have an underlying structure that organizes experiences. Without this process of dealing with information, we would be catatonic because our conscious mind would need to constantly ask questions: What are all the possible responses I could make? What are all the possible consequences of each action? How will others possibly respond? For most of our everyday life, these questions and many others are not given conscious attention. As Goffman points out, "The routines of social intercourse in established settings allow us to deal with anticipated others without special attention or thought. When a stranger comes into our presence, then, first appearances are likely to enable us to anticipate his category and attributes, his 'social identity'—to use a term that is better than 'social status' because personal attributes such as 'honesty' are involved, as well as structural ones, like 'occupation.'"[3] Racism is only possible because skin color is a social identity and is stigmatized.

Stigmatizing any attribute involves establishing a "normal" against which an attribute is compared. Goffman didn't try to explain why, and it isn't necessary to know why, in modern society the definition of normal becomes universally held across all social groups. He postulates that possibly it's because the medical profession needs to define a normal or healthy person. He also wonders about education standards. Possibly they universalized the concept of a normal human as someone who passed the test. One of the powers of stigmas is that because normal is universally accepted, a stigma impacts the person who is stigmatized. The person who is stigmatized can't just say, "I am going to ignore the stigma." It is known to everyone as an abnormality. It needs to be managed, just like William was trying to manage the stereotyping he experienced.

African American sociologist W. E. B. Du Bois wrote about the damaging psychological impact of stereotyping in 1903. To describe the results of racial stereotyping, he introduced the concept of "double consciousness." After describing the stereotypes experienced by blacks, he writes,

> There is a patent defense at hand,—the defense of deception and flattery, of cajoling and lying. It is the same defense which peasants of the Middle Age used and which left its stamp on their character for centuries. To-day the young Negro of the South who would succeed cannot be frank and outspoken, honest and self-assertive, but rather he is daily tempted to be silent and wary, politic and sly; he must flatter and be pleasant, endure petty insults with a smile, shut his eyes to wrong; in too many cases he sees positive personal advantage in deception and lying. His real thoughts, his real aspirations, must be guarded in whispers; he must not criticize, he must not complain. Patience, humility, and adroitness must, in these growing black youth, replace impulse, manliness, and courage. With this sacrifice there is an economic opening, and perhaps peace and some prosperity. Without this there is riot, migration, or crime. Nor is this situation peculiar to the Southern United States, is it not rather the only method by which undeveloped races have gained the right to share modern culture? The price of culture is a Lie.[4]

Du Bois's social theories have been largely ignored by mainstream social science until recently. He describes the impact of white-imposed stereotyping as a world "which yields him no true self-consciousness, but only lets him see himself through the revelation of the other world. It is a peculiar sensation, this double-consciousness, this sense of always looking at one's self through the eyes of others, of measuring one's soul by the tape of a world that looks on in amused contempt and pity. One ever feels his twoness,—an American, a Negro; two souls, two thoughts, two unreconciled strivings."[5] Du Bois also described the impact of this stigma:

> For the beauty revealed to him was the soul-beauty of a race which his larger audience despised, and he could not articulate the message of another people. This waste of double aims, this seeking to satisfy two unreconciled ideals, has wrought sad havoc with the courage and faith and deeds of ten thousand thousand people,—has sent them often wooing false gods and invoking false means of salvation, and at times has even seemed about to make them ashamed of themselves.[6]

Recently social psychologists have made important discoveries about managing stereotypes and stigmas. In *Whistling Vivaldi*, Claude Steele shares the story of how he and others came to understand the power of stigmas. Research has demonstrated that for people with stigmas, "by imposing on us certain conditions of life, our social identities can strongly affect things as important as our performance in the classroom and on standardized tests, our memory capacity, our athletic performance, the pressure we feel to prove ourselves, even the comfort level we have with people of different groups." Steele says that this stereotype threat is rooted "in the fact that as members of society, we have a pretty good idea of what other members of our society think about lots of things, including the major groups and identities in society."[7] This means that although stigmas are defined at the level of the larger society, they cannot be ignored at a personal level.

Steele describes how Jeff Stone performed a psychological experiment on white Princeton students. The stereotype of white Princeton students is that they are academic and not athletic. Stone set up an experiment where the students were asked to play golf in a controlled setting. Some of the students were just asked to perform the task. Others were told that the golf task was part of a standardized sports psychology measure called the Michigan Athletic Aptitude Test (MAAT). As Steele reports, "They found something very interesting: white students who were told the golf task measured natural athletic ability golfed a lot worse than white students who were told nothing about the task." It took them on average three strokes more to complete the task. This suggested that being reminded of the stereotype just before the task had an impact on their outcome. Stone conducted the same experiment with black students. In this case, both groups performed exactly the same. He concluded that they were not impacted by the stereotype because black students at Princeton are not stereotyped as being nonathletic. To test this hypothesis further, Stone experimented with other Princeton students where the instructions just before the task included telling the students they were testing "sports strategic intelligence." In this case, the white students were not impacted by the instruction, but the black students who were reminded in a very subtle way of the stereotype that blacks are not intelligent had a dramatic decrease in their score. It took them an average of four extra strokes to complete the task.[8]

These experiments conducted at Princeton in 1999 and hundreds of other studies were largely stimulated by a paper published by Claude Steele and Joshua Aronson in 1995 titled "Stereotype Threat and the Intellectual Test Performance of African Americans" in the *Journal of Personality and Social Psychology*.[9] This paper introduced the term *stereotype threat*. Steele and Aronson observed a negative impact on performance when stereotypical expectations become part of a situation. The Princeton students experienced a stereotype threat when they were reminded that white students are not good at athletics. It is not surprising that stereotypes, such as *blacks are poor students*, can have a negative impact on the performance of black students when white students use the stereotype to bully blacks. What is surprising is that even an indirect reminder of the stereotype can impact performance.

The research on stereotype threat in education stimulated research into the conditions in which the threat has an impact. Mary Murphy and Valerie Jones Taylor studied the circumstances when the situation becomes a stereotype threat. They point out that each person has multiple social identities. When there is a signal that a particular identity may be an issue, the person enters a "vigilance phase" of assessing the potential for an identity to be the "source of stigma, devaluation, or mistreatment." Cues to a possible stereotype threat can be very subtle. Things like the race or gender of people in the surroundings can be cues that a threat is possible. Murphy and Taylor discovered that the amount of vigilance processing varies by individuals, and the same clues will impact individuals differently, but they conclude, "It is clear, then, that the psychological and behavioral experiences of stereotype threat are grounded in an environment's situational cues."[10]

Stereotyping partially explains why racism is difficult to eradicate. Once racial categories have been embedded in our process of participating in everyday life, they become real in the sense that we take them for granted. Every time we encounter a person of a different race, we quickly fit our experience into the pattern we have already established. Whites have stereotypes of Mexicans. Mexicans have stereotypes of African Americans. And African Americans have stereotypes of whites.

It should not surprise us that neither Alger nor any of the other participants in Secretary Duncan's session picked up on William's description of his own struggle with a double identity. To do so would have required a shift in the agenda of the meeting. William was offering an opportunity to discuss the impact of racism on students at a much deeper level than they were prepared for. The stated agenda for the meeting and Alger's presentation was how to respond to racial harassment on college campuses. Alger didn't come prepared to discuss racism. This illustrates one of the realities of race relations in 21st-century America. Whites do not come prepared to discuss racism. Since the 1960s, a number of sociological theories have been developed to help us understand racism and to provide a language to talk about it. One example is microaggressions.

MICROAGGRESSIONS AND CODING

William's experience at the Department of Education was an example of what social scientists call a microaggression. Derald Wing Sue defines *microaggressions* as "the everyday verbal, nonverbal, and environmental slights, snubs, or insults, whether intentional or unintentional, that communicate hostile, derogatory, or negative messages to target persons based solely upon their marginalized group membership."[11] William experienced a microaggression when Alger refused to recognize his presentation. I left the meeting with William and rode the elevator to the first floor with him. When I asked him about the meeting, he said he felt like he had not been heard. It was an insult that his presentation was ignored, a microaggression.

One might ask, "What is the big deal with microaggressions?" Sue explains, "These everyday occurrences may on the surface appear quite harmless, trivial, or be described as 'small slights,' but research indicates they have a powerful impact upon the psychological well-being of marginalized groups and affect their standard of living by creating inequities in health care, education and employment."[12] Stereotyping is not a trivial matter. Microaggressions delivered by well-intentioned people who are not aware of their harmful conduct are the most harmful to people on the receiving end.

Sue identified three types of microaggressions: microassaults, microinsults, and microinvalidations. Microassaults are explicit attacks. They include the use of racial epithets and violent verbal attacks. Microassaults are explicit in the sense that their intent is to denigrate a person of color. They include name calling and purposeful discrimination. They are purposeful but are often expressed so that the perpetrator is not exposed as a "bad person."[13] Whites who claim a belief in equality can still perpetrate a microassault. This is possible under three conditions. The first is that the perpetrator feels some sort of anonymity. Actions like racist graffiti fall into this category. Second, a perpetrator may feel that he or she is in a safe environment. For example, white students in a college fraternity may believe that other members will not be offended by their use of racial epithets. Finally, a perpetrator who is under stress or intoxicated may respond to a situation with a microassault. In this last situation, the person loses self-control and acts from an unthinking emotion.

An example of a microassault is the clearly racist pronouncements of Obama Haters. In 2015, Algernon Austin says that there were about 25 million Obama Haters. Austin's analysis "shows that race is a motivating factor for this group of people. In addition to this hatred of blacks, many Haters see whites as an oppressed minority group in the United States." Many of them believe that whites face more discrimination than blacks and that whites are a politically weak group confronting a country with politically powerful blacks. Their hatred of Obama is just a specific example of their hatred and paranoia about black people." Austin says that this traditional racism is not limited to African Americans: "Haters are also motivated by anti-immigrant and anti-Muslim sentiments."[14]

Extreme racism appears when race becomes an obsession for a white person. For these white Americans, racism provides an organizing principle for their personal identity. Unlike most Americans, they do not even give lip service to the value of equality for all. For example, Louis Beam is reported to have said, "The founding fathers shed their blood to give you this country, and if you want to hold on to it, you're gonna have to shed some of yours. Never let any race but the white race rule this country."[15] Beam is a proponent of what he calls "leaderless resistance."[16] He discouraged organized racist efforts and promoted "lone wolf" terrorism. Historian Walter Laqueur says that the extreme racist groups are not highly organized or disciplined. They are "more of a breeding ground from which individual terrorists and small terrorist groups have emerged and continue to develop." He explains that the splinter Klan and Aryan Resistance groups share a belief in the superiority of the white Aryan race. In addition, they "want to destroy or at the very least reduce the influence of all others. But they also hate liberals and Democrats, even if they are of pure Aryan stock, lesbians and homosexuals, policemen and women, tax collectors, politicians, especially those located in Washington and New York, bankers, the media, and, generally speaking, everyone who disagrees with them."[17]

Extreme haters are part of American racism's tapestry, and they need to be taken seriously as Americans work to overcome racism. Most white Americans, however, reject the irrational arguments, false interpretation of history, and emotional appeals of extreme racism. We don't have a good way to count the extreme haters, but they are a minority that is well below 10 percent of the white population. In the 21st century, the majority of Americans believe that racism is wrong. Microassaults are not the most common microaggression for most Americans.

Microinsults convey a stereotype, rudeness, and insensitivity that is demeaning. Unlike microassaults, where insulters usually can recognize that they are insulting, perpetrators of microinsults may be unaware of the impact of what they are saying or doing. Yet the message is sent that the recipient is dehumanized. The content of a microinsult can convey a variety of suggestions or assumptions. Among them are expressing surprise that a person is intelligent, suggestions that a group is less worthy or important or deserving, and assuming criminality. A white valet assuming that a Hispanic man would only go to a restaurant to look for a job is a microinsult.

A microinsult is illustrated by an experience that Teya told me about. When she was an undergraduate at Ball State University in Indiana, she took a world history course. This was a large introductory lecture class with about 100 students. Teya was one of four African American students. At the end of one of the lectures, the professor announced that the next assignment was to read a section of Frederick Douglass's *Narrative of the Life of Frederick Douglass, an American Slave*. There were loud objections from the class. The professor responded with, "How hard can it be? He was only a slave."

Microinvalidations involve excluding, ignoring, negating, or nullifying the thoughts, feelings, or experiences of people or groups. William was a victim of a microinvalidation when his feelings and experiences were ignored. In his case, there was a blindness to the racism that he experienced. Microinvalidations can also include suggesting that someone or a group is an alien in their own land. An example of this is when Hispanics are told, "If you don't like it here, go back to Mexico." When whites deny that they are racist or that racism exists, it is often in a context that invalidates the experiences of people of color. Microaggressions are not only part of our day-to-day interactions between whites and nonwhites; they play a role in the political and public discourse.

Ian Lopez discusses microaggressions in political discussions with the metaphor of a dog whistle: at one level, what is said is not explicitly racist, but the people who are tuned in to hear it recognize the clear racial intent. It is coded language. He explains,

> The new racial politics presents itself as steadfastly opposed to racism and ever ready to condemn those who publicly use racial profanity. *We fiercely oppose racism and stand prepared to repudiate anyone who dares utter the n-word.* Meanwhile, though, the new racial discourse keeps up a steady drumbeat of subliminal racial grievances and appeals to color-coded solidarity. *But let's be honest: some groups commit more crimes and use more welfare, other groups are mainly unskilled and illiterate illegals, and some religions inspire violence and don't value human life.* The new racism rips through society, inaudible and also easily defended insofar as it fails to whoop in the tones of the old racism, yet booming in its racial meaning and provoking predictable responses among those who immediately hear the racial undertones of references to the undeserving poor, illegal aliens, and sharia law. (italics in original)[18]

In politics, this involves "three basic moves": The first is to introduce the race issue through "thinly veiled references to threatening whites"; second, "a parry that slaps away charges of racial pandering, often by emphasizing the lack of any direct reference to a racial group"; and finally, by accusing critics of "opportunistically alleging racial victimization." Lopez claims that the whites who respond positively to this rhetoric are often not sensitive to the explicit racist nature of the politicians who use it. They do not hate every black person, yet they are motivated by racial fears. "Dog whistle entreaties often hide racism even from those in whom it triggers strong reactions."[19]

An example of this coded political discourse is a speech that Newt Gingrich, a former speaker of the House of Representatives, gave at a National Federation of Republican Women luncheon in 2007. As reported in the *Washington Post*, Gingrich said, "The American people believe English should be the official language of the government. . . . We should replace bilingual education with immersion in English so people learn the common language of the country and they learn the language of prosperity, not the language of living in a ghetto." Certainly, there is a place for public debate about the merits of bilingual education. However, saying that Spanish and all other non-English languages are the "language of living in a ghetto" insults without contributing to the public debate. The *Washington Post* asked Peter Zamora, cochair of the Washington-based Hispanic Education Coalition, for his reaction. Zamora said, "The tone of his comments were very hateful. Spanish is spoken by many individuals who do not live in the ghetto."[20]

Identifying the mechanisms of stereotyping and microaggressions answers some of the questions about how racism is perpetuated. The mechanism of perpetuating racism, however, does not explain why the stereotypes exist in the first place. This is a question that sociologists in the last half of the 20th century asked. A British sociologist, Anthony Giddens, was one of the sociologists who looked with fresh eyes at the relationships between everyday activities and the structures of society.

STRUCTURATION

In books published in 1976 and 1979, Giddens criticized earlier social theory. What was missing "was a theory of action."[21] Giddens did not replace traditional sociology theory; rather he added to it. The first generation of modern sociologists, Max Weber, Karl Marx, and Émile Durkheim looked for underlying forces that created a framework to interpret human society. They were particularly interested in understanding industrial European society and the social forces that brought it into existence. Max Weber looked at large-scale organizations. He was interested in the role of religion and how charismatic individuals create change. Karl Marx thought that the economic organization of work creates social structures. Émile Durkheim studied the division of labor, religion, and suicide. He believed that the role of society is to create normality and a common consciousness. For Durkheim, changes come as new structures and relationships are needed. These are oversimplified summaries of intellectuals who brought creative, complex, and useful concepts to the academic study of societies. Yet they illustrate one thing that the theories had in common: they saw the individual as the recipient of the social order.

Giddens's critique of traditional sociology is very direct. He says, "Since actors do what they do for reasons, they are naturally likely to be disconcerted if told by sociological observers that what they do derives from factors that somehow act externally to them."[22] This includes the suggestion that we are controlled by our unconscious mind. Of course, Giddens is aware that we often do things without thinking about what we are doing. And sometimes we speak without thinking. To account for this, he identified three levels of consciousness: unconscious, practical consciousness, and discursive consciousness.

In Giddens's explanation of our social actions, the unconscious is unimportant for most of our everyday activity. In our day-to-day life, we don't worry about what is happening in the unconscious mind of other people or in our own unconscious mind. This is because, as Giddens says, "It is expected by competent agents of others—and is the main criterion of competence applied in day-to-day conduct—that actors will usually be able to explain most of what they do, if asked."[23] It is our ability to successfully navigate our everyday activities that allows other people to evaluate us as competent. And for the most part, we think we know what other people expect, so we are careful not to make them suspicious about our actions. If we can produce an explanation for what we do that others will accept, then they will considered us competent.

The unconscious is much more difficult to uncover. Ever since Sigmund Freud described the role and functioning of the unconscious mind in the late 19th and early 20th centuries, psychologists and other social scientists have had to consider the unconscious mind as part of their theories. Freud's observations seem obvious to us today because they have become a part of our everyday understanding of the world. He recognized that our minds sometimes hide things from us. These hidden memories and ideas are there; we just don't have access to them in our conscious thoughts. Freud observed that these unconscious parts of our mental activity can be observed in our dreams and when we misspeak. In Giddens's framework, the unconscious is limited to those things that are beyond our reach to explain our behaviors. Racism can be very deeply buried in our unconscious. If someone has an emotional commitment to the idea that whites are superior to all others, and this idea is held emotionally without an explanation, then it is unconscious. Freud discovered that it is possible to uncover what is hidden in our unconscious. The process is remembering what happened. Simply put, our experiences cause our mind to hide things, so when we search our experiences, we can uncover the source of unconscious thoughts and actions.

Giddens called the second category of consciousness "practical consciousness." It seems like it is unconscious because we don't process why we say something or act in a particular way. But the difference between unconscious behavior and practical consciousness behavior is that with practical consciousness we are able to explain our action if we need to. Before stopping at a red traffic light, we don't consider who made the law that says red means stop. Who benefits from the law? Is the system that created the law representative of the will of the people? Would there be a more efficient way to control traffic at an intersection? In times of high unemployment, should we hire people to direct traffic at every busy intersection? We stop at the red light just because we do. It is part of our practical consciousness. Most of our everyday conversation is just saying what comes into our head. No one says to us, "Why did you say that?" or "What do you mean?" If they did, we could tell them.[24] In this way, practical consciousness differs from activities that come from our unconscious mind. A slip of the tongue is an example that Freud used of the unconscious control of our words. When we are asked, "Why did you say that?" we reply, "I don't know. That isn't what I meant."

Interracial interactions in the 21st century usually result in exchanges that are governed by our practical consciousness. Whites, having internalized the rules of how to avoid appearing racist, process racist comments or microaggressions in their practical consciousness. Nonwhites have a practical consciousness that allows them to survive day-to-day life without becoming catatonic from the constant processing and reflecting on the impact of racism. Racism is baked into our everyday life just like stopping at a red light.

The third category of consciousness that Giddens described is discursive consciousness. He observed that most of us don't use discursive consciousness on a day-to-day basis. As Steven D. Levitt and Stephen J. Dubner point out in their book *Think Like a Freak*, most of us spend very little time really thinking.[25] We are capable of thinking and talking about the big questions of why and how; it just isn't necessary. Unless someone asks us, we don't explain to others or to ourselves why we act the way we do in everyday life.

The boundaries between the three kinds of consciousness are porous. Something that was part of our practical consciousness can be raised to our discursive consciousness when someone else asks us to explain an action, as already mentioned. Contradictions in our practical consciousness can also force us to reflect and use discursive consciousness. For example, Tom generally dismisses the opinions of Latinas/os without thinking about it. Then one day he has an appointment with a Latina doctor, and he discovers that he respects her knowledge and advice. If Tom reflects on the experience and decides because of the doctor to consider the opinions of Latinas/os in the future, for a time he will use discursive consciousness whenever he interacts with Latinas/os. Eventually the new behavior will become part of Tom's practical consciousness.

Sometimes we do or say something and it has a surprising result—an unintended consequence. This happens, for example, when someone points out to us that a comment we just made is based on a racist assumption. Surprising results can cause us to adjust our practical consciousness. We can also come under the influence of people around us and adopt new patterns of behavior. Or we might be in a situation where someone teaches us how to act, just like someone taught us that a red light means stop.

We can consider all of our practical consciousness regarding interactions between races in our discursive consciousness when we choose to, and we can discuss and reflect on the reasons for our actions. In the other direction, we can begin with a discussion or reflection about our interactions across racial lines and decide to experiment with new ways of acting until they become second nature to us—part of our practical consciousness.

Giddens's break with the academic sociology of the pre-1960s was to apply the various kinds of consciousness to an understanding of the structures of society. This ability to reflect on our actions and to make decisions inserts the individual into the preservation and formation of social systems. To talk about this way of understanding society, Giddens needed to invent a new word to describe it. He chose the word *structuration*. Structuration theory explains the way that the characteristics of organizations, cultures, and societies are constantly re-created by the activities of people.

Social structures are re-created every day through a process that involves the actions of people who are part of that social organization. As Giddens says, "The structuration of institutions can be understood in terms of how it comes about that social activities become 'stretched' across wide spans of time-space."[26] By "stretched across wide spans of time-space," he means that the institutions, norms, and customs of a society take on a reality of their own. This social reality provides a framework for individual actions. Our practical consciousness is a product of this social reality. More precisely, our practical consciousness is both the producer and the product of the social structure. And the social structures are both the producer and the product of the actions of individuals. This means that we perpetuate racism through actions based on stereotypes because those stereotypes are part of the racialized social structures of 21st-century America. It also means that we have a way to address racism that both diagnoses and treats it. The activity that perpetuates racism can be brought to the level of discursive consciousness. We can think and talk about racism. And we can change what we do, which will change the social structures of racism.

HABITUS

Giddens was not the only scholar looking for a new direction for the social sciences. In 1977, the English translation from French of anthropologist Pierre Bourdieu's *Outline of a Theory of Practice* appeared. Like Giddens, he argued that current social theory was inadequate in part because it didn't take time into account. An example he used from his own anthropological study is the custom of gift giving. When one receives a gift, the decision about reciprocating involves many considerations, such as the nature of the gift and the relative social status of the giver and receiver. A previously overlooked critical factor in studies of gift exchanges is time. If one responds immediately with a return gift, it is not a gift—it is a transaction. If one waits too long, it appears that the gift was not appreciated or, worse, it becomes an insult. So gift exchanges require strategy. Bourdieu proposed that we should interpret social actions as the application of strategies rather than following rules. The way stereotypes are applied in social settings illustrates the usefulness of thinking of them as strategies rather than rules. The stereotype that women are bad drivers is not universally applied as a rule would be; rather, it is strategically applied depending on whether the woman is a stranger and other circumstances. Bourdieu's useful observation is that social interactions are not the applications of rules; they are developing strategies.[27]

Once time and strategies are introduced into the discussion of social structures, a whole range of possibilities emerge to understand the issues of social change. Bourdieu's and others' approach to social science was a complete break with the sociology previously taught in college and university classrooms. During the early 20th century, sociology was usually based on an assumption that understanding the structures of societies and how they change makes it possible to see the future. In the natural sciences it was taught that natural laws are there for us to discover. The science of biology was particularly influential because, looking back, we can see history "evolving." It can appear that there is a guiding hand. Social scientists wanted to discover the rules and forces that govern society.

Harvard sociologist Talcott Parsons created complex theories about the way societies function and change in an attempt to identify the essential elements that a society needs to survive. These elements then guide the evolution of society. Parsons saw that humans are actors in society, but he did not recognize the day-to-day role of human activity. He claimed, "There is a sense in which all action is the action of individuals. However, both the organism and the cultural system involve essential elements which cannot be investigated at the individual level."[28] Today we can see the folly in his attempt to use a biological model of evolution. When Parsons followed his ideas to their logical conclusion, he determined that the United States of America is the highest point of human development. Thus, sociology became a strategy to justify the state of American society.

The new generation of social scientists found the language of social science inadequate to describe social reality. Just as Giddens introduced the word *structuration*, Bourdieu introduced the word *habitus*.[29] This is what each individual possesses "in their incorporated state, the instruments of an ordering of the world, a system of classifying schemes which organize all practices." Language is one component of this shared knowledge, but Bourdieu says it is much more. Habitus includes "the sense of necessity of balance and the sense of beauty, common sense and the sense of the sacred, tactical sense and the sense of responsibility, business sense and the sense of propriety, the sense of humour and the sense of absurdity, moral sense and the sense of practicality, and so on."[30]

Habitus is the content of each person's socially constructed reality that Peter Berger and Thomas Luckmann described,[31] while William James described the individual world. Habitus is the content of the unconscious, practical consciousness, and discursive consciousness mind in Giddens's theories. It is our identity, who we are.

A clear example of how habitus operates is stereotype threat experienced by stigmatized individuals. We saw how students who are reminded of their stigma will perform differently from students who do not have a stigma. Ideas about race are embedded in the habitus and provide the resources to determine activity. In the case of a stereotype threat, the habitus processes the information about the stereotype and develops a strategy for action.

Habitus differs from culture in that it is unique for each individual. Because the habitus develops out of the shared social experience, it overlaps with others and makes social interactions possible. We might say that British culture has a particular type of humor, but that does not mean that every Brit has exactly the same sense of humor.

There is a certain amount of the habitus that we share, which is taken for granted by everyone. A boundary separates that which can be discussed or questioned and that which cannot even be conceived. The boundary that limits the possibility for individual habitus is the unthinkable. The person who pushes the boundary too far is considered by others to be abnormal or mentally ill. Habitus incorporates the paradigms that are available in the society. As Giddens explains, "Madness is the suppressed, sequestered, dark side of human awareness and passion, which Enlightenment and modern thought is unable to conceive of in any other way save as 'unreason.'"

At the unconscious level, the shared habitus justifies the arbitrariness of social structures. Habitus provides a justification for the naturalness of social structures and in so doing hides the fact that everything is arbitrary. This is true for trivial matters that are arbitrary, like red means stop. It is also true for more sinister arbitrary social structures, like white is pure and black is evil.

The habitus hides more than the arbitrary nature of taken-for-granted "facts"; it also hides social stratification. Everyone has the ability to conduct their day-to-day lives with the power of the elite hidden in the activity. By defining the things that cannot be considered because of our habitus, the stratification of a society is supported. Stratification in society is arbitrary. Different societies have different systems of stratification. Yet Americans in their everyday life don't think about how strange it is that some people live in poverty while other Americans are extremely wealthy. As Bourdieu observed, in a stratified society, those who are oppressed have an interest in "exposing the arbitrariness of the taken for granted."[32]

Social creativity is not limited to pushing the limits of the taken-for-granted world, important as it is for transforming social systems like racism. Even within the shared taken-for-granted experience there are opportunities for social innovation. The habitus allows for social creativity by recognizing both orthodox and unorthodox social behavior. This means that in a racist society, individuals can push the limits of unorthodox behavior. The double consciousness that Du Bois talked about is a case of oppressed people living with the experience of both the orthodox and unorthodox expressions of a social system. Even without breaking through the wall of considering the unthinkable, strategies for testing antiracist activity can grow out of the habitus when unorthodox activity is experimented with.

We are not born with habitus; we acquire it in our interactions with other people. One of the strategies of racism is to limit opportunities for nonwhite children and adults to develop habitus. So a Hispanic girl born into poverty in a poor neighborhood has limited exposure to a broad range of people and experiences. She may not have any relatives who are engineers, ever meet an engineer, or even know that engineers exist. It is impossible for her to decide that she wants to become an engineer and design beautiful bridges. If none of her family members have gone to college, she knows that there are colleges, but she is not able to think about what it would mean to go to college herself. At the same time, the habitus of whites attributes her lack of initiative to attend college to laziness. In the white and nonwhite case, expanding experiences will help both develop an expanded habitus.

The difference in the habitus between races currently has two consequences. The first is that whites and nonwhites grow up learning strategies that allow them to coexist. Just as a white person might commit a microaggression without thinking because of that person's habitus, the nonwhite person receives it without responding angrily because of his or her resources of habitus. The second consequence is that the divergence in habitus make cross-racial communication very difficult. This is what we saw when William and Alger were asked to share in the same presentation. They could each describe reality as they saw it, but they could not discuss it with each other.

To summarize, social structures legitimize everyday activities, and everyday activities preserve social structures. If we intentionally change everyday activities, we can have an impact on racism. Two activities that depend on stereotyping are microaggressions and the stereotype threat. They have their roots in habitus. If whites and nonwhites work on communicating with each other, they can both find ways of acting that do not depend on racism. The social science that helps us understand stereotyping, microaggressions, structuration, and habitus can also help us recognize racism in our everyday life. But there are also institutions that sustain and preserve racism. The next chapter considers institutional racism.

Chapter 8

Institutional Racism

In 2014, I met Alberto Morales at Saxbys Coffee in the Georgetown neighborhood of Washington, D.C. Morales's parents moved from Acambaro, Guanajuato, Mexico, to the southwest side of Chicago where he was born. He was surrounded by an inspiring Latino urban culture that also had its challenges, such as limited quality public schools and gangs, but his parents kept him focused. He attended Cristo Rey Jesuit High School and graduated from Georgetown University. Morales worked for Georgetown University, supporting over 600 first-generation, low-income undergraduates. When we visited, he was excited to talk about the program he administered as assistant director through which Georgetown University has been able to counter the national trend of Latinos completing college at a lower rate than any other racial group. Morales told me that at Georgetown, almost every Latino student who enters as a freshman graduates; the program boasts a 97 percent graduation rate for its students, higher than the Georgetown average.

Morales explained that at Georgetown, they discovered that Latino students were just as well prepared as other students, and when they arrived they had the financial resources to pay tuition and expenses. Then, somewhere on the way to their degree, they ran into an obstacle. It was these obstacles that the program sought to help students overcome. Each case was unique. A student's grandmother unexpectedly died in California, and the program covered the cost of the plane ticket. The program also secured housing for nontraditional students who didn't have anywhere to go during school breaks. When students left Georgetown prematurely, it was because they encountered barriers that they could not figure out how to overcome. The barriers were not academic; they were financial.

The Georgetown solution was to establish the program that Morales administered. The university raised money to fund Morales's work with students to overcome the emergency or unexpected barriers of having insufficient financial resources, thus removing their financial obstacles and allowing them to focus on their college experience.

The difference between what happens at Georgetown University and higher education in general illustrates how racism is baked into most institutions of higher education. On average, white students have more sources for emergency financial support. Because college students in America are responsible for putting together their individual plan to pay for college, white students on average have fewer barriers. Hidden in the institutional structure are policies and practices that make it easier for white students on average than for Latino students on average. This is called institutional racism.

A theme of this book is that advances in the study of sociology since the 1960s provide insights that give us new and better tools to address racism. When it comes to understanding modern institutions and racism, a great deal of relevant social theory was developed before the 1960s. Sadly, however, American academics largely ignored much of the sociology that interpreted the role of institutional racism because it was produced by an African American, W. E. B. Du Bois. Du Bois was born on February 23, 1868, in Great Barrington, Massachusetts, and his life spanned the period of Jim Crow racism in America. Although he grew up in New England, his academic career was spent at Atlanta University. Before settling in Atlanta, he earned degrees from Fisk University, Harvard University, and the University of Berlin. In 1961, he moved to Ghana to work on a history of Africa project and died there in 1963.

For Du Bois, the most critical system impacting blacks is economic. In 1899, he published *The Philadelphia Negro*, which includes statistical data and the results of interviews with blacks in Philadelphia. Du Bois concludes his study by offering suggestions for change. He says that "the centre and kernel of the Negro problem" is "the narrow opportunities afforded Negroes for earning a decent living." In his direct style, he goes on to explain, "Such discrimination is morally wrong, politically dangerous, industrially wasteful, and socially silly." American sociologists ignored this recognition of the ways economic structures limit opportunity for blacks, but the idea was influential in Europe. Du Bois's contemporary, German sociologist Max Weber, changed his views about race and developed many of his theoretical perspectives in response to his exchanges with Du Bois.[1]

Du Bois was not only a pioneer in the development of scientific sociology, he was also a political activist. He was a founder of the Niagara Movement in 1905, which organized African Americans to struggle for civil rights. In 1909, he was a cofounder of the National Association for the Advancement of Colored People (NAACP). His recognition that the American economic system is stacked against nonwhites naturally led him to an interest in the alternatives offered by sociologist Karl Marx and the Communist Party.[2] As young leaders emerged in the late 1950s and early 1960s to pick up the civil rights struggle, Du Bois chose to move to Ghana, where his past associations with Communism would not be a burden to the movement. Also, just before the civil rights movement developed momentum, Du Bois had grown discouraged that America would face racism. In Ghana, he could continue to work on the global struggle against colonialism and racism. By the 1960s, anticommunism in the white establishment had reached such a fever pitch that leaders like Martin Luther King Jr. were very careful to assure white supporters that they were not part of the international struggle led by Socialists and Communists. The choice of the term *civil rights* is just one illustration of this intentionality. In the international community that included Communists, the preferred term was *human rights*.

Although racism in academic institutions continues to deny Du Bois the credit he deserves, many of his insights have moved into the mainstream of American sociology through the works of Max Weber. Translations from German into English of Weber's writing began to be available in the late 1940s, but a full English translation of his major work, *Economy and Society*, was not available until 1968.

According to Weber, there are two categories of organized social structures: communities and institutions. In their pure forms, which they never are, they are distinguished by the bonds that hold people together. Communities are held together by a shared knowledge of reality: history, values, and emotions. In a community, individuals have a large amount of overlapping habitus. While an individual feels an emotional attachment to a community, institutions are rational. Weber talked about the bureaucratic nature of institutions. An institution functions according to an explicit logic that is mostly driven by the opportunities within the economic system. The economic system is the arena where the use and benefits from resources are negotiated. In its abstract sense, we can think of the economic system as a market where all the inputs of human time and labor, environmental resources, and unconsumed previous production (capital) are available. The possible benefits are human leisure, human consumption, and excess production (capital). The economy in this sense includes the shared activity related to producing everything. The arts and culture are part of this economy, as are schools, hospitals, and jails. With the exceptions of government organizations and community organizations, all organizations are institutions in the Weberian sense.

Institutions regulate everyday activity. For Weber, the drive to rationalize human activity through increasing rule- and custom-bound institutions is the defining characteristic of modern society. The benefits of rules and procedures in institutions is something we experience every day. We expect there are people following procedures to make sure our food is safe. We know how the grocery store works. We don't look for spaghetti sauce mixed in with the breakfast cereals. We trust that the manufacturer of a marinara spaghetti sauce will not change the recipe and put alfredo sauce in a jar with the label that was previously used for marinara. The woman checking us out expects that her paycheck will be calculated according to the same formula that was used the previous week. Life would be much more difficult and maybe even unbearable if items were randomly displayed in a grocery store, there were no relationships between labels and the content of jars, or we needed to negotiate our pay every week.

Written rules and regulations are not the only way institutions control people. Participants also develop a habitus that allows them to act appropriately in each institutional setting. The institutions themselves take on a socially constructed reality as Berger and Luckmann described: In 21st-century America, institutions are legitimized by the white paradigm and the modern structure of social life based on the institutional model. Because this is all socially constructed, it is also arbitrary. While it appears to us that the practices of institutional racism are necessary, it only appears that way because of our socially constructed understanding of reality.

We learn how to live in this institutionalized environment. The best employee is one who knows exactly what the boss wants even without being told. The best patient is one who will sit for an hour in a waiting room without even thinking that it is strange. According to Weber, we become programed to meet the rational needs of the institution. He says, "The human being is stripped of his personal biological rhythm, and then is reprogrammed into the new rhythm according to the prerequisites of the task."[3]

Weber worried that the benefits of institutions are so great that organizations that might be communities are driven to take on aspects of institutions. Churches and other religious organizations are primarily based on a shared habitus of beliefs, rituals, and emotion. In their pure form, they are communities. The habitus necessary to participate in a religion is passed from parents and other adults to children. Or, in some cases, a person makes a choice to join a particular religious community. These organizations, however, seldom remain fellowships of like-minded people who practice shared rituals. They write a statement of beliefs so they can determine who really accepts their true religion. They institutionalize the roles that leaders play and establish rules for exactly how their rituals are to be performed.

In Weber's view, the danger is not only that faith-based organizations are driven to institutionalize but that they support individual acceptance of participation in institutional life. In his book *The Protestant Ethic and the Spirit of Capitalism*, Weber explains how Christianity has strong traditions of asceticism and the value of work. These were the values of the monastic movement. With Protestantism, these values moved out of the monasteries and into the world of institutions. In the monasteries, the work provided discipline and glorified God. The excess production went to expand the monastery and support the poor. Released into the world, asceticism and hard work produce individual material prosperity. That prosperity makes it difficult to practice asceticism. Few people can resist what Weber called an "iron cage," by which he meant that it is extremely difficult to escape from the power that institutional life has over us as individuals. We all become part of an economic system driven not by asceticism but by consumption. Weber explained it this way:

> For when asceticism was carried out of monastic cells into everyday life, and began to dominate worldly morality, it did its part in building the tremendous cosmos of the modern economic order. This order is not bound to the technical and economic condition of machine production which today determine the lives of all the individuals who are born into this mechanism, not only those directly concerned with economic acquisition, with irresistible force.[4]

We become loyal to the institutional way of being in relationship with each other. The values of institutions become our way of being in society.

Weber points to a second consequence of the Christian monastic tradition moving into everyday life. In the monastery, the individual has a calling from God to the vocation of being a monk. At first, the Protestants attempted to carry on this concept that working in institutions is a calling. This is still a theme in some faith-based organizations, where hard work in the economy is affirmed as glorifying God. The Catholic Church makes a distinction between two vocations. There is the religious vocation of priests, monks, and nuns, and there is also the personal vocation that values participating in the secular economy. Pope Paul VI explained, "Within the Christian community, each person must discover his or her own personal vocation and respond to it with generosity."[5] In the early 20th century, Weber believed that these attempts to hold on to the community values of asceticism and support for the poor had already been coopted by the forces of institutionalization.

Weber, the German friend of Du Bois, wrote, "In the field of its highest development, in the United States, the pursuit of wealth, stripped of its religious and ethical meaning, tends to become associated with purely mundane passions."[6] While Weber was concerned about modern life with its institutions, in his sociological writing, he described them as the nature of modern society. The resistance of institutions to deviate from a path dictated by pursuing rational structures means that the organizing principle is not what is right or fair or moral. For Weber, this is disappointing, but it is just the way that modern society is. The institutions are the way the modern economy functions so that people have shelter and food.

As noted, communities in modern society adopt the values and practices of institutions. We call it institutionalization. We don't have a good word for the opposite of institutionalization. Weber had to make up a German word to describe when an institution attempts to adopt some of the characteristics of communities. For example, managers of a factory may decide that they want all the employees to share a commitment to each other, so they set aside a day for team building with a consultant organizing activities. The community value of valuing everyone's contribution sometimes pushes its way into the culture of an institution with employee appreciation days. Since institutions organize modern life, the exceptions prove the rule. Companies like Alphabet and its subsidiary Google claim to include characteristics of community in their corporate structure. But their public presentation hides the rational structure where responsibility for productivity is placed on each employee who is required to have a work plan. As Jordan Newman, a Google spokesperson, explained to the *Washington Post*, "It should probably be obvious at this juncture, but Google doesn't require employees to work from the office. It doesn't even keep track of who's there. The notion seems to have never occurred to anyone. . . . 'I don't think we've ever had a policy on that.'" Newman went on to explain, "We do expect employees to figure out a work schedule with their team and manager. It's not a free-for-all."[7]

According to Weber, one enemy that institutions have is charismatic leadership. Du Bois talked about the talented tenth of the African American community who could bring leadership to the black community as well as the nation.[8] Charismatic leadership is "authority that is based on a special personal Spiritual gift (charisma), and which is reflected in a personal dedication to, and a personal trust in revelation, heroism, or other traits characteristic of a Leader."[9] This leadership stands in opposition to the leadership that is found in institutions, where the role of the leader is to make the institution more rational. The institutional leader's success depends on the success of the institution, while charismatic leadership depends on the loyalty of followers. The charismatic leader requires community. In an institution, when a president or other leader leaves the institution another person comes in and takes over. Charismatic leaders depend on the personality of the leader and the nature of the community.

Charismatic leaders like Frederick Douglass, Mahatma Gandhi, Martin Luther King Jr., John Kennedy, and Nelson Mandela come to mind. They called others to join them in a community based on shared values. Weber used the concept in a much broader sense. He saw the potential for charisma in everyday life. Charisma is claiming the authority that comes from values that cannot be rationalized and that have a supernatural source. When the founders wrote the Declaration of Independence, they identified the value of equality that they said is established by a higher power beyond human rationality. This irrational source is always the basis for charismatic leadership, and it can be the source in everyday life of interventions that challenge institutional practices that support racism.

One of Weber's most famous observations is that in modern societies the government claims power through the exercise of a monopoly on violence. This makes political organizations a special case of organizations. Weber points out that this means that the task of government is very limited. Government can accomplish "tasks that are only solvable with the coercive power." Therefore, government can exercise power over both communities and institutions. But nongovernment organizations do not have the tool of violence. Each entity (community, institution, and government) has its own source of power. The power of communities is the possibility of exclusion from the community. The power of institutions, according to Weber, is the discipline that results from being the rational response to the economy. Discipline is enforced in institutions because the "rationalized orders are executed when received in a predictable fashion."[10]

Because institutional demands make rational sense, people accept the expectations of institutions. "What is key is that the rational uniform obedience occurs across a multiplicity of people and [situations]."[11] For this reason, institutions are extremely stable. When they do change, it is because they establish greater rationalized practices. They accommodate themselves to succeed in the competition of the economy. Weber is pessimistic. He says, "As domination congeals into a permanent structure, charisma recedes as a creative force, and erupts only in short-lived mass emotions with unpredictable effect, during elections and similar occasions."[12] This is the story of racism described in chapter 2, but the 1960s demonstrated that progress can be made when the power of government joins forces with the charismatic power of a movement.

IMPLICATIONS OF DU BOIS AND WEBER'S ANALYSIS

The Du Bois–Weberian analysis suggests three approaches to eliminating racism from institutions. The first approach is to form an alliance between government and charismatic community groups that are committed to the goal of full participation of all people. In this way, the power of the government compels institutions to adopt practices that are consistent with antiracist values. The second is to use the logic of institutions and promote the idea that racism adds inefficiencies to the economic process: rooting out racism makes the economy more effective in satisfying the materialistic cravings of Americans. The third approach is for participants in institutions to use their charisma to bring about reform to institutions from the inside. This involves identifying racist practices and working to change them.

Each of these approaches involves people taking bold actions, sometimes at great risk. The white paradigm is ready at every turn to justify white privilege with traditions and its own charisma. None of these are a strategy that by itself can end racism. All three approaches need to be pursued.

GOVERNMENT GUIDED BY CHARISMATIC COMMUNITY

The abolition movement joined with the federal government to end slavery. This is a good example of when the government's monopoly on the use of violence was guided by the charismatic leadership of abolitionists. As we saw in chapter 2, the government was reluctant to pick up the cause. Lincoln explained in his second inaugural address that the "government claimed no right to do more than to restrict the territorial enlargement of it [slavery]." As the war progressed, the abolition of slavery became the purpose, and the community of abolitionists provided the justification. And following the Civil War, the presence of federal troops throughout the South protected the civil rights of the freed slaves.

The legislative and judicial activism of the 1950s and 1960s provides another example of what can be accomplished when the government is pressured by charismatic leaders and a community that supports them. In the 1950s, the NAACP led a legal battle to integrate schools in Little Rock, Arkansas. Their success in the courts resulted in a plan to enroll nine black students in a previously all-white high school. Governor Orval Faubus sent the Arkansas National Guard to support white segregationists who attempted to block the black students from attending. In response, President Dwight Eisenhower sent federal troops to Little Rock and nationalized the Arkansas National Guard. This show of force resulted in nine students— Ernest Green, Elizabeth Eckford, Jefferson Thomas, Terrence Roberts, Carlotta Walls LaNier, Minnijean Brown, Gloria Ray Karlmark, Thelma Mothershed, and Melba Pattillo Beals—attending Central High School.

In 1963, the University of Alabama was ordered by a federal judge to admit two black students, Vivian Malone Jones and James Hood. When they arrived in Tuscaloosa accompanied by federal marshals to register for classes, Alabama's governor, George Wallace, stood in their way. President Kennedy was contacted, and he federalized the Alabama National Guard. The Guard ordered Wallace to make way, and he complied. Because of this show of force, the university was integrated.

Presidents Eisenhower, Kennedy, and Johnson were all supported by a community of Americans who in various ways participated in the civil rights movement. The support from the charismatic movement resulted in civil rights laws that put the power of the federal government behind the goals of the movement. The use of federal troops is not always necessary. With the civil rights laws, injunctions, civil penalties, civil suits, fines, and imprisonment are used to force compliance.

Another example of charismatic leadership working in tandem with government structures is the Southern Poverty Law Center's use of the court system to disrupt and bankrupt individuals promoting racism and racist organizations. Cofounder Morris Dees grew up in Alabama, where he worked side by side with blacks on his father's cotton farm and became incensed by their treatment under Jim Crow racism. He went to law school motivated to work for justice, but after graduating he was lured by the possibility of making money.[13] He and a friend—Millard Fuller, who later founded Habitat for Humanity—opened a mail-order business. They both became millionaires. Dees continued to grow wealthy living in Montgomery, Alabama. Surrounded by the civil rights movement, in 1962, he negotiated a large fee to defend a member of the Ku Klux Klan, Claude Henley, charged with attacking Freedom Riders. In 1967, he happened to pick up a copy of Clarence Darrow's *Story of My Life.* Darrow was a successful lawyer in Chicago who stopped defending the railroads in order to support striking railroad workers. Darrow's story inspired Dees to sell his share of the mail-order business and dedicate his life to using the law to support racial justice.

Dees uses the civil courts to claim damages for the families of victims of racism. He has a dual purpose in going to court: to compensate victims and their families and to financially bankrupt hate groups and people who promote hate crimes. This combination of Dees's antiracist commitment and the power of the government has proven extremely effective. In one case documented in Dees's book *Hate on Trial,* Ethiopian immigrant Mulugeta Seraw was beaten to death by skinheads in Portland, Oregon. Dees put together a team of researchers and lawyers who made an argument to a jury that the murder was connected to Tom Metzger, the leader of White Aryan Resistance, a neo-Nazi group. The jury agreed and gave Seraw's family an award of $7 million. The judgment virtually crippled the Ku Klux Klan.

These are all examples of charismatic movements and communities cooperating with the power of the federal government. State and local government power can also team with charismatic leaders to work on antiracist agendas.

PROMOTE THE RATIONAL ARGUMENT FOR ANTIRACIST PRACTICES

Institutions are not organized around a commitment to a value other than the commitment to rationalize economic social relations. Since British settlers arrived in North America, this has meant that all institutions serve the needs of whites. Nonwhites' role in institutions is to serve whites. Institutional racism continues from generation to generation without needing to be reinvented by each generation of whites. And the activities of institutions that provide special benefits to people with white skin can be performed by people of any color. Institutional racism does not depend on stereotypes, although stereotypes can be part of the justification for an institution's practice.

The white paradigm not only claims that white skin deserves to be treated better but that nonwhites are to serve whites through institutions. This is one of the reasons that after the passage of civil rights legislation in the 1960s, institutional racism continued. The laws required that institutions not discriminate in hiring, for example, but a grocery store owner might hire nonwhites as clerks and stockers but continue to stock items that appeal to a white clientele. Even if a person of color is hired as the buyer, the store's practice of serving the preferences of whites does not change.

Since practices and policies are implemented by whoever happens to have responsibility in a particular role, changing attitudes about race have very little impact on institutions. In institutions, people do not have the option of ignoring practices. This is one reason that cultural sensitivity training in the workplace does not end institutional racism. A workplace can become a more pleasant place to work for all people if there is mutual respect, but pleasant exchanges at the copy machine or in the lunchroom do not change the impact of the institution in perpetuating racism.

Can a case be made that institutions would be more efficient if the practices that support racism were eliminated? Through the 20th century, the answer has been no. The drive to rationalize the economic system supporting the white paradigm where whites managed and nonwhites served them was too strong. In 1970, when I lived in Harlem, New York, I banked at the Freedom National Bank, the only black owned bank in New York. When I visited the bank to open an account, it looked like any other New York bank branch except there were brochures explaining that the goal of the bank was to support the people in Harlem with banking services and loans to develop the community.

With Wall Street, the largest financial center in the world, just a few miles south, Harlem was part of the economic system. The black and other nonwhite population provided a source of low-cost labor. And what money they had to deposit in banks was used by the white-controlled banking institutions to provide loans to develop white businesses. As I learned when I joined a community effort to get landlords to make needed repairs in an apartment building, Harlem housing was viewed as a profit source for white landlords. In this case, we confronted a white landlord at his downtown office; he made it clear that his plan was to continue to collect rent without making the building safe or habitable until the building was condemned. He would continue to expel tenants who did not pay rent, and we all knew that his lawyers would ensure that the building did not get condemned.

In 1990, 20 years after I banked at the Freedom National Bank, "a team of Federal agents strode into the bank, plastered the automatic teller machine with masking tape and padlocked Freedom's doors forever. After a quarter-century of some success and much more struggle, the bank had failed."[14] It turned out to be irrational to think that a bank supporting the nonwhite population of Harlem could survive. The bank was an institution that stood against the rationalizing forces of the society. Racism was more efficient.

As chapter 5 explained, soon whites will no longer be a majority of the American population. America in the 21st century has an opportunity to transform the logic of institutional racism. Before there was efficiency in keeping people of color from full participation in the economy because they provided a source of labor to serve white interests. As people of color become the majority, institutions will begin to benefit from the full participation of everyone. The bank in Harlem may have been founded 25 years too soon.

PARTICIPANTS IN INSTITUTIONS IDENTIFY AND CHANGE RACIST PRACTICES

Institutional racism is sometimes called *systemic racism* because it is part of the structure of organizations. Individual acts of racism usually occur within a socially supportive context of family, friends, associates, and even strangers. The specific acts of institutional racism are also committed by individuals. The difference is that with institutional racism, participation in the institution requires participation in racist practices.

The practices of institutional racism fall into two categories: practices that discriminate and practices that discourage. Practices that discriminate are the easiest to see because one only needs to ask the question, Is there a difference in the experiences of whites and nonwhites? If so, does it limit the opportunities or participation of nonwhites?

Practices that discourage are illustrated by failing schools predominantly attended by students of color. These are "drop-out factories," where the senior class is at least 40 percent smaller than the freshman class. Efforts in both the G. W. Bush and Obama administrations to address the issues at these schools reduced their number from over 2,000 to well under 1,000, yet there are still thousands of students attending schools where they know that they and those around them are not succeeding.

In the afterword to Richard Sennett and Jonathan Cobb's 1972 book *The Hidden Injuries of Class*, Cobb points out that for Americans, even self-value is determined by economic contribution: "The degree of worthiness granted a person has come to be, in other words, a measurement of his productivity, a personal reflection of the social uses he makes of his time."[15] The primary learning for kids of color at these schools is that they are not smart enough to succeed in white American society. Because the kids fail in school, they learn that they should accept the various consequences of being a person of color. The importance of the research conducted by Sennett and Cobb is that the result of nonwhite students underperforming in comparison to white students goes much deeper than reducing their ability to compete. Nonwhite students accept their position of inferiority in society because they come to understand that it is their own fault. For nonwhite students, the lesson is that whites are superior.

Once we recognize racist practices of discrimination or discouragement in the institutions that we participate in we can attack them from two directions. First, arguments can be made that racism is counterproductive and actually works against efficiency because of demographic shifts. Second, specific practices that support racism can be named and proposals made to modify them. Even in situations where logic will not win the day, charismatic leadership provides an alternative to the power of institutions. Charisma is available to everyone. We all can raise a prophetic voice that points to a racist outcome from an institutional practice. The third section of this book includes examples of people who have raised their voices and worked for changes in policy and practice in specific institutions.

Chapter 9

Disciplinary Institutions

American Indian boarding schools are a very sad chapter in American racial history. Native Americans were removed from their families and communities, sometimes being transported for miles to an unfamiliar place. The stated goal was to "civilize and Christianize" young Native Americans. The method was harsh discipline.

By the 1880s there was a consensus among white Americans regarding Indians. It was expressed by Carl Schurz, who had served as Commissioner of Indian Affairs. He said that Native Americans were confronted with "this stern alternative: extermination or civilization."[1] Well-meaning philanthropists and Christian missionaries, with the support of the federal government, took on the project of civilizing. Changing Native Americans into individuals with values and practices of white Americans was the stated goal of the boarding schools. This was based on the unquestioned belief in white superiority.

Discipline was the order of the day at Indian boarding schools. For example, at Chilocco Indian School, a bugle sounded 22 times a day to govern student activity. Uniforms were worn, and the students marched from place to place and in drills. "Discipline was based on a system of demerits, which lost a student privileges and/or earned them a place on a work detail waxing the hallways or cleaning bathrooms. Serious offenses such as drunkenness or running away might result in time spent in the lockup room or, for boys, assignment to the rock pile, breaking down big rocks with a sledgehammer to go into the rock crusher."[2] Corporal punishment was common at boarding schools.

The Indian boarding schools supported the white paradigm. They were racist as *racism* was defined in chapter 1: "Racism imposes identity. In a racist society, value is assigned to various identities." Institutions like the Indian boarding schools are very different from the institutional racism described in the previous chapter. The most important difference is that institutional racism is found in organizations that have a primarily economic function, while the boarding schools had a goal of changing people. Institutional racism results in legitimizing and preserving the white paradigm, but this is not the primary focus or purpose of the organization. The goals of most organizations could be accomplished if the racist policies and practices were replaced.

NATIVE AMERICAN CIVIL RIGHTS INITIATIVES

In the 1960s and early 1970s, Native Americans joined the civil rights movement. Clyde Howard Bellecourt was one of the leaders. Bellecourt's first response to the racism he experienced growing up in Minnesota in the 1940s and 1950s was to rebel. When he was in the second grade the public elementary school he attended tired of his truancy and sent him to the reservation mission school of the Catholic Order of St. Benedict. He continued to rebel against the religious curriculum and strict discipline. He ended up in juvenile detention.

As a young adult Bellecourt found himself in Stillwater Prison near Minneapolis. His experience of the Minnesota Department of Corrections was similar to his experience with the education system. The prison used strict discipline in an attempt to change him. He responded with rebellion and was placed in solitary confinement. Then in 1961 Eddie Benton-Banai, a Native American from Wisconsin who was also incarcerated at Stillwater Prison sought out Bellecourt. Together they organized other inmates and Benton-Banai taught Native culture and history. It was a turning point in Bellecourt's life.

When Bellecourt and Benton-Banai left prison they joined with other Native Americans in Minneapolis including Dennis Banks. Banks had personally experienced the harsh discipline of an Indian boarding school where his Native language and culture were taken away from him. In 1968 they participated with others in organizing AIM, the American Indian Movement.

As well as bringing attention to the abuses of the criminal justice system, AIM leaders organized "survival schools" that were designed to meet the needs of Native Americans. In 1972 AIM opened the A.I.M. Survival School in Minneapolis and Red School House in St. Paul.

Julie Davis summarized what they accomplished in her book, *Survival Schools: The American Indian Movement and Community Education in the Twin Cities*: "While they crafted an alternative institutional structure, governing system, and environment, survival school people also created an innovative curriculum, one that was deeply embedded in AIM's founding mission and political philosophy and consciously departed from the public school model. The AIM organizers and Indian parents who created the survival schools, and those who shaped them most profoundly throughout the 1970s and early 1980s, all worked toward a central goal: to nurture the identity development of Native youth through an educational system grounded in traditional Indigenous knowledge, infused with a contemporary political consciousness, and anchored by a commitment to family and community."[3]

DISCIPLINARY INSTITUTIONS AND EMPOWERING INSTITUTIONS

Indian boarding schools are examples of disciplinary institutions. The concept of disciplinary institutions was introduced by French sociologist Michel Foucault, whose extensive study of discipline and prisons was published in French in 1975. An English translation, *Discipline and Punish*, appeared in 1977. Foucault used historical data about the development of punishment to analyze the social forces that led to the current prison system. From his in-depth study of criminal justice, Foucault was able to discover how institutions that are based on changing people promote and preserve oppressive social systems such as racism.

Foucault's insights make it possible for us to distinguish between institutional racism and disciplinary institutions. It is important to be able to recognize the difference because the two vehicles of racism require very different approaches to treating the racism that they support. Addressing institutional racism requires changing practices and policies, but it is not necessary to change the goal or purpose of the organization. As we have seen with racism in general, disciplinary institutions adapt over time to meet the needs of the white paradigm. In this chapter, Foucault's insights will be described so that the characteristics of disciplinary institutions can be used to identify them in 21st-century America institutions.

The ability to recognize specific characteristics of disciplinary institutions is important because many disciplinary institutions are organized and supported by people who are well meaning and often believe that they are addressing racism. To identify disciplinary institutions that are sustaining racism it is necessary to look carefully at what they are doing. It is not enough to simply ask if an institution claims to be antiracist. For both whites and people of color, the white paradigm makes it difficult to distinguish when an institution is creative in helping people or working against the civil rights goal of full participation of all identity groups in American society.

The challenge of transforming disciplinary institutions is more complicated than addressing institutional racism. In most institutions the policies and practices of racism are not essential for the success of the institution.

As we saw with Native American education, some schools are disciplinary institutions and other schools are not. Also, in many cases the people who work in and support disciplinary institutions believe that they are involved in antiracist work.

There are other cases where the motives of those who organize and support a disciplinary institution are far less honorable. Politicians who played on white racial anxiety, invented the war on drugs, and incarcerated large numbers of nonwhites did not always claim that their goal was to change nonwhites into better people. Yet as Michelle Alexander documents in her book, *The New Jim Crow*, the criminal justice system in 21st-century America has the characteristics of a disciplinary institution. The unacknowledged goal of mass incarceration is that it "marginalizes large segments of the African American community, segregates them physically (in prisons, jails, and ghettos), and then authorizes discrimination against them in voting, employment housing, education, public benefits, and jury service."[4]

Leaders of the civil rights movement in the 1960s did not have the benefit of Foucault's social analysis. Yet there were people in the 1960s, 1970s, and later who gave a great deal of thought to how institutions like prisons, schools, and hospitals could be transformed into institutions that empower people rather than oppress them. Educators, particularly, theorized and experimented with developing institutions that are empowering rather than disciplinary. Examples such as the survival schools demonstrate that it is possible to create a future with schools and prisons and other institutions that support group identity formation. Today we can address the characteristics of disciplinary institutions and institute practices that are empowering.

The characteristics of disciplinary institutions will be described and illustrated using schools in the Boston area, where their policies and practices are well documented. This is followed by considering how each characteristic can be addressed to create empowering institutions.

CHARACTERISTICS OF DISCIPLINARY INSTITUTIONS

Because of our collective social construction of reality, disciplinary institutions such as prisons and schools as they exist in the 21st century seem to us to be both essential and unavoidable. It might be argued that schools such as Indian boarding schools are a mistake of the past; today schools need to be improved, but they are never vehicles for racism. I argue that schools and prisons that are disciplinary institutions do not need to be improved. They need to be transformed. Realizing the civil rights dream will require serious attention to identifying where the characteristics of disciplinary institutions exist and intentionally implementing strategies of empowering institutions.

Foucault used examples from French prisons to explain disciplinary institutions. I will describe Foucault's observations of prisons and add examples from five charter schools that are promoted by Katherine Merseth in her book *Inside Urban Charter Schools: Promising Practices and Strategies in Five High-Performing Schools*. The schools that Merseth describes are part of a movement without coordination in urban education that is sometimes called the "No Excuses Movement." These schools illustrate how disciplinary institutions promote and preserve racism. The point is not to criticize the schools that Merseth describes. I chose to use them to illustrate disciplinary institutions because Merseth has provided a great deal of detailed description of what happens at these schools. I also wanted to be able to provide illustrations from someone who is a supporter of the No Excuses Movement.

Using descriptions of disciplinary institutions is the technique that Foucault used to introduce how disciplinary institutions function. He quotes M. Berenger, who describes how prisons function:

> It is a principle of order and regularity; through the demands that it imposes, it conveys, imperceptibly, the forms of a rigorous power; it bends bodies to regular movements, it excludes agitation and distraction, it imposes a hierarchy and a surveillance that are all the more accepted, and which will be inscribed all the more deeply in the behaviour of the convicts, in that they form part of its logic: with work the rule is introduced into a prison, it reigns there without effort, without the use of any repressive and violent means. By occupying the convict, one gives him habits of order and obedience; one makes the idler that he was diligent and active . . . with time, he finds in the regular movement of the prison, in the manual labours to which he is subjected . . . a certain remedy against the wanderings of his imagination.[5]

The characteristics that Foucault identified in disciplinary institutions can be summarized as:

- intending to transform the individual
- controlling the body
- controlling time
- being watched
- separating from family and competing social supports
- dehumanizing

Intending to Transform the Individual

The most important characteristic of disciplinary institutions is that they intend to transform the individual. Foucault describes this as a "hold" on individuals, "not only on what they do, but also on what they are, will be, may be."[6] He points out that this characteristic makes these institutions seem natural or commonsensical. It is just common sense that we need to transform sick people into healthy people, criminals into good citizens, and young people into productive adults. Of course, hospitals, prisons, and schools are arbitrary institutions. If we look at all human cultures in all of history, they did not all have schools, prisons, and hospitals, yet we cannot imagine a modern society without them. Because of their intimate connection with the fundamental powers and racism in modern society, we talk about reforming them but not about eliminating or transforming them. Their goal of changing people is never questioned.

The five charter schools in Boston described by Merseth provide useful examples because they are all founded by people who noted difference in achievement between white and nonwhite students on the state-mandated standardized tests. They are motivated by what they believe is an antiracist desire to help the nonwhite students perform on tests at the same level as white students. With their stated goal of changing nonwhite students so that they are like white students, they are similar to the Indian boarding schools. While intending the opposite, they are preserving racism and the white paradigm.

After she approvingly quotes Peter Drucker, the organization guru who claims that "nonprofit institutions are human-change agents," Merseth explains that the five high achieving charter schools she describes share that they can advertise "that they offer students a chance to achieve high scores on state tests."[7]

Community Day Charter Public School's use of data illustrates how even when individual students are considered, they become data measured against the expectation of state standards. According to Merseth, "this school is, in some respects, a highly effective, very organized enterprise, fueled by a coordinated and intricate system—use of student data. . . .They ensure comprehensive coverage of state standards."[8]

The characteristic of intending to transform individuals is a goal of disciplinary institutions even in situations where it is not clearly stated. The four following characteristics are strategies used to accomplish this goal. The final characteristic, dehumanizing, is a consequence that supports racism.

Controlling the Body

Controlling the body is an essential component of disciplinary institutions. Foucault explains that controlling the body is required to make a person accept discipline. He calls this process "an apparatus intended to render individuals docile and useful, by means of precise work upon their bodies."[9]

With disciplinary institutions, the body is controlled with a rationale that the student, prisoner, or patient benefits from the control of his or her body. Merseth claims that "systems that enable classrooms to be places of intense productivity are the student management systems."[10] The Roxbury Preparatory School student handbook says that "The disciplined environment is largely responsible for the school's academic success." The rationale is not only that the student who is disciplined benefits but the system of discipline is also justified because of the benefit for other students. The handbook goes on to explain, "Students who fail to meet the clearly defined standards for appropriate and acceptable conduct are not allowed to disrupt the education of others. Students are held accountable through clear consequences for violating the school's rules."[11] The handbook then provides a list of 53 prohibited behaviors.

Some of the prohibitions are very general: "Misbehavior inside or outside of class (at school and/or on school grounds; participating in a school-sponsored activity; walking to or from school or a school-sponsored event; walking to or from, waiting for, or riding on school-provided transportation; or walking to or from, waiting for, or riding on public transportation to and from school or a school-sponsored activity) is not permitted. Students may not engage in any willful act that disrupts the normal operation of the school community." Other prohibited activities are very specific: "Students may not expose the private parts of the body in a lewd or indecent manner."[12]

The use of discipline to control every movement of the body is also illustrated by MATCH, another school described by Merseth. But as she points out, "All of the secondary schools [in her report] outline their behavior management systems in a written handbook for students and families." Merseth continues, "At MATCH, the 22-page Code of Conduct provides explicit rules in areas ranging from tardiness and absences to dress code and procedures for expulsion . . . by offering a written code or handbook that outlines rewards or sanctions, these secondary schools communicate their expectations clearly and unequivocally."[13]

Being docile is one result of discipline, but the mechanism is different from the control of the body in slavery. With slavery, social custom and physical violence are used to completely control the bodies of slaves. The slave master only wants to extract labor from the slave. In disciplinary institutions the careful attention to controlling the body expects that the body will internalize the behaviors so that external reminders or discipline are not necessary. The purpose of the discipline in disciplinary institutions is to accomplish the goal of changing individuals. Jon Valant spent time observing what actually happens at Boston Collegiate Charter School. He visited a fifth-grade history class where the teacher tells the class, "There will be a time when I don't remind you to sit up." Valant then visits a high school class where he reports, "Indeed, the eleventh-grade students are not reminded to sit up straight."[14] Foucault pointed out that the attention to details like how the body sits in a disciplinary institution is related to improving the individual.[15]

The purpose of controlling the body in disciplinary institutions is also very different from discipline in economic institutions. A plant that manufactures batteries will have many rules and expectations of employees. There will be rules about arriving at work on time, rules about safety, rules about conduct during work. There may be written policies about the consequences for not following the rules. The factory has expectations about the behavior of employees, but the reason for rules and discipline is to make the factory successful, not to change the employees. As we saw in the last chapter, a battery factory may have policies and practices that are based on the white paradigm, but the goal of the factory is not to change people and preserve the white paradigm.

Controlling Time

Foucault explains that the control of the body and time are interconnected: "In the correct use of the body, which makes possible a correct use of time, nothing must remain idle or useless: everything must be called upon to form the support of the act required."[16] Foucault says that disciplinary institutions "exhaust" time. By this he means what we might call making the most of time. Every minute is managed with planning and intentionality. Foucault says that discipline "arranges a positive economy; it poses the principle of a theoretically ever-growing use of time: exhaustion rather than use; it is a question of extracting, from time, ever more available moments and, from each moment, ever more useful forces. This means that one must seek to intensify the use of the slightest moment, as if time, in its very fragmentation, were inexhaustible or as if, at least by an ever more detailed internal arrangement, one could tend towards an ideal point at which one maintained maximum speed and maximum efficiency."[17] Almost echoing Foucault, Merseth says, "Allocating time in schools is more than just logistics. It is a philosophical and pedagogic decision and an investment of a critical resource."[18]

In a video posted by MATCH on their website, the connection between "a victory in the battle against wasted learning time" and discipline is made explicit.[19] The rationale for the strict discipline is to ensure learning time is not wasted.

At Roxbury Preparatory, Chris Wynne reports, "During class several procedures help lessons run smoothly and efficiently. For example, as students work on the Do-Now at the beginning of each class, teachers circulate between rows and collect student's homework and distribute handouts for the day. This system is simple, but it prevents students from sitting idly as they wait to submit or receive their work, which gives them fewer opportunities to drift off task and ultimately preserves more time for teaching and learning."[20]

Disciplinary institutions not only exhaust time, they also attempt to monopolize time. In a prison setting the time of inmates is already completely at the disposal of the prison. But for a school, it is necessary to take time away from alternative activities. At Roxbury Preparatory, on Mondays through Thursdays structured academic time begins at 7:45 and ends about seven-and-a-half hours later at 3:10. On Fridays students are dismissed at 1:20. From 3:10 to 4:15 there is an enrichment period during which students who are struggling can receive tutoring from one of the teachers. Those who are not required to attend tutoring participate in art, music, and physical education classes from 3:10 to 4:15. "There is also a Homework Center from 4:15 to 6:00 daily, which students are required to attend if they struggle regularly to complete their work." As well as structuring time for the whole day, a teacher may "hold a mandatory Saturday school session."[21]

In addition to the extended hours, all the schools in Merseth's study extended the school year. She estimates that with increased days and hours each day students at Boston Collegiate spend 23.1 percent more time in school than students in Boston Public Schools.[22]

Being Watched

In order to transform the student by giving special attention to the body of the student and the use of time, a system of watching and monitoring is essential. In describing the disciplinary institution of a prison, Foucault says, "The prison, the place where the penalty is carried out, is also the place of observation of punished individuals. This takes two forms: surveillance, of course, but also knowledge of each inmate, of his behaviour, his deeper states of mind, his gradual improvement; the prisons must be conceived as places for the formation of clinical knowledge about the convicts."[23]

All of the secondary schools that Merseth describes have both types of monitoring that Foucault identifies as characteristics of a disciplinary institution. First, they watch the students and monitor actions. Second, they collect data so that they have knowledge about each student.

The monitoring of student behavior is based on a disciplinary system of merits and demerits. For example, at MATCH the extensive set of rules described above are complemented with specific rewards and punishments for each infraction. The *Student Handbook* explains: "The Match High School Merit and Demerit System is used to give our students feedback on what behavior creates a safe, productive, and professional learning environment. It also provides data for Match High School staff to identify if a student needs extra support in meeting these expectations." The system requires constant monitoring of the activities of each student with clear consequences for both approved and not-approved behavior.[24]

Watching students is not limited to the classroom. Chris Wynne observed teachers dismissing students from class at Roxbury Preparatory. Then teachers "assume various posts in the hallway to ensure that students make a silent transition to their next classes."[25] The constant collection and analysis of data on each student complements the more subjective observation of student behavior so that students are being watch constantly.

Separating from Family and Competing Social Supports

Foucault points out that one of the powers that has been given to disciplinary institutions is the power to define what is "normal." He observed, "The judges of normality are present everywhere. We are in the society of the teacher-judge, the doctor-judge, the educator-judge, the 'social worker'-judge; it is on them that the universal reign of the normative is based; and each individual, wherever he may find himself, subjects to it his body, his gestures, his behaviour, his aptitudes, his achievements."[26]

Defining "normal" is the characteristic of disciplinary institutions that is the source of their support of racism. By claiming that it is normal to be able to pass examinations that are designed by departments of education in every state, schools like those described by Merseth are promoting the idea that the tests that white students score well on are a normal criterion of success. Because there is well-publicized evidence that nonwhite students do not do will on these tests, the family and social setting of the nonwhite students appears to be the problem. This provides a justification for separating the students from the values of their families and attempting to impose values that come from the white paradigm.

At the schools that Merseth describes, the role of parents and the family is clearly articulated. Parents have chosen the school. After that their role is to follow the requirements of the teachers and staff. Parents are not part of evaluating the success of the school. Success is defined only in terms of test scores.

According to Merseth, an important role for school leadership is "attracting the 'right' families and students."[27] She explains, "These schools approach the process of attracting and preparing students and families with the same deliberate consideration they give to teacher hiring practices and the development of teachers and leaders. This attention parallels the teacher hiring process, in that getting the right people is dependent on both the recruitment process that matches a family with a school and the development process that occurs once a family has been accepted."[28]

Merseth notes that there are forces that pull the student toward connection with the community, but she observes that the schools determine what is needed and values "high expectations for families and how they support the student." Some of the schools value or even demand parental involvement, but the involvement is to support what the school does rather than to participate in determining the goals or methods used by the school.[29]

Dehumanizing

In describing the prisoner, Foucault says, "He is seen, but he does not see; he is the object of information, never a subject in communication."[30] This could also describe the students at the schools studied by Merseth. The schools begin with the goal of making a student successful according to the white paradigm. They prove that students of color can be disciplined and managed so that they will pass a state-mandated examination. And students of color can gain admittance to colleges at the same or better rate than white students.

The design of disciplinary institutions is not just to transform people but to transform them in such a way that they accept the social order. The is the distinction between the goals and methods of disciplinary institutions and empowering institutions described in the next section. It is the difference between the Indian boarding schools and the Survival schools organized by Native Americans in Minnesota.

The loss for students in disciplinary institutions is that they are separated from the identity group of their families. The loss for America is the students lose their ability to contribute to the future of America by bringing the gifts that come from their families and identity groups.

EMPOWERING INSTITUTIONS

Each disciplinary institution requires its own evaluation and the development of a transformation strategy. Americans need a mechanism to respond to individuals who pose a danger to society. For example, we need protection from serial killers, rapists, and child molesters. Therefore, criminal justice transformation involves several strategies. First, a top priority is modifying those practices that have a racial bias. This includes things such as laws that are more likely to criminalize people of color and enforcement that focuses on nonwhites. The second priority is to limit those activities that are defined as criminal. In some cases, problematic activities like public drunkenness or purchasing marijuana can simply be decriminalized. Other cases, like alcoholism or drug addiction, can be treated outside the criminal justice system. Finally, the criminal justice system needs to reduce its disciplinary function and increase its empowering role.

The idea that education supported by the government is essential in a democratic nation has a long history. Partly driven by the needs of the industrialization of the United States, education became a national concern beginning in the middle of the 19th century. Following the Civil War, Northern philanthropists and religious organizations invested in the education of former slaves. President Ulysses S. Grant is best known as a military hero, but during his presidency he was an advocate for universal education. He believed "free public education lay at the root of the nation's liberty." In 1875, he proposed a constitutional amendment to guarantee a free quality public education for every child in the United States.[31] Congress did not pick up on his proposal. More recently, Robert Moses proposed amending the Constitution to say that receiving a quality public education is a right of every American.[32]

Each of the practices of disciplinary institutions has a parallel practice in an empowering institution. By adopting the practices of empowering institutions, we can dismantle the role that disciplinary institutions have in preserving racism:

- intending to transform the individual
- controlling the body
- controlling time
- being watched
- separating from family

- dehumanizing

○ supporting development
○ expanding the environment
○ supporting history making
○ entering into shared learning
○ supporting cultural enrichment and pluralism
○ empowering communities and individuals

Supporting Development

Empowering institutions begin with the student, patient, or inmate. The assumption is that every individual has a starting point. And there is literally a next step. Considering parents of preschoolers illustrates how development is supported. Parents or their surrogates teach children how to understand language and speak. They teach them how to walk. They teach them hygiene and how to control their bodily functions. All of this is done with the purpose of ensuring that the child has skills to function in the world.

All of these skills are learned because parents understand development. The goal is to humanize the child so that the child can participate in human society. Most important, no two children develop in exactly the same way. Parents and other adults talk to a child, encourage the child to repeat sounds and words, and practice making socially appropriate verbal responses. There are a variety of child development strategies promoted in books, videos, and websites. Yet whatever the child-raising approach used, children learn to talk, walk, and use the toilet.

Most children walk by the time they are 18 months old. When a child is 17 months old and is not walking, parents don't say, "My child is a failure." They understand that children develop at different paces. They have every confidence that the child will learn to walk. When institutions adopt this developmental approach, they become empowering institutions.

Jean Piaget was a French educator and psychologist whose ideas became well known and popular in the United States in the 1960s. During the first half of the 20th century, he made an observation that children respond to some questions consistently differently than youth and adults do. This led him to investigate the development of the mind and eventually to propose a theory of cognitive development. As he investigated further, he determined that to master certain concepts a child must have developed to the cognitive level to master the concept. Even more important, he developed a theory of learning based on "assimilation." He uses this word to describe how a child (or adult) constructs knowledge from within. In an empowering school, children are allowed to do their own learning in a social setting where they are able to exchange ideas. Finally, Piaget argued that each child has an understanding that organizes the environment. He claimed that learning happens when the child is confronted with new information. For children, this usually involves engagement with the physical world. For adults, this engagement is with social situations as well as physical objects.

Many social scientists, educators, and others have taken Piaget's ideas and applied them. MIT professor Seymour Papert was interested in how we learn science, mathematics, and computer science. He took from Piaget the idea that we learn something new when it is a small step away from what we already know. Then he showed how, in an empowering education setting, children learn mathematical concepts by experiencing physical objects and taking small steps toward new learning.[33]

Piaget was extremely influential in an educational movement in the United States called *constructivism* because the child constructs knowledge from experience. Although Piaget focused on education, the concept of human development has applications in other disciplinary institutions, such as prisons and hospitals. In prisons, the goal changes from turning a criminal into a law-abiding citizen to helping a person develop greater habitus to live successfully in society. In the hospital, the goal changes from making people have normal health to helping people discover how they can work with healers to meet their health goals.

Expanding the Environment

The development of increased habitus requires having options, making choices, experimenting, and learning from experiences. This is the goal of many middle-class American parents in the 21st century. Parents provide a diverse environment with toys and books for young children, and they enroll children in clubs and lessons according to their interests as the children grow older. This is the approach advocated by Shannon Helfrich in her book *Montessori Learning in the Twenty-First Century: A Guide for Parents and Teachers*. She writes, "If parents can support and encourage their child to reach for his or her fullest development as a human being, this is the ultimate gift. In turn, parents will reap the reward of one day witnessing their child as an adult with his or her own life and path, participating in the furthering of humanity."[34]

Maria Montessori graduated from the Faculty of Medicine at the University of Rome in 1896. She was the first woman to practice medicine in Italy. In 1907, she opened a small school in a poor neighborhood in Rome. In 1909, she started teaching courses that explained her methods of supporting children as they learn. Her idea is to provide children with an environment appropriate for their physical, intellectual, and moral development.

Helfrich explains that Montessori "believed that the child who grows and sees him/herself as a productive member of a positive society would grow into an adult who would desire a world that allows for similar experiences. This is the hope for the future. This is the basis for a world society of peace and tranquility. This is the start of a global society based upon an inherent respect for all others, recognizing the commonalities of our humanity and the richness of our differences."[35] From this perspective the body is seen as something that engages the environment rather than something that needs to be controlled.

Supporting History Making

In the 1960s, Paulo Freire was the director of the Department of Cultural Extension of Recife University in Brazil. There he developed a program where he taught literacy to adults and empowered them to participate in democracy. He called his educational methodology "the development of critical consciousness" and based it on an understanding of what it means to be human.

The beginning point for Freire is the distinction between human beings and animals. Humans have reflexes just like animals, but we differ from animals in that we "engage in relationships with others and with the world." These relationships are not limited to stimulus and response engagement. We relate in what he calls "a critical way" through reflection. He points out that as we respond, we discover that time has a past, present, and future. This consciousness of history is what makes us human. Once we are conscious of history, we can become history makers. Freire argues that this makes it possible for us to "integrate" with our context. He distinguishes integration from adaption. Adaption is the goal of disciplinary institutions where one "is subjected to the choices of others, to the extent that his decisions are no longer his own because they result from external prescriptions."[36]

Freire says that because we recognize history, we can participate in the themes of our times and the issues that engage us.[37] For empowering institutions, time is not something to be used; time is what we live in that progresses and makes the future, which is created by our participation in the present.

Entering into Shared Learning

In 1970, I was living in New York City and saw that Neil Postman was teaching a graduate course on education theory at New York University. I had read the book that he wrote with Charles Weingartner titled *Teaching as a Subversive Activity*. I registered for the course and arrived for the first class to see Postman sitting on a stool with a clipboard containing the class list. He opened the class by explaining that he didn't see how grades were helpful, but he needed to turn in a grade for everyone at the end of the semester. He then passed around the clipboard. We were instructed to find our name and put the grade we would receive next to it. He hoped that some of us would volunteer to receive a B because the dean gave him trouble if he gave everyone an A. I was taking the course just to see what I could learn, so I volunteered for a B. For the first time I experienced what it feels like to be in a college classroom where there is a commitment to shared learning rather than the presumption that the professor has wisdom to pass on to me and I will be judged by whether I meet the professor's expectations.

Postman and Weingartner provide an outline of what it looks like when a teacher uses an inquiry style of education. In keeping with the commitment of not prescribing, but discovering, they make a list of what one might generally see in the exchanges between students and teachers:

- The teacher rarely tells the students what the teacher thinks they ought to know.
- The basic mode of discourse with students is questioning.
- Generally, the teacher does not accept a single statement as an answer to a question.
- The teacher encourages student-student interaction as opposed to student-teacher interaction. And generally, the teacher avoids acting as a mediator or judge of the quality of ideas expressed.
- The teacher rarely summarizes the positions taken by students on the learnings that occur.
- Lessons develop from the responses of students and not from a previously determined "logical" structure.
- Teaching success is measured in terms of behavioral changes in students.[38]

An empowering institution has a culture of seriousness about discovering a shared understanding of truth. Discovering truth or reality is the goal. The difference between empowering and disciplinary institutions is that in the empowering institution no one claims to have a monopoly on the truth. In a school, the teachers don't claim to know everything while the students know nothing. Lisa Bloom wrote about how this can happen in a classroom. She calls on teachers to "become learners in their classrooms."[39] In empowering institutions, everyone's contribution is respected and encouraged. And the civil rights dream of full participation is supported.

Supporting Cultural Enrichment and Pluralism

There is a long tradition in the United States of using schools and other disciplinary institutions to devalue nonwhite culture. As recently as 1998, the California electorate passed a citizen-initiated statute that made it illegal for public schoolteachers to teach in Spanish. This follows a long tradition of disrespect for the variety of cultures in America. In 1864, Congress made it illegal for Native Americans to be taught in their own language.

The survival schools are a good example of empowering institutions. Indigenous people in the United States and across the world have traditions of empowering institutions. Anthropologist Angeles Arrien looked at empowering practices in indigenous cultures and identified four universal components: (1) showing up and choosing to be present, (2) paying attention, (3) telling the truth, and (4) surrendering attachment to an outcome. She calls these the Four-Fold Way.[40] This is a good summary of what it means to create an environment where all traditions and cultures are honored.

Empowering Communities and Individuals

This chapter has been about how institutions, even those that claim they are promoting equity, can hide racism in their practices. Disciplinary institutions provide cover for racism that permeates the whole society. While the focus has been on institutions themselves, institutions act on individuals. When institutions are disciplinary, they attempt to make people uniform. In a nonracist society, there is not just respect for difference of race and culture; there is celebration of those differences. Therefore, institutions that empower will not only allow differences to exist but will enjoy and celebrate those differences. Difference, however, can only be celebrated with integrity when difference is seriously engaged. To say, "OK, if that is your opinion" is to disrespect difference. Celebrating individuality means trying to understand other people's perspectives and accepting and expecting that our own ideas, customs, and habits can be questioned by others.

This celebration of individuality is made possible in a context of community where our identity is formed. Freire described how this is possible in an educational setting. In *The Politics of Education: Culture, Power, and Liberation*, he describes a strategy of adopting a questioning perspective, recognizing the shared struggle to humanize, and embracing hope. Freire explains that a questioning perspective "is the same as that required in dealing with the world (that is, the real world and life in general), an attitude of inward questioning through which increasingly one begins to see the reason behind fact." The purpose of a critical perspective, Freire claims, is that "maintaining this curious attitude helps us to be skillful and to profit from our curiosity."[41]

Since to be human is to participate in a culture, the questioning perspective leads to empowerment within a social context. Freire describes a Chilean peasant who told him, "Now I know that I am a cultured man." When asked what he meant, the peasant replied, "Because through work and by working I change the world." This recognition of one's power is a psychological event of recognizing the power of an identity group. In this case, the peasant was part of Chilean culture where he was "not only in the world, but *with* the world" (italics in the original).[42] And he recognized that he has "a right to have a voice."[43]

We need to decrease the impact of disciplinary institutions. In some cases we need to completely eliminate them because they are vehicles of racism. We also need to cultivate empowering institutions because they are vehicles for creating and sustaining a society without racism. Creating and supporting empowering institutions is an important part of an overall strategy for realizing the civil rights dream. The next chapter looks at how individual behavior and stereotypes, institutional racism, and disciplinary institutions combine to preserve racism.

Chapter 10

A Framework to Overcome Racism

In section 1, the civil rights dream for the 21st century was defined as a dream that America will be a nation where every race, ethnicity, and identity group has full participation in the political, economic, and cultural life of the nation so that the barriers to fulfilling individual aspirations are no greater for one person than another. The question was asked, Why, more than half a century after the civil rights movement of the 1960s, are we still so far from realizing that dream?

The short answer is that our understanding of racism was inadequate in the 1960s. Social science had not provided the tools necessary for us to develop strategies individually or collectively to end racism. Today we are in a very different place. The previous four chapters described the advances made in social science theory. Social psychologists understand how social structures relate to the way we act, and sociologists have developed theoretical systems that provide ways for us to better understand the role of institutions in supporting racism. Putting this all together gives us a framework to use to become a nation with a history of racism rather than a nation with a culture of racism.

We make a diagnosis of racism based on its symptoms—things like economic inequalities, housing segregation, and differing rates of college graduation. To move from its diagnosis to its treatment, however, we must understand the processes involved in the disease. We must understand the underlying causes and the factors perpetuating the chronic disease of racism. This chapter presents a framework for understanding how and why racism in America exists and persists. The framework is based on the theories about race that were presented in the preceding four chapters. Treating symptoms has its place in an emergency, but understanding the underlying causes makes it possible to cure a disease. As we have seen in the past 50 years, treating the symptoms only allows the underlying structure of racism to mutate and present different symptoms.

Once a disease has been cured, it is important to put into place strategies that will sustain health. These are the structures of health. There are processes that support a healthy, nonracist, patchwork quilt nation. The underlying structures and processes for this healthy condition have also been considered by sociologists since the 1960s and are described in the previous four chapters. A patchwork quilt framework uses social science theories to show how a patchwork society is supported.

After the underlying processes of disease and health are understood, some treatments for the disease appear obvious. But the shift from one paradigm to another is particularly difficult for societies. The previous chapters also describe what social scientists have learned about paradigm shifts. These insights are extremely important. One of the reasons for our past failures to realize the civil rights dream is that we have underestimated the complexity of making a paradigm shift. This chapter ends with a description of what it will look like as we make a shift from a white paradigm to a patchwork paradigm.

FRAMEWORK OF RACISM

Figure 10.1 shows the factors that provide the social structure necessary to preserve racism and the relationships between them. This represents a society that is sick with racism.

The "white paradigm" is the social foundation of American racism. Racism is based on the shared reality that there are social benefits for those with white skin. This is not a biological reality. There is not a gene that makes whites more intelligent, more hard working, or more deserving. The social preference for white skin is socially constructed with a social history. To say that the white paradigm is a reality means that it is part of Americans' commonsense understanding. It does not need to be explained because it is "the way things are." As long as white skin is preferred and given social value, it will be impossible to end racism.

The arrow running from "Individual Actions" to "White Paradigm" in the figure indicates that the white paradigm is socially constructed. It depends on the day-to-day actions of people. Actions include what we say, what we do, our body language, the decisions we make, what we decide not to do, and everything that is sometimes called human agency. The connection between paradigms and everyday activity is structuration, which Anthony Giddens described. What we do every day preserves the already existing, socially constructed reality.

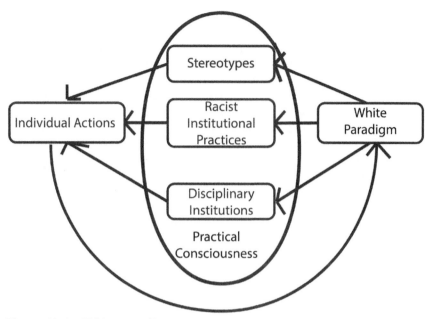

Figure 10.1 White paradigm

Civil rights leaders in the 1960s called on people to recognize the immorality of racism and to change their ways. They realized that there are individual acts of racism. It was not understood, however, that everyday conversation and actions provide social and cultural support for racism. Because racism is part of our day-to-day conversation and interactions, it has a social reality. And because the complexity of this process was not understood, "changing their ways" became equated to not using racial epithets.

As soon as being called a racist became an insult, it was very difficult for everyone, whites and nonwhites alike, to point out racist activity. Whites quickly learned to use the strategy of starting a very racist comment by first saying, "I am not a racist, but . . ." This was a clear signal that the speaker wanted a "get out of jail free card." In safe settings, whites continued to support each other with racist interpretations of experiences. As long as there were no nonwhites listening or the nonwhites could be trusted for some reason, white conversation continued to support white racism. The removal of racial epithets from public conversation and their restriction to segregated or safe settings did not address racism. The adoption of polite conversation sustains racism.

A result of the 1960s civil rights movement was that race disappeared from political discourse. After the passage of civil rights laws in the 1960s, and a small amount of judicial support, politicians hid behind the possibility of equality, and they only talked about equality if they could not avoid racial disparities. Equality sounds like a lofty goal, but it is difficult for politicians to deliver on. They can create opportunities or barriers. They can incentivize actions, but equality is an end result. The focus on equality provided a cover for ignoring political discussion about the sources of inequality and racism. Everyone knew that it would take a long time to achieve equality. Talk about equality became coded language for "don't worry, I am not going to bring up racism." Coded language appeared in other places. TV commentators and editorial writers joined politicians in using coded language. For example, nonwhite women were called "welfare mothers," and nonwhite men were called "drug dealers."

Segregation, and especially economic segregation, continued to be the practice. Housing covenants had previously been used to ensure new housing developments excluded people of color. These were replaced by expanding suburbs with housing developments where only a small number of people of color could afford the housing or wanted to subject themselves to the restrictive white culture of the suburbs.

A lack of will to continue a civil rights struggle, coded language in political discourse, social segregation, and other strategies were part of the environment that supported the white paradigm through the early 1970s. These strategies soon settled into a new set of social structures to replace Jim Crow racism. Social scientists identified three social structures that evolved and became particularly effective in the 1980s. They are represented by the three boxes in the center of figure 10.1: stereotypes, racist institutional practices, and disciplinary institutions. When the judicial and legal tools that whites had used to oppress nonwhites were greatly reduced in the 1960s and early 1970s, whites adopted these social structures to redirect and justify racist activities. All of them had existed before, but now they took center stage in preserving racism.

The top box indicates the important role that stereotypes play in preserving the white paradigm. When individual nonwhites excelled, they became the exceptions that proved the stereotypes. Stereotypes were not directly confronted. Even in workplaces where races often mixed, race, like religion, was not an acceptable topic for conversation. Sports, television, and movies occupied the conversation at lunchtime and during breaks. Whites learned how to avoid saying anything that would appear racist in the new environment. At the same time, nonwhites worked out their own strategies for adapting to the new racial environment where explicit name-calling was replaced by more subtle comments and actions called microaggressions. Microaggressions are the everyday verbal, nonverbal, and environmental slights, snubs, or insults, whether intentional or unintentional, that communicate hostile, derogatory, or negative messages to target persons based solely on their being nonwhite. Stereotypes were already in place. The only change was that now whites made less use of direct reference to the inferiority of others and more use of microaggressions.

The second box represents all the ways that whites benefit from the culture, policies, and practices of institutions. Like whites who stopped using racially explicit language around people of color, institutional cultures made certain accommodations for nonwhites but still gave special privilege to whites. For example, there are colleges that have very few nonwhite alumni, but they give special admission consideration to the children of alumni. The admissions officer who processes applications is carrying out a racist practice because it gives advantages to whites. The practice is subtly—rather than explicitly—racist because no one says that the purpose of the policy is to limit the number of students of color. Often racism is deeply hidden in the culture of an organization. Grocery store chains that close or do not open new stores in neighborhoods with nonwhite populations will justify their decisions on economic or other grounds.

Racist activities based on stereotypes are usually conducted by one race against another. Racist activity based on an organizational culture or practice can be conducted by anyone. A Hispanic admissions officer may be responsible for enforcing the preference for children of alumni even though the practice reduces opportunities for Hispanic students.

The third box is the most creative strategy to provide support for the white paradigm. A disciplinary institution is established for the purpose of making people better. By defining good or better people, these institutions play a role in establishing the understanding that white is better. Disciplinary institutions include criminal justice, education, health, and other institutions. The most egregious example of this is the expansion of the criminal justice system and the war on drugs. Politicians proposed and promoted the idea that drugs were a source of crime in African American neighborhoods. Urban police support this idea by concentrating their drug enforcement in urban areas. The media helps by exaggerating the dangers and extent of drug usage, particularly among blacks. While the use of drugs by whites is no less than among other groups, nonwhites are targeted for incarceration. Following incarceration, blacks are "supervised" by a parole system and discriminated against in hiring. The criminal justice system claims to be helping black communities rid themselves of the harmful impact of drugs, but it is actually limiting black participation in American society and supporting the idea that white skin is better.

Police officers and teachers who work in these disciplinary institutions do not intend to support racism. Their actions are seldom consciously motivated by racism. People of all races are teachers and police officers. While they are certainly participants in the culture of stereotypes, their activities in the disciplinary institutions take on a different character. A black teacher working in an inner-city school may be personally committed to preparing students for college or a career, yet the very structure of the school is teaching students that they are disadvantaged because of the color of their skin. In the same way, a white police officer who is assigned to make drug arrests may hold stereotypes and use microaggressions, but the drug arrests are just doing a job. The officer is not intending to establish a system that oppresses nonwhites.

Stereotyping, institutional practices, and disciplinary institutions are part of our practical consciousness as described by Giddens. This is indicated by putting them inside a practical consciousness circle. We act without reflection because of the influence of the white paradigm. For all three of these vehicles of racism, we can usually provide a justification for our actions and the policies and practices. We do not think, "I am rolling my eyes because the Hispanics are always late for work," but if someone asked us why we rolled our eyes, we could tell them the stereotype that justifies our action. The racist effects of institutional practices are usually overlooked and replaced by other explanations when we are asked to justify them. For example, the criminal justice system is justified on law-and-order grounds.

This practical knowledge makes it possible for us to get through the day because we are just doing what is natural. Our participation in racist activity is not thought about, but it is not unconscious in Giddens's sense. When we act because of unconscious motivation, we are not able to give an explanation for our actions when asked, "Why did you do that?" With most racist actions, we don't think about them, but we could explain our actions in a way that others could understand.

As figure 10.1 indicates, the influence of stereotypes, institutional racism, and disciplinary institutions provides the environment in which people of all races say things and take actions that support the pervasive white paradigm. This is indicated by the arrows pointing to the box labeled "Individual Actions."

The interconnections of racism are more complex than the figure suggests. The supports of racism interact and overlap. For example, stereotypes provide the justification for many institutional racist practices, and the disciplinary institutions justify stereotypes. Also, the arrow indicating that individual actions support and preserve the white paradigm oversimplifies the process. The actions of people also create and support institutions, then institutions support the white paradigm.

The complexity of the web of interactions between the underlying paradigm and all social structures partly explains why it has been difficult to recognize, diagnose, treat, and eradicate racism. Each time we have made strides to advance civil rights, we have been unable to finish the work. Looking back at chapter 2, we see the vehicles of stereotyping, institutions, and disciplinary institutions playing various roles during the history of racism in preserving the white paradigm. For example, since racism was established by the British settlers, the education system played various critical roles: During the time of slavery, keeping slaves illiterate was part of the disciplinary institution of slavery. In southern states and elsewhere, Jim Crow racism was based on well-established stereotypes that justified unequal schools and limited access to higher education for all people of color. In the 21st century, education is permeated with institutional racism. Education policy ensures that white students have more and better educational resources available to them.

The framework explains what happened to America when the civil rights dream of the 1960s disappeared into a period of racial stability in the beginning years of the 21st century. An important accomplishment of the 1960s civil rights movement was establishing racism as something that is wrong. Use of the noun *racist*, as in "He is a racist," however, implies that racist behavior is limited to individuals who are immoral. This made it possible to dismiss most racist behaviors by saying, "He is a good person—he didn't really mean it." Since immorality is a personal defect, it became very difficult to talk about racist activity. Support for stereotypes continued through microaggressions. And the microaggressions could not be challenged since it would amount to calling the perpetrator immoral.

WHY WE FAILED

We are now ready to answer the question of why we still have a nation with a racist foundation in the 21st century. There are two reasons. First, the arrow that goes from the box labeled "Individual Actions" was not understood. We did not fully appreciate the power of everyday activity in preserving the white paradigm that white skin has added value. Second, we did not appreciate the adaptability of the three vehicles of racism. Without an adequate understanding of the social forces and the vehicles they use, it was not possible to develop comprehensive strategies to address racism.

Looking back, we can see what happened. Martin Luther King Jr. called on us to judge each other by the quality of our character. The white paradigm found a way for us to adjust the way we talk about each other. We changed our language, but we didn't stop judging by skin color. The expressed racial judgments of the Jim Crow–era stereotypes became microaggressions. Institutions adapted by focusing on diversity, making it possible to avoid full participation. Disciplinary institutions were expanded through experiments in founding elementary and high schools that use disciplinary strategies. And the criminal justice system was vastly expanded to support racism. As the arrows from the vehicles of racism to "Individual Actions" indicate, the everyday practice of racism took on new forms that reinforce the white paradigm. The civil rights movement of the 1960s was hijacked, and America continues to have a racist foundation where we don't mention stereotypes out loud, our institutions focus on diversity not participation, and disciplinary institutions have been expanded.

Before looking more closely at each of these shifts in the application of the white paradigm, it is important to point out that no one would ever want to return to the days of Jim Crow racism. Things are not just different; they are better. The fact that things are better for people of color should not be taken as a sign that everything is fine or that racism is no longer an issue. Racism causes hardship and suffering in the 21st century, particularly for people of color.

VEHICLES OF RACISM HAVE MUTATED

The three vehicles of racism have each mutated from the racism of the Jim Crow period to their use in the 21st century. Developing strategies to end racism requires recognizing the current forms of these vehicles. Chapter 7 described the power that stereotyping has in preserving racism. Characteristics ascribed to groups of people were well established during Jim Crow racism. In the 1950s, it would not be uncommon for a white person looking over a job application from a person of color to say, "It is surprising that a black student would graduate at the top of her class at such a good high school." Whereas, in the 21st century, a white human relations manager might say, "Your class rank is very impressive." The shift is not in meaning; it is in avoiding a direct reference to the stereotype.

Many stereotypes have been carried over from the past, but the use of stereotypes has not only evolved—new stereotypes have also been constructed. For example, a new stereotype is the "pushy black man." This stereotype was created in recent years so that whites have a way to dismiss legitimate requests for equal treatment. Another stereotype invented by whites since the 1960s is the "angry black woman." Like all negative stereotypes, the new stereotypes are used to dehumanize and to preserve racism.

While stereotypes are seldom used explicitly in mixed-racial settings or generally in public, whites still refer to nonwhites using stereotypes when they think it is safe. So the prohibition on mentioning stereotypes out loud only applies to some situations.

Racist institutional practices have also mutated. Jim Crow policies stating that an organization or service is for "whites only" have largely disappeared. Official published policies that exclude people of color from organizations like golf clubs are extremely rare. But there are golf clubs where the all-white membership has not raised questions about racism. Sometimes racist policies and practices of institutions are not challenged because to do so requires pointing out specific racist actions that imply the participants are immoral. Institutional racism is sometimes ignored because institutional traditions justify practices that make no explicit reference to race. Also, institutions exchanged the explicit racist justification for policies and practices that do not mention race. In some cases, institutional policies have been changed so that there is at least a reference to diversity. There can be diversity, however, without full participation.

An example of how diversity does not equate to equal participation is the Department of Education in the Obama administration. Diversity was a high priority for the Obama administration. The Office of Presidential Personnel made a concerted effort to hire a diverse group of people to work at the Department of Education. The Obama administration appointed women and people of color to 53 percent of political positions requiring Senate approval across the government. In comparison, George W. Bush appointed women and people of color 26 percent of the time and President Clinton 37 percent of the time.[1] Comparing the diversity of the Obama and Bush administrations shows that a great deal of progress was made to address diversity, but this hid the fact that women and people of color did not have full participation. The key leadership included a higher percentage of whites, while the lower ranks had a larger percentage of people of color. Even where people of color had job titles that indicated responsibility, there was an environment of taking the ideas of whites more seriously. Participation in decision making favored white ideas. Racism was not addressed at the Department of Education because the inequity in hiring no longer existed; the people appointed by the president were a diverse group. This gave cover to the managers and supervisors to avoid allowing the full participation of women and nonwhites. And most importantly, the department continued to privilege white skin. Racism was seldom mentioned until the last two years of the Obama administration, when Secretary Arne Duncan was approached and supported several initiatives to raise racial awareness.

Disciplinary institutions have expanded greatly since the Jim Crow period. The most obvious is the criminal justice system. Michelle Alexander described how the system has been racialized:

> The War on Drugs is the vehicle through which extraordinary numbers of black men are forced into the cage. The entrapment occurs in three distinct phases. . . . The first stage is the roundup. Vast numbers of people are swept into the criminal justice system by the police, who conduct drug operations primarily in poor communities of color. They are rewarded in cash—through drug forfeiture laws and federal grant programs—for rounding up as many people as possible, and they operate unconstrained by constitutional rules of procedure that once were considered inviolate. Police can stop, interrogate, and search anyone they choose for drug investigations, provided they get "consent." Because there is no meaningful check on the exercise of police discretion, racial biases are granted free rein. In fact, police are allowed to rely on race as a factor in selecting whom to stop and search (even though people of color are no more likely to be guilty of drug crimes than whites)—effectively guaranteeing that those who are swept into the system are primarily black and brown.[2]

This is just the beginning of a process where, after being swept into the system, nonwhites are incarcerated, labeled as criminals, and monitored by a parole system. The practices of disciplinary institutions have also been expanded since the 1960s into systems like education and health care.

A NEW FRAMEWORK: THE PATCHWORK QUILT NATION

An important step was taken in the 1960s of reminding us that racism is not fair, not right, and not necessary. Now we have an understanding of how racism persists, so we can develop strategies to eliminate it. The framework of a healthy paradigm is described here. This is followed by summarizing what social scientists have learned about how paradigms change and the process necessary to bring about this change.

Figure 10.2 shows the factors that support a patchwork quilt paradigm. This is the paradigm of a nation where the civil rights dream of the 21st century is realized. The barriers that people of color and other identity groups experience have been eliminated, and there is full participation of all races and identity groups in the economic, cultural, and political life of America.

The arrow running from "Individual Actions" to the "Patchwork Quilt Paradigm" reminds us that the larger social structures that surround us are completely dependent on the day-to-day activity of every American. Overcoming racism is not something that is done once and finished. The support of the patchwork paradigm depends on continued vigilance to identify

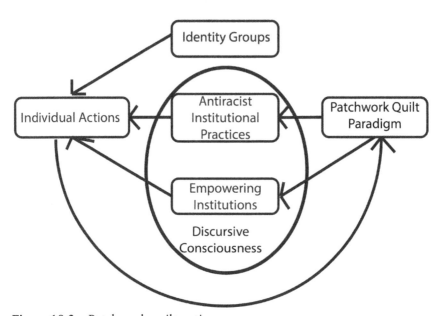

Figure 10.2   Patchwork quilt nation

new expressions of racism. When the white paradigm becomes a topic of history, new racist paradigms may appear to compete with the patchwork paradigm.

The top box in the center section labeled "Identity Groups" replaces the box in figure 10.1 labeled "Stereotypes." In the patchwork paradigm, identity groups are not defined by others. An arrow is not drawn from "Patchwork Quilt Paradigm" to "Identity Groups" because they are self-selecting. The group itself, not stereotypes, determines the characteristics of the group. Usually people don't get together and decide the characteristics they want to adopt. Rather a group like Mexican Americans meet socially, share common child-raising practices and cultural practices, and call themselves Mexican Americans. They develop a shared understanding of reality. It is this shared understanding of reality that makes them an identity group. Native American tribes are a good example of groups that have sustained identity. Rather than claiming that white is better, the patchwork paradigm claims that every identity group has its own construction of reality that is true for it. By recognizing the social construction of these identity groups, the characteristics of every group have equal value. Whites are just another identity group. And there is no justification for saying that any group is better or deserves special privileges. This will open the opportunity for Native Americans to pose questions about the sovereignty of identity groups in American society without negative stereotypes clouding the issue.

Once white identity does not have special privileges, then the role of group identity changes. With the patchwork paradigm, whites have lost their ability to say what it means to be black or Asian. Whites will be expected to answer the same question that every identity group is asked: What makes you special or different, and what gifts do you bring to the life of the nation? Without the categories forced by racism, identity groups may form around a variety of self-identified social, historical, or cultural categories. For example, an identity group may develop of people who continue the traditions of the black churches, keep alive the memory of the oppression of color-based racism, take a special interest in Africa, and share cultural traditions like music and food. But, and this is important, a person with dark skin and some ancestors who came from Africa is not required to identify as black.

Identity groups have a socially constructed shared culture that is important in the self-identity of members of the group. This differs from interest and issue groups, which are independent of the self-identity of the participants. An example of an interest group, in contrast, might be a group of people interested in Zulu culture. They could form an online community where they share what they know or are learning about the Zulu people of South Africa, but they would not intend to adopt Zulu culture or to become Zulu.

The patchwork paradigm allows for individuals from different identity groups to join together when they share a concern for a specific social issue.

Issues that are not associated with identity can be addressed with equal participation by all groups. With some issues, like human trafficking, the perspectives from different groups help address the issue.

There will always be boundaries to negotiate. Questions will need to be asked. Does a particular practice by an identity group do harm to themselves or to others? When does the common good require limits on what individuals or an identity group can do? These can be complicated issues, but this is not new for Americans. For example, the issue of polygamy forced discussion about when a group can participate in a practice that is outside the norm of the majority. With the patchwork paradigm, there is more diversity in the political process. All questions that concern the common good are considered with full participation from all groups.

The arrow running from "Identity Groups" to "Individual Actions" signifies the importance of identity groups in the development of self-identity. The self-identity that results from relating to identity groups is the primary determiner of individual actions. This is a critical difference between the white paradigm and the patchwork paradigm. When the white paradigm claims superiority for whites, it implies inferiority for nonwhites. Making identity groups free to define themselves provides an independent source of self-identity. This self-identity is untainted by stereotypes imposed by the white paradigm.

The middle box labeled "Antiracist Institutional Practices" represents the work that needs to be done to eliminate the effects of institutional racism. The penetration of racism in American society and institutions is so deep and entrenched that we will need to be vigilant in looking for vestiges of racism and rooting them out. Just like the heritage of slavery or the detention of Japanese in World War II are part of our history, racism based on the white paradigm of the 21st century should never be forgotten. The arrow from the "Patchwork Quilt Paradigm" box to the "Antiracist Institutional Practices" box represents the resource that institutions have to evaluate new and existing policies and practices: *the civil rights dream of full participation by all groups and the removal of barriers that limit individuals' ability to achieve their aspirations.* This civil rights dream becomes the articulated and discussed criteria for evaluating policies and practices. The dream replaces the unspoken assumption of white superiority.

"Empowering Institutions," the third box, are described in chapter 9. They replace disciplinary institutions designed to make people better. Empowering institutions are designed to support the development of each person. In the patchwork paradigm, empowering institutions, like all institutions, are inspired by the patchwork paradigm to help each person find and pursue personal aspirations. They are distinct from other institutions because their primary purpose is to support the development of individuals. Other institutions have purposes like providing goods and services, moving people from one place to another, and supporting communication. Empowering institutions in a patchwork nation have increased importance. They include more than schools and the criminal justice system. The health care system will be empowering when it helps individuals become and stay healthy. The entertainment industry, for example, becomes empowering as it provides opportunities for artistic expression that are not controlled by the white paradigm.

The "Discursive Consciousness" circle around institutions is a reminder that institutions cannot be left to practical consciousness where racism is not considered. The patchwork paradigm requires that we think about our participation in institutions and reflect on how our participation might perpetuate stereotypes or privilege whites. With the patchwork paradigm, reflection is necessary to identify racist language and actions.

Like figure 10.1, figure 10.2 is incomplete in showing the interconnections between all of the factors involved. "Identity Groups" play an important role in supporting "Empowering Institutions." "Individual Actions" not only support the patchwork paradigm, they also create and sustain identity groups.

ADOPTING THE PATCHWORK PARADIGM

Changes in paradigms do not happen overnight. Social theorists like Giddens and Pierre Bourdieu emphasize the important role that time plays in social theory. The history of racism in America reminds us that expanding civil rights is often a painful and time-intensive process. In order to move from the white paradigm to the patchwork paradigm, we need to consider methodically walking through the following steps:

Step 1—Recognize the power of the white paradigm.

Step 2—Question the white paradigm and see an alternative.

Step 3—Embrace the patchwork paradigm sufficiently to indicate an end of the dominance of the white paradigm, the turning point.

Step 4—Preserve the patchwork paradigm as the dominant paradigm.

Avoiding the first step has resulted in our failure to take the civil rights movement of the 1960s to its logical conclusion. History is always made by individuals, and the movement to a patchwork paradigm requires individual action, but we will also need to act collectively to end racism.

Step 1: Recognize the Power of the White Paradigm

Figure 10.3 shows the white paradigm as the dominant paradigm in American society. The cage of the white paradigm surrounds everyone. It is the black box that everyone in America lives inside. The circles represent

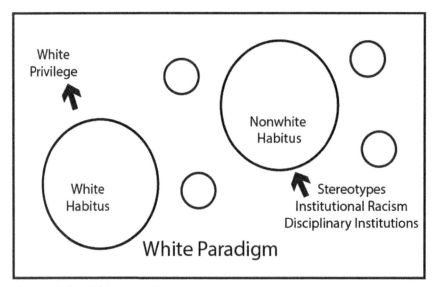

Figure 10.3   White paradigm cage

individuals. In this cage of racism, there are more than 300 million circles. This is the starting point. Whites and nonwhites have different experiences of living in the white paradigm. Like fingerprints, every person has a unique habitus—all of the resources that an individual has in all levels of consciousness to decide what to say and how to act. Other figures could be drawn that show the impact of wealth inequality, place of residence, gender inequality, and many other factors that impact the development of each person's habitus.

Even when we don't recognize it, we take actions that support the white paradigm. Stereotypes are part of the environment of the white paradigm. As we saw in chapter 7, stereotypes have a particularly strong impact on nonwhites. White privilege is also an important component of the environment of the white paradigm. Privilege impacts the habitus of whites who come to expect benefits from having white skin.

Nonwhite Americans have their experiences limited in many ways. The arrow points toward the example of a nonwhite person because the white paradigm works to limit possibilities and the expansion of the habitus. One way the white paradigm limits nonwhites is through institutional practices that isolate nonwhites from a variety of experiences that are open to whites. This has been well documented regarding the experiences of school-age children during the summer months. White children living in the suburbs have multiple enrichment experiences available, but children living in the inner city watch television or hang out with friends on the street. The result is that the children in the inner city have less experience to develop a rich repertoire of knowledge to navigate situations when they move beyond their setting.[3]

Another form of oppression is the result of disciplinary institutions, which limit the expansion of the habitus with structures like the criminal justice system. The criminal justice system targets nonwhites, labels them as criminals, enrolls them in a restrictive system called parole, and provides a justification for discrimination in jobs and other opportunities.

Oppression in North America began when British settlers saw themselves as morally and culturally superior to Native Americans. As chapter 2 describes, British settlers expanded this oppression to include black African slaves. They settled on white supremacy as the basis for this oppression. Having established the white paradigm, Americans were able to apply it as the basis for the oppression of Mexicans when Texas became part of the United States. Since then, the white paradigm has been successfully used to oppress successive waves of immigrants. For example, a rationale for excluding and oppressing Asians did not need to be created because the white paradigm was already firmly established.

The white paradigm not only restricts nonwhites. While the primary role of the white paradigm is to support white superiority and preserve special privileges for whites, it also limits the range of experiences open to whites. The taboo on sharing across racial lines about the personal experience nonwhites have of oppression is an example. It limits whites' understanding and the possibility of developing a habitus that is sensitive to oppression. In short, the white paradigm is a bad idea for everyone.

Step 2: Question the White Paradigm and See an Alternative

Figure 10.4 shows the first movement toward the adoption of the patchwork paradigm. Step 2 is stimulated by a few individuals and institutions that recognize there are problems with the white paradigm. Whereas step 1 is a period of stability of race relations, step 2 begins a period of action. There is a recognition that the white paradigm is not working. Some people notice that striving for diversity does not produce full participation. Others wonder why even basic equality is an elusive goal. This is important because it raises questions about whether the white paradigm is common sense. The idea for a new paradigm comes from an individual or group who first recognizes a better alternative. These are represented by the circle inside the area of the patchwork paradigm.

Individuals expand habitus in three ways. First, they recognize the contradictions that exist in their understanding of reality. For example, it may become impossible to ignore the firing of a Hispanic coworker so that a white person can be hired. This internal force for change coexists with the

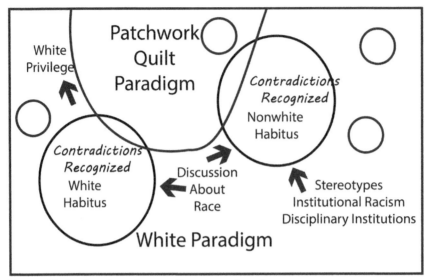

Figure 10.4 Patchwork paradigm introduced

habitus. Second, other people stimulate consideration of race. This discussion about race has an impact on habitus. Chapter 12 includes stories from people about their experience of racism. These are examples of the kind of conversations that expand our habitus. Third, some people and organizations begin to experiment with alternatives to race-based practices. This is represented by the patchwork paradigm intruding into the dominance of the white paradigm. The patchwork paradigm also begins to penetrate the consciousness of individuals.

Figure 10.4 represents race relations in the early years of the 21st century. The white paradigm is the dominant paradigm for race relations, but there are some people who are committed to alternatives.

Step 3: Embrace the Patchwork Paradigm

At some point, the patchwork paradigm becomes a large influence in the day-to-day lives of enough people that a turning point is reached. Step 3 occurs when the patchwork paradigm is sufficiently embraced to indicate an end of the dominance of the white paradigm.

At this point, the habitus of many people includes everyday knowledge about interacting with people who are different. Those interactions are not based on the assumption of white superiority or assigned stereotypes. Most importantly, there are more resources available to individuals to develop and pursue their aspirations. Just as the range of strategies available to individuals is changing, institutions are also changing. This turning point is critical. Disciplinary and other institutions are under pressure to adjust. It is impossible for them to continue under the assumptions of the white paradigm.

It is not predetermined that this period of transformation or turning point will result in the full adoption of the patchwork paradigm, the end of racism, and the realization of the civil rights dream. The white paradigm is still part of the social environment with strong institutional support. As we saw in chapter 2, southern states after the Civil War experienced a period of transformation where the previous paradigm of slavery that had defined race relations was abandoned. The occupation of the United States military ensured that former slaves could exercise their right to vote, to serve in elected offices, and to access educational opportunities. There were experiments with social integration, but rather than embrace this new paradigm, as soon as the troops left, whites developed new strategies to impose white superiority. In a short time, Jim Crow racism was firmly established as the paradigm that structured race relations.

In the same way, the fragility of the new social order and the strength of the white paradigm can cause a backlash that results in a transformation of the white paradigm and the preservation of a system of oppression. While it is difficult to predict what form this backlash might take, there are already signs of one possible alternative paradigm. Since whites control economic power, stereotypes might be shifted so that poverty becomes the primary criteria used to define hierarchy in American society. This would not be good news for people of color because such a shift would only make it possible to drive skin-color racism deeper underground in disciplinary institutions, where it will become even harder to eradicate. A paradigm based on economic success defined by white values would also make it particularly difficult for immigrants to establish a place in American society.

Step 4: Preserve the Patchwork Paradigm

The final step is illustrated in figure 10.5. This shows the patchwork paradigm as the foundation for American society. When this step is reached, vigilance will still be required to preserve the participation of all in American society, but institutions will support the empowerment of individuals. The barriers that inhibit people of color from full participation will be removed. Everyone will benefit from expanded habitus. This includes the habitus of whites, who are no longer restricted by race relations that inhibit sharing across racial lines. People of color will experience even greater possibilities for expanded habitus because of the elimination of social structures created by racism.

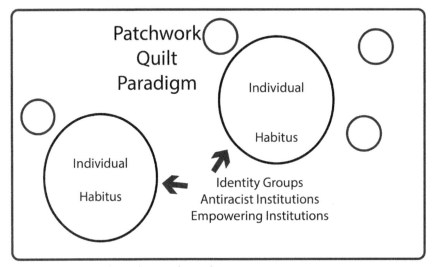

Figure 10.5   Patchwork paradigm dominates

In figures 10.3 and 10.4, there was a distinction between whites and non-whites. When the patchwork paradigm is dominant, white privilege will disappear. Figure 10.5 includes six individuals who represent that every person in America has unique aspirations as well as unique habitus.

It is one thing to recognize the process of paradigm transformation. It is another to put it into practice. The next part points to specific strategies and lifts up real examples of individuals and institutions who are taking antiracism seriously.

Section 3

Realizing the Dream

Chapter 11

Being Antiracist in Everyday Life

When my family and I lived just north of Seattle in the 1990s, we attended the Ronald United Methodist Church in Shoreline, Washington. The pastor was of Filipino descent, but he had prepared for the ministry at a seminary in Columbus, Ohio. His style was very welcoming. He appeared to be well received by the whites who had been members for years. The congregants included Filipinos, Africans, West Indians, Japanese, Koreans, South Americans, Europeans, and others. The pastor would go to great lengths to explain the cultural context of music from all these cultures, but he never explained the European music. For example, the church had a beautiful organ. A white member who was an accomplished organist sometimes played a piece of sacred music written by Johann Sebastian Bach. No one pointed out that Bach was the director of music at the Lutheran churches in Leipzig, Germany, for 27 years before he died in 1750. Music written by Bach has a cultural context just as a beautiful song from the Philippines does. The assumption that white culture, behaviors, values, and lifestyles are normal is a foundation of racism in America.

The pastor and congregation did not have a racist intent. I didn't see the racism in what was happening until I reflected on the church services several years later. The racism was unintentional and without reflection. This experience raised for me the question of what it means to be white in 21st-century America. If, as I have argued, the civil rights dream is for full participation of all racial groups, what is the role of whites in this patchwork paradigm nation? How can I be part of facilitating the full participation of all groups in American society? What do we all need to do—regardless of our racial identity?

The framework in chapter 10 shows us the role of identity in preserving racism. Treating racism requires intentional adjustment in our approach to identity. In a patchwork society, everyone benefits from being part of identity groups that sustain them. This is a critical step in treating racism, but it is only a step. Another important step in the transition to and preservation of a patchwork nation is that everyone needs to develop a strong awareness—or sense—of racism. A sense of racism will be described more fully later, but in a nutshell, it is the ability to recognize racism in everyday life, institutions, and government.

It is possible that we could become a pluralistic nation of individuals committed to their own identity groups. This appears to be the approach taken by societies in the past who experimented with being multicultural. One example is Cordoba, a city in what is now southern Spain that thrived in the 10th and 11th centuries. It was an important cultural center where Muslim rulers supported educational institutions and protected Christians and Jews. Eboo Patel, the author of *Sacred Ground: Pluralism, Prejudice, and the Promise of America*, claims that "Cordoba predicted America. It was a civilization that experimented with a partial pluralism, extended limited rights to diverse communities, and allowed some degree of civic and political participation."[1] As we look back 1,000 years, Cordoba appears to be a society where individuals participated in identity groups of Muslim, Christian, and Jewish. It also appears that the Muslim Moors were clearly in charge, and everyone must have been very aware that the Moors had special privileges. While Cordoba may have predicted America, it did not fully achieve the goal of the patchwork society I have proposed. Our goal is the civil rights dream of full participation. Achieving this goal requires taking actions in our everyday lives.

The importance of what we all do every day is the basis for social theory developed since the 1960s: everyone, every day, unintentionally and intentionally, communicates and acts in ways that preserve racism. This chapter focuses on what we do as individuals in our everyday lives that supports racism. Three areas are considered: our identity, our sense of racism, and our interactions with others. This is not a comprehensive list of ways the framework of racism can help us in our daily life. Our most important tool for identifying antiracist activities is to test a proposed thought, word, or action against the civil rights dream. Do we promote full participation, and do we support individuals in achieving their personal aspirations? We are not alone as we each find our path to pursue antiracist work. Chapter 12 and 13 provide specific examples of individuals and organizations that are taking action to treat racism. Chapter 14 considers several antiracist strategies that specifically address institutions and government.

ADOPTING AUTHENTIC IDENTITY

For everyone, adopting authentic identity means rejecting the claim that America is a white nation. It means rejecting that white culture and values define normal. This is the lesson of the Ronald Church. In a patchwork nation, white culture needs to be explained to others with the same seriousness and pride as every other culture. White is not the "normal," and all people can be considered to be colored. This is the most important lesson we can learn from social science since the 1960s. It is the basis of American racism: racism persists because the idea that white skin is normal and better is supported by everyday thoughts and interactions.

To quickly review the importance of everyday life, everyone's everyday activity is possible because thoughts and interactions are organized, given meaning, and justified with the support of a personal organization of past experiences called *habitus*. Each person's habitus develops over time in the context of a socially constructed societal paradigm that white is better. The white paradigm influences the habitus through stereotypes, institutional racism, and disciplinary institutions. This brings us full circle because each person's habitus is the source of the idea that white skin is better and defines what is normal.

Thinking about what the Ronald Church would look like under the assumption that everyone has color helps us see how we all benefit from abandoning the white paradigm. With opportunities to express the cultural source of worship activities, each member would be challenged to think more deeply about the gifts that can be offered to the whole community from her or his identity. The question of what is normal or traditional is abandoned along with the idea that white practices are better. Everyone is asked, "What is there about my identity group that I can offer to the whole community? What are the gifts that my group and I can bring?" We can imagine the Ronald Church where everyone brings gifts from their identity group, and every identity group has full participation in a shared worshiping community.

In modern society, every person finds her own route to an identity that avoids as many internal contradictions as possible. We do this in the context of social interactions with different groups. Because of the diversity of American society, we can identify with the shared values and customs of more than one identity group. I find the example of the Hispanic American community helpful. There is an emerging Hispanic American identity, but it is growing out of a Peruvian Hispanic American identity, a Mexican Hispanic American identity, a Puerto Rican Hispanic American identity, and many more. Whites also come from a variety of historical contexts.

As chapter 7 described, we each develop a habitus with our values and preferences. In racist America, whites aren't required to struggle with finding and claiming an identity because whites simply claim supremacy of the white paradigm. There are whites who grew up in a very racist family and environment. There are those who grew up in a whites-only environment. There are whites who have a white Italian American experience, yet the question of identity is seldom raised.

My friend Jon O'Bergh, who has written a book about his own journey to claim an identity as a gay man,[2] helped me understand this. He pointed out that, as whites, we can each find an identity that is a starting point. In his case, it is the southern California beach culture that he grew up in. For me, it is the liberal college setting of the 1960s. It was there that I had Jewish and Hindu roommates, I became committed to racial justice, I began to think about war and violence, and I decided that I wanted to learn more about Christianity. I arrived at college with a feeling that there were contradictions in what seemed fair to me and the American social and economic system; it was during college that I discovered language to talk about sexism, militarism, racism, and economic exploitation. O'Bergh helped me recognize that when I ask myself, "Who am I?" I always go back to the questions I had in college. It is my starting point for looking back from that point to the values and opportunities that my parents and small-town Iowa environment gave me. It is also the starting point for the continuing evolution of who I want to be and where I fit in to my environment. This book is an example of my personal journey by starting in the 1960s and moving forward and backward to understand and address racism.

In a workshop led by Michelle Molitor in 2016, I became aware of how important it is for everyone, including myself, to claim a racial identity. Molitor asks participants who they are to themselves, to others, and in their work. She explains, "That sounds simple, but many adults, particularly white adults, have not spent extensive time considering their identity in society. They haven't needed to—their identity is often the norm."[3] Molitor calls this thinking about "the skin you're in." It is claiming participation in one of the patches of a patchwork nation. For whites, this is particularly important because it not only provides integrity when engaging with others but also ensures that they do not assume that their identity defines a normal or preferred identity.

For whites, thinking about the skin we're in also involves recognizing the role of all whites in creating and perpetuating barriers for people of color. In the 21st century, white skin continues to carry institutionalized benefits. It is impossible to live in America as a white and not benefit from having white skin. Yet a majority of whites ignore or deny this fact. The opinion of some whites—that America has become a land where people of color have political power that is used to disadvantage whites—is contrary to economic and political data. Stereotyping, institutional racism, and disciplinary institutions all play a role in supporting the falsehood that racism has disappeared.

Categories of race are imposed by the social construction of reality where whites use their social power to define stereotypes. For people of color, reflecting on "the skin we're in" involves managing racial stereotypes. This can be a long and painful process of standing against the stereotypes and claiming an identity that is authentic. Barack Obama wrote a book titled *Dreams from My Father* about his journey to find and claim an identity.[4]

The complexity of claiming an identity should not be minimized. It is impossible without a reference to the historical context. White identity includes Bach's music, but it also includes slave masters, segregation, and Jim Crow racism.

It is tempting to decide that it is too difficult to deal with the question, "Who am I?" It may seem that it is easier to live one day at a time and get by. Paulo Freire warns us, "If I lose myself in the details of daily life, I lose, at the same time, a vision of the dramatic meaning of my existence, I become either fatalistic or cynical." Freire goes on to point out that claiming our identity cannot begin with the moment and ignore the past. "In the same way, if I try to escape from the daily demands and details to take up my life's dramatic character—but without at the same time becoming historically involved—I can have no other destiny than to fall into an empty intellectualism, equally alienating. I shall then see existence as something impossible and hopeless." Becoming historically involved means recognizing that, as individuals, we are part of time that has a past and a future. History is a process, and we are a part of it. We make history. Being historically involved is saying, "I cannot permit myself to be a mere spectator. On the contrary, I must demand my place in the process of change." The process of claiming an identity that Freire proposes is not once and done. The question "Who am I?" is constantly before us. The question comes with our shared humanity. Freire calls it a permanent challenge: "So the dramatic tension between the past and the future, death and life, being and nonbeing, is no longer a kind of dead end for me; I can see it for what it really is: a permanent challenge to which I must respond."[5]

For whites who benefit from racism, reflecting on "the skin you're in" can be a starting point for claiming an authentic identity. It puts the question clearly in the context of historical racism. For both whites and nonwhites, the first step is to reject stereotypes and to ask ourselves, What is important to me? What communities do I belong to? What makes me who I am? In the end, the goal of claiming our identity for everyone is to claim the meaning that our identity gives to our lives. Another benefit of reflection on our identity is that our identity is the foundation for cross-racial conversations.

As Molitor explains, one benefit of clarifying our own identity is that "we are much more capable of putting ourselves in the position of someone different from us."[6] It is not just that cross-racial conversations are improved when participants have given thought to their own identity. Honest conversations are impossible when whites see their identity as the normal way to be human. While we can look forward to a time when stereotypes are no longer imposed on any group, until that time every American's self-identity has a racial component. The other side of that coin is that every American has an identity with gifts to offer to others. The Ronald Church illustrates what it means when nonwhites offer the gifts that their racial and ethnic identities bring to a community. A patchwork community abandons the idea that white is normal so that both nonwhites and whites bring gifts from their identity to share on equal footing.

The Ronald Church also illustrates what happens when people do not recognize racism. I didn't think about it until years later, after I had moved to Ohio. The organist might have wondered why all the other music was explained. He could have requested a few minutes to explain the cultural context of the music he played, but he probably didn't notice what was happening. Because no one pointed out the racism, there was no antiracist response.

A SENSE OF RACISM

Before we can take an intentional antiracist action, we need to recognize the racist actions that surround us. The goal for ourselves and our children is to increase our habitus so that we have a sense of racism. A sense of racism is similar to a sense of humor. It develops in our habitus as we participate in society. Every time we hear another person make a statement, it gets filtered through our habitus and checked to see if it is funny. Sometimes we are in a setting where we know that other people are joking around. We expect what they say to be something they think is funny. At other times, we are surprised by a statement and start to laugh. Other times we consider in our discursive consciousness whether a statement is meant to be funny and whether it is polite to laugh. Finally, there are times when our habitus runs a screen and we know that it is not funny. It is never funny to yell "fire" in a packed theater.

Our sense of humor seems natural, but like all of the habitus, it develops as we interact with the surrounding environment and society. A sense of humor can be cultivated, and so can a sense of racism. Since we are not born with a sense of humor or a sense of racism, both develop as we go through childhood and later.

Because of the white paradigm, it is possible for whites to develop a self-identity that is based on an unstated assumption of white superiority. Even when presented with a multiracial environment, a white racial identity is not always recognized because the identity is assumed to be normal. The white paradigm protects whites from the necessity of developing a sense of self with a strong racial component. Therefore, most whites need to intentionally develop a sense of racism. In all cases, developing a strong sense of racism requires the support of others who will help make sense of our experiences.

As we saw in chapters 6 and 7, there are two ways that a sense of racism can be enhanced. The first is through the social construction of our reality where other people exhibit racial sensitivity; we pick up an ability to recognize racism from them. The second way occurs because our habitus not only recognizes what is orthodox or expected but also what is unorthodox. By considering the unorthodox, we can see racism where others around us miss it. So we both learn to recognize racism from others and we figure it out for ourselves.

Even when we figure out for ourselves that a particular action or institution is racist, we still need confirmation from other people. The double consciousness that Du Bois identified is only possible when there are two communities where reality is defined

The theory of paradigm change explains the importance of a community that supports the new paradigm. The white paradigm is supported by societal structures. As we begin to adopt a new patchwork paradigm, we need a community of support. The white paradigm uses segregation to protect whites from engaging in pluralist institutions and communities. Developing a habitus that is sensitive to racism is facilitated by participation in interracial communities. This presents a problem because there is little reason for people to trust others across racial lines. Without trust, community is impossible.

John McKnight is an advocate for revitalizing neighborhoods. In his book *The Abundant Community: Awakening the Power of Families and Neighborhoods*, he observes that "competent community is a place where that which is most personal can be manifested. The loss of the personal connection with a neighbor is more of a crisis now because the extended family has disappeared." This is not a call for a return to an idealized neighborhood; rather it is a recognition that our individual development of healthy self-identity depends on a trusting community. McKnight goes on, "The purpose for reinvesting caring capacity in neighborhoods and communities is to replace the loss of the extended family."[7]

EVERYDAY INTERACTION

Even with a support system, when we recognize an act of racism or a racist institution, we may avoid antiracist activity due to social pressures. For example, we might avoid a simple thing like discussing racism with a relative. As long as the white paradigm is dominant, there will be pushback. There are risks when racism is named or challenged, and it is only logical to consider the cost. There are circumstances where we need to be strategic in confronting racism. There are times when confronting a racist situation benefits from planning a response with supporters. Three examples of ways that individuals can be intentional about antiracist activities are (1) paying attention to the words we use and their meaning, (2) being honest about our history, and (3) supporting our neighbors or the people who are around us.

OUR WORDS

Studies that show the power of stereotype threats are described in chapter 7. Even an indirect reminder of a stereotype impacts the target. Americans know that we can pay attention to what we say and change the language we use regarding racism. Once we understood in the 1960s that racism is immoral, we decided not to use racial slurs in the presence of people who are different from us. Everyone learned this. Whites learned not to use racial slurs related to nonwhites. People of color learned not to use slurs related to other groups. This is called being politically correct because it is used to hide racial beliefs rather than to address them. As we saw in chapter 7, replacing words that had previously been offensive with microaggressions did not address racism. An antiracist step is to develop a sensitivity to microaggressions so that interracial exchanges are not based on unstated stereotypes.

Our discussion about racism will also benefit from our attention to words like *equal*. In some situations, the word *equality* has been coopted to support racism. *Equal* can easily become a verbal microaggression that conveys a commitment to white supremacy. Making things equal could mean that oppression is addressed, and it could also involve addressing the special privileges of whites in America. However, the equality language has made it possible to avoid discussion about both oppression and privilege. Calling for equality in education is a good example of the use of the word *equality* to avoid addressing racism. Most education reform discussion begins with pointing out the "achievement gap" between white students and others. Then a proposal is made to "help" the others catch up to the white students and close this gap. This is called *working for equality*. The approach supports a racist perspective that white education is the best education one can obtain. The implication is that what needs fixing is nonwhites. Or worse, it is heard by nonwhite students as "you are not as good as white students."

When equal education means white education, we are not addressing the goal of full participation. An education system with full participation would include participation of people of color in working out a curriculum that is sensitive to the cultural gifts that nonwhite students, teachers, and administrators can bring. Calls for equal opportunity or equal access also have a racist subtext. Equal opportunity can mean inviting nonwhite students into an education environment where they are at a disadvantage compared to white students. When equal access means access to an education environment defined by the white paradigm, the civil rights agenda is not advanced. Rather than using the words *equal* and *equality*, we can use the words *pluralist* and *pluralistic*. This will help us develop a strong antiracist habitus and will help those we talk to realize that our antiracist goal is not to make everyone equal to whites. Rather, we want pluralism, where everyone has full participation.

The word *tolerance* has also been hijacked to support the white paradigm. This is partly because of a problem with the English language. Tolerance sounds like it is the opposite of intolerance. Since intolerance is one of the sources of racist activity, tolerance becomes a goal. The problem is that both intolerance and tolerance allow the white paradigm to remain unchallenged. A white can be intolerant of native Spanish speakers. And another white can tolerate native Spanish speakers while still holding to the position that native English speakers are superior. The word *pluralism* is the opposite of both tolerance and intolerance. Unlike *intolerance*, *pluralism* does not include a negative judgment of others. Unlike *tolerance*, *pluralism* does not imply that one position is better than another even though other positions are respected. Pluralism says, "my position is true for me" and "other positions are equally valid for other people."

Talking about full participation and pluralism is shifting our language so it is consistent with the civil rights dream; it is not adopting politically correct language. Talking about pluralism is not using coded language; it is promoting a vision for a nation that is nonracist. Abandoning racial slurs in polite conversation turned out to be an easy way to support the white paradigm. This is because words like *blacks* and *Indians* or *Native Americans* replaced the previously used objectionable words, but the stereotypes were carried over to the polite word. Moving beyond the white paradigm requires not only thinking about our language but also using the language to express an antiracist perspective. Giddens's theory of consciousness is helpful in defining the task. Until we establish a fully antiracist habitus, our use of words like *pluralism* and *equality* need to be brought to the level of our discursive consciousness every time we use them.

OUR HISTORY

In 1967, Martin Luther King Jr. pointed out in his book *Where Do We Go from Here?* that we need to tell each other the truth. He wrote, "It is time for all of us to *tell each other the truth* about who and what have brought the Negro to the condition of deprivation against which he struggles today" (italics added).[8] He goes on to explain that most groups deceive even themselves. Groups that oppress rationalize their beliefs and look for scapegoats. He points to blindness of individual and collective sins. King said that people who live with untruth are living lives in spiritual slavery. The necessity of talking to each other about racism is as important today as it was in 1967. Only by talking to each other will we be able to come to a common understanding of the truth about racism in our own time.

One of the strategies that preserves the white paradigm is that whites are committed to relational segregation. This has been particularly true for housing and education. In 1967, the Supreme Court case of *Loving v. Virginia* made interracial marriages legal in all states. Marriages across racial lines are an indication that things are changing. By 2016, more than 10 percent of marriages were across racial lines. As this continues, families will become integrated in ways that open up opportunities for conversation. Yet even in families with members from more than one race, race can be a taboo subject for conversation. A common microaggression is for whites to refuse to hear the stories of oppression. When a nonwhite begins to describe an experience of being excluded or denied opportunity, a white person can always offer an alternative explanation for the incident. For whites, denying oppression can be an unconscious strategy to preserve the white paradigm. Often the objection is expressed verbally so that it adds another layer of microaggression. The white person says, "I am sure that wasn't intended," or "That happens to everyone," or "You should have just said something." An important step in overcoming racism is to encourage people to tell their stories of oppression and for everyone to listen to them. By telling and discussing our stories, we help each other uncover the unconscious sources of racist actions. Our story sharing also helps us develop strategies for responding in the future to the racism we encounter.

Whites also need to share their stories of experiencing privilege. I worked with a young woman, Anna Leach, who told me about feeling uncomfortable about her privilege. She had obtained a position as an intern in the office of a member of Congress because of family connections. Then, because she had sufficient family financial resources, she was able to volunteer as an intern in the Department of Education. She was ultimately hired after college to work at the Department of Education. Leach talked about how she didn't know how to feel as a white person benefiting from all her advantages. This is the sort of storytelling and discussion that moves us all forward. We all have stories about oppression and privilege. Whites have stories of observing oppression and sometimes stories of experiencing oppression. Nonwhites observe privilege and sometimes have stories of experiencing privilege. All of these stories are important to share and talk about.

As previously noted, too often whites shut down sharing stories about oppression and privilege with the comment, "I am not a racist, but . . ." Since *racist* is not an identity group, there is no reason to claim not to be a racist. As sociology shows, we are all immersed in racist institutions, and we all participate in racist actions. We can open our story sharing by explaining, "This is how I felt when . . ." or "I was confused when . . ." or "This really happened to me . . ." or "When you said that it made me uncomfortable because . . ." The best stories are about how we feel and what we experience.

Just as stories are important in discovering and clarifying what it means to live in the patchwork paradigm, stories are also a tool to support stereotypes and racist practices. Telling stories about a drunk Indian or a black manager who was fired or a Latino who stole a car supports racist stereotypes. This is a reminder that when we hear or tell stories, it is important to run them through our discursive consciousness to test them against our sense of racism. When we hear ourselves or others telling a story that includes a reference to a stereotype, we have an opportunity to bring into a conversation the relevance of the story to antiracist conversation.

The following chapter includes examples of people telling their stories of how they became aware of the racism that surrounds them and their responses to it. Everyone has a story. Those stories are helpful to us as we share them and helpful to others who hear them.

OUR NEIGHBORS

Helping the young people around us is one place where we can, as individuals, participate in antiracist activity. Parents play an important role in helping young people both claim their identity and develop a sense of racism. Other adults have opportunities to engage with young people who live nearby. Adults can play many roles, including as role models, tutors, coaches, and mentors.

A role model is simply a person who demonstrates positive behaviors. If young people only see adults ignoring racism, they will learn this behavior. Stereotypes are passed from one generation to the next by adults. Bold examples of antiracist activity provide youth with possibilities for their own antiracist activity.

Tutors are adults who have a particular skill that they offer to teach someone. The tutor enters into an agreement to pass on the skill to another person. Part of the antiracist work ahead of us is to remove the barriers that young people of color face. The barriers that nonwhite students face are often systemic, but they can be personal. When adults provide support for a young person that addresses a specific barrier he faces, it helps the young person. It also helps the adult gain a greater understanding of the structures of racism so that institutional racism can be addressed. As the structuration theory shows us, it helps the nation become a patchwork nation.

A coach is like a tutor in that the goal is to help a young person increase in skills or accomplish a goal. The difference is that the tutor's work is defined by the skill to be transferred. The coach begins with the student. The coach helps the student succeed, while the tutor passes on a skill.

A mentor is a person with experience who offers to help a young person with her aspirations. Being supportive of aspirations begins with listening carefully. This is the basis for true mentoring: listening until a young person discovers an aspiration, helping the young person learn what is required to fulfill that aspiration, supporting the identification of barriers and resources, and making sure the young person knows that she is not alone—someone else is committed to her success.

Margo Murray is a business consultant who specializes in helping businesses develop mentoring programs. She points out that the best mentors are trained. One of the components of a mentoring process is the use of "strategies and tools for diagnosing the developmental need."[9]

Not all mentoring is antiracist mentoring. If a white mentor with a commitment to white superiority works with a student of color, the relationship can be filled with microaggressions. If white professionals are recruited to mentor students of color and the mentors are not provided extensive training, the whole program is based on a racist assumption that just because someone is a white professional, she is equipped to help a student of color. Yet mentoring that is designed to assist a young person find and attain her aspiration is an effective antiracist strategy.

PARTICIPATING IN CHANGE

Paying attention to our words, being honest about our history, and helping our neighbors are just some examples of antiracist activities. Being a member of society is the only requirement for you and me to play a role in realizing the civil rights dream. The opposite is also true. If individuals are not intentional about eliminating racism, then the social structure of racism will stay in place. Everyone needs to find a way to participate in antiracist activity. The more people who participate in antiracist behaviors, the sooner the paradigm shift will occur. Everyone can do a little or a lot of antiracism work, but unless a lot of people do a lot of antiracism work, the white paradigm will continue to be the foundation of American society. The advances in social science theory not only show the way racism functions but also that the task of doing away with racism is complex. The lesson of the last half of the 20th century is that racism will not just wither away.

Everyone has reasons or excuses for not being intentional about standing up to racism. Even with a strong self-identity and a good sense of racism, it is difficult to initiate antiracist activity. Probably the most common excuse used by both whites and nonwhites is that their actions will not make a difference. The framework that sustains racism makes it clear that actions do make a difference. Because every racist action supports the white paradigm, every antiracist action makes a contribution to building the patchwork paradigm.

Chapter 12

We All Have Stories

Finding our way in a racist environment requires a personal journey. Except for Cheryl Crazy Bull, whom I met in the process of writing this book, all of these stories are from people who have inspired me over the years. I found that even though I knew them, there was more to their stories than I knew before. I have learned from all of them in the past, but I learned even more when I sat them down and asked them to tell me their stories, which are shared below. I was reminded of how important it is to take time to listen to the stories even of people we think we know.

These stories share a common feature: each person, in some way, came to a self-understanding that she or he is a person of worth in a racist society. When this happened, they all found themselves with a life path, both personal and profession, that addresses racism.

In the context of this book, the stories illustrate the connection between developing a sense of racism and developing a self-identity. They also illustrate what we can learn from each other when we listen carefully to the experience of other people as they confront racism. Because overcoming racism requires changing the nature of our social interactions, talking about racism with each other is an important step.

Several of the people I interview told me, and I know from my own experience, that sharing our stories helps us develop our self-identity and learn things about ourselves. So when we listen to others' stories, we are giving them a gift.

RALPH SINGH[1]

Like most Sikh men, Ralph Singh has a full beard and wears a turban, but he hasn't always been a Sikh. In the summer of 1970, he had just finished his degree in Japanese studies at Columbia University when a spiritual being appeared to him with a diamond-like light shining from his head. The man instructed him to meditate on something that looked like an atom. Taking the money his parents had intended for him to use in graduate school, he set off on a quest that took him to India. There, in February 1971, six months after the vision, he found himself in Delhi and face to face with the man he had seen in his vision. He became a disciple of Baba Virsa Singh.

Baba Virsa Singh does not read or write any language, but those who met him would attest that he could answer any question on any matter from personal issues to the state of a nation to the nature of the cosmos. Everything came to him through revelation. He was a saint in the Sikh tradition, following a series of Sikh gurus dating back to the 15th-century teachings of Guru Nanak. Sikhs believe in one God that is present in everything in the universe. The gurus encourage a life based on meditation, belief in the unity and equality of all humanity, hard work, and the practice of selfless service based on social justice. They celebrate the wisdom that comes from the prophets and teachers of all faith traditions, enshrined in the scripture they revere as the eternal guru, Guru Granth Sahib. When I visited Singh at his home in upstate New York, he showed me the shrine he built in his backyard garden where there are pictures of Sikh gurus, images of Baba Siri Chand ji, Buddha, and the Virgin Mary as well as other symbols of faith.

Since meeting Baba Virsa Singh, Singh has spent time in both India and the United States. He established a successful business in Syracuse, New York. There he has participated in numerous civic activities, including serving as the chair of the City County Human Rights Commission and helping establish the local model UN and the North American Interfaith Network. He is also one of the founders and leaders of the Gobind Sadan USA, a Sikh temple located just north of Syracuse.

On November 18, 2001, after the September 11 attacks, four teenagers who had been drinking set fire to the Gobind Sadan temple. They knew nothing about Sikhs. They thought that the turbans indicated that Sikhs were followers of Osama bin Laden. The Sikh community rose above their grief and offered a prayer of forgiveness. They reached out to the arsonists after their arrest. As Singh says, "No one is an enemy. They were our children and our responsibility to heal and teach." The Sikhs then shared Babaji's message of forgiveness with the youth at their sentencing. The message was that although setting fire to the temple was wrong and based on hate and fear, Sikhs are called on to forgive the person. They wanted the teens to hear that there is another narrative. Sikhs see no one as an "other" or outsider; no one is an enemy. The arsonists responded by writing from jail that they would not have set the fire "if we had known your story."

Singh says he disagrees with those who say we need a new narrative to replace the racist narrative of hate and fear. He thinks that we already have stories that counteract the dominant paradigm narrative and we need to claim those stories and share them with each other. There are many ways that Singh promotes this. For example, he and his wife, Joginder, transformed a soup kitchen into a community dinner. Rather than being an occasion that symbolizes the failure of some who need food and the success of those who have more food than they can eat, the meal became a time for everyone to share their stories with each other.

Singh is the founder of the Wisdom Thinkers Network, which works to connect the world through the sharing of stories, particularly by children. Singh believes that there are universal values in the stories of our faith and secular traditions. He has developed resources and curriculum material so that children can hear the stories of others. Equally important is that the children learn to share the stories from their own traditions. As children recognize the shared values in the stories of children of different races and backgrounds, stereotypes start to melt away. When children share their own stories, they learn a narrative that is different from the narrative of hate and fear that supports racism.

As Singh explains, older children and adults see in traditional stories that "the battle between good and evil is part of human existence." He thinks of "darkness as the stage for the light to play on." When things become particularly dark, we need to tune in to the teachable moments. It is at those moments when prophets appear. While we may all yearn, Singh doesn't think we should wait for prophets: "We all have to be prophets." He is concerned that too often the media creates false narratives around events to justify particular positions. They frame the information to create conflict as opposed to promoting the common good. He says that dialogue should be driven by a desire be in community. In community, every person is respected and accepted rather than being judged.

I asked Singh about injustices and those who have perpetrated injustice. He says that the perpetrators need to be accountable for their actions, and the victims need to forgive. He believes that serious attention needs to be paid to developing modern rituals that create and heal community. As an example, he pointed to the celebration the temple had one year after the fire. They called it "gathering around the light." "One of the arsonists, Cassie, felt that our forgiveness had transformed her life. She felt welcomed as part of our community and came with her baby and family."

Other examples of rebuilding community can be designed around a narrative of shared humanity, where we honestly honor each other's stories. Singh illustrates this with the current trend of telling the stories of slave labor building institutions of higher education. They are willingness not just to share those stories but to offer opportunities to move past "confession and forgiveness," and enter into community. If we start with an understanding that we are part of one community, Singh says, "the narratives of hatred and prejudice that smolder beneath the surface can be released into an atmosphere of love."

NAOMI COTTOMS[2]

Naomi Cottoms was born and grew up in Helena, Arkansas, in the rural Mississippi Delta. Her black parents were extremely protective of their two daughters. She says they had to stay in the yard when they were not at church or school. Cottoms's mother worked in the houses of whites, which resulted in Cottoms's limited contact with whites while she was growing up. She also remembers that there was a white boy who walked past the house to go fishing. Sometimes he stopped on his way home to give the family fish he had caught. This made an impression on her because he didn't use honorific titles like Miss or Mrs. Her parents didn't correct him, but she knew they would have corrected a black child at school or church. It was her introduction to a world where people are treated differently.

After high school, Cottoms went to Philander Smith College, a historically black college in Little Rock, Arkansas. She graduated with a degree in social work and stayed on as a secretary at the college. Soon the college tapped her to be the director of the Upward Bound program, a federally funded program where she worked with more than 100 high school students and their families. Students were selected from low-income families where the parents had not attended college. The program is designed to provide students with extra academic and counseling services to prepare them so that they will attend and graduate from college. Cottoms says that she loved working with the students and their families. The Upward Bound program provided a setting for her to develop what would become a centerpiece of her anti-racist work: community and other support systems, which are essential for the success of every individual. For whites in Arkansas, governmental and educational structures are in place, but people of color need community and family supports, she explained. With Upward Bound, she worked with families to help them see what was possible for their children. The result was not just that the children benefited; the parents benefited also. Cottoms estimates that about 15 percent of the parents decided to pursue higher education after participating in the program. For her, this is an example of how the whole family benefits from supports like Upward Bound.

At Philander Smith College, Cottoms met a white woman, Dr. Mary Olson, a United Methodist minister who came to the college to be the executive assistant to the president. They formed a friendship, and Cottoms took Olson home to meet her family. According to Cottoms, Olson soon convinced her that they should both move to Helena and work on antiracist and economic development projects. So Cottoms returned to her childhood home.

One of the projects Cottoms worked on when she returned home was a job training program. This involved recruiting people who were not working and providing training on how to get and keep a job. Some of the things she learned there served her later. Because the training didn't promise a job at the end, motivation was very low when people knew how few jobs were available. She also became aware that with a job, you need a support system, especially if you have children. The relationships that people have as they enter the workforce can determine whether they are able to keep a job.

Later she became the director of the Tri-County Rural Health Network, where she developed the concept of *community connectors*. Community connectors met with groups in churches and schools and sometimes went door to door to tell people about resources available from Medicaid. Cottoms credits Olson with suggesting that the experiences in the job training program could be applied to this grant-funded project. She used mostly word of mouth to recruit more than 30 people from the same population that had been eligible for the job training program. Cottoms provided a job training program as part of the orientation to be a community connector. Since the participants in this training already had a job, they were not discouraged by the prospect of not being able to find a job. Recognizing the importance of a support system, the job training included helping people identify or build the support systems that they needed to be successful.

MARCO DAVIS[3]

Marco Davis's father came by himself to the United States from the island of Jamaica when he was a young man. Without support from his family, he ended up at the Seventh-day Adventist Union College in Lincoln, Nebraska. After graduating, he went to medical school in Mexico because the schools were less expensive there, which is where he met Davis's mother. They married and moved first to New Jersey and then to the Bronx, New York. After they had Davis's two older sisters, they moved to Mount Vernon, New York, just north of the Bronx, which they felt would be a better school environment for the children.

People didn't know what to make of Davis's family. His father was from the Caribbean and was finding his way in the African American community of New York. His mother was Hispanic but not part of the New York Puerto Rican or Cuban communities. For Davis, this meant that he felt like he didn't fit in. He says, "People didn't know what to do with us as kids." He was often asked, "What are you?" He claimed that he was half and half—half Mexican and half Jamaican. It may have helped other people in the 1970s to put him in a category, but he always felt like he was "other." During elementary school, the Mount Vernon school became predominantly black, but he was not like the other black kids because his mother spoke English with an accent and was from Mexico.

Education was always a priority for Davis's father. As the quality of the Mount Vernon schools slipped, his sisters led the way in moving into private schools. So, after middle school, Davis was enrolled in a private prep school.

As in many New York City prep schools, Jews, not blacks or Hispanics, provided the only diversity there. In Davis's class of 100 students, there was only one other black child.

In high school, Davis tried to fit in with white culture by learning about the music and movies that the other students preferred, but he also liked the music he had grown up with, which his classmates were not interested in. As he looks back, he doesn't remember the students or teachers being explicitly racist. In fact, only one incident stands out: He was with a group of friends from the football team and someone used the N-word, which made everyone feel uncomfortable.

As a teenager, he noticed that the teachers were all white and the custodians and cafeteria workers were all black and Latino, but he didn't know what to do with that observation except to ignore it. Davis discovered that he enjoyed skiing while on a school ski trip and would go on ski trips to Vermont with his friends. He noticed the small number of people of color who skied but wasn't sure what to do with that observation. Music was another place where he tried to fit in by learning about and listening to the music the other students liked, but he recognized that his tastes made him different. Today Davis makes a distinction between the teenage experience of insecurity, awkwardness, and wanting to be like everyone else and his experience. He was very sensitive to being "other."

Until Davis was 12, he spent two months every summer with his relatives in Guadalajara, Mexico. When the family decided that he could do other things, like work instead of vacation in Mexico every summer, his family stopped sending him. Then the family went to Mexico for Christmas when he was 15. On this trip, he fell in love with Mexico as a teenager and returned on his own when he was 16, 18, and 20. He hung out with the children of people who had gone to medical school with his father and stayed with aunts and uncles. He loved the music and culture and being with people his own age. In the 1980s, Mexican youth culture was evolving with its own music. In Mexico he didn't experience racism. He suggested this may have resulted from being perceived as part "American" and therefore advantaged.

A turning point came for Davis when he visited Yale University as a prospective student. He spent a weekend hanging around with students of color and went to a dance at the Afro-American Cultural Center. For the first time in his life, he realized that he could just have a good time at school. He didn't have to feel uncomfortable about being different. He decided to attend Yale, where he became active in both the Chicano and Afro-American student groups. Becoming a leader in both groups, he encouraged them to schedule their meetings and events so they didn't conflict. His own self-identity changed from half black Jamaican and half Mexican American to being both fully black and fully Latino.

Davis became interested in understanding more about African American and Latina/o culture. Because he wanted to dig into his heritage, he took classes in African American and Latino history and ultimately decided to major in history. Also, he was invited to a meeting of the Alpha Phi Alpha Fraternity, Inc. He'd had no idea that there was an organization of African American college students who were eager to learn about their culture, to support each other, and to serve others. After learning more about it, he joined the fraternity. At Yale, he connected with the cultural centers that supported Puerto Rican students and Chicano students. He took it upon himself to learn more about the experiences of Latinos/as from predominantly Latino areas like the southwest. In the process, he became committed to an idea that he shares with young people: you can be fully part of more than one identity group. And equally important, each identity group has important positive characteristics.

By claiming both Hispanic and black cultural heritage, he has been able to reflect on each from the other perspective. He has observed that one difference between African Americans and Hispanics is that everyone largely accepts that African Americans are in America to stay; they are a part of American society. Hispanics have not achieved that status. The question is still being asked, Are Hispanics here to stay? Not everyone answers with a resounding "yes." Davis believes that it is important for the various Hispanic communities to cooperate to develop a shared Hispanic American identity that is unquestionably part of America's future. He doesn't want Puerto Ricans or Mexicans or others to give up their unique identities; rather, people can claim full participation in multiple identity groups, and one of those identities is a Hispanic American identity.

After his sophomore year in college, Davis spent the summer in northern California. His middle sister had gone to Stanford and stayed in California, and she made arrangements for him to apply for a job as a dorm counselor at a summer program for migrant youth. He worked with three consecutive groups of mostly Mexican American and a few Central American high school students who attended a two-week camp sponsored by the Santa Clara County Department of Migrant Education called Summer Institute for Leadership and Computer Awareness. The experience was another important turning point because he became aware of the tremendous potential that these young people had, but he also saw how they had been let down by poor teachers, limited opportunities, and unlucky circumstances. This led him to direct his growing sensitivity to his own identity into a commitment to work in education. Since then, he has followed a personal and professional path of supporting kids who are, to use his words, "brilliant and hard-working, but did not have a chance because of the system."

At first, he considered becoming a classroom teacher but eventually decided to work in the nonprofit sector. After college, Davis went to work for an organization called Prep for Prep. Founded in the 1970s, this nonprofit identified fifth-grade students who had exceptional potential and drive but lacked the family resources to be able to attend a New York City prep school.

The students were offered an intense education enrichment program that started with full-time summer school after fifth grade, included two nights a week of classes during the school year, and finished with summer school after sixth grade. The graduates of this program were promised a place in a private school, regardless of ability to pay tuition. Unlike Davis's experience of being one of two black students at his prep school, these students go as a cohort so they have peer support. Part of Davis's job was to meet with the students until they graduated from high school and went on to college. He talked to them about college, but he also helped them understand that even though they had a different life than many of their classmates, they could succeed academically and socially and make their own future.

Davis has worked for several education and civil rights nonprofit organizations. With each transition, he has increasingly moved toward working for systemic change. For example, he worked for National Council of La Raza, which has been the leading nonpartisan voice for Latinos since 1968. They coordinate national advocacy efforts based on research and policy analysis and are also an umbrella for a network of local service-providing nonprofit agencies. He also served in the Obama administration as the deputy director of the White House Initiative on Educational Excellence for Hispanics.

Today Davis works both personally and professionally with organizations that support the development of particularly Latino communities. As he has learned in his own life, developing a Latino American identity does not require giving up a Mexican identity. We can identify fully with multiple identities.

CHERYL CRAZY BULL[4]

Cheryl Crazy Bull is Sicangu Lakota and was born on the Rosebud Indian Reservation in south central South Dakota. She remembers her young years as a time of being surrounded by extended family and calling many others by relative names even though they were not her blood relatives. This was a nurturing environment that provided the foundation for her understanding of kinship among the Lakota. Her school experience from the early 1960s until she graduated from high school in 1973 didn't give her a specifically Native American identity because very little of the school curriculum included Native knowledge and there were almost no Native teachers.

Crazy Bull shared that her parents valued education and were very entrepreneurial. They had a restaurant and store at a time when it was unusual for Natives to own businesses. Her dad had also gone to a couple of years of college prior to World War II when that was very rare.

When she was young, Crazy Bull didn't think about racial differences or her own identity as a Native American, but now that she is acutely aware of identity she credits her parents, especially her father, with instilling in her a respect for all people.

For example, she remembers that when an aunt who was a member of a Pentecostal church died, the family decided to hold the wake and funeral service in a Catholic community hall in the town where her aunt lived. Members of the Pentecostal church came to her parents' home to complain to her father because they did not believe in the Catholic teachings. She remembers her father, who practiced Native spirituality and was Episcopalian, talking to the visitors about "God being the god of all of us." Her parents' acceptance of diverse religious beliefs made it possible for her to feel comfortable with her own spirituality.

During Crazy Bull's senior year in high school, she became aware for the first time that there were people who didn't do everything like her family did. In her family, the only difference between people was whether they attended church and, if so, what church they attended. Her family included people who followed traditional practices and those who participated in Catholic, Episcopalian, Pentecostal, and other churches. She was friends with a white classmate who had grown up on the reservation and spoke Lakota fluently. She didn't think of him as being any different from her family or other classmates. When his father died, arrangements were made for the funeral, and there was not an all-night wake. For the first time, she realized that everyone is not the same.

After graduating from high school, Crazy Bull went to a couple of different colleges before entering the University of South Dakota College of Business. There she not only stood out because she is Native American but also because there were very few women studying business. This was a very formative time when she was supported by the community of Indian students and the Indian community beyond school because of the small number of Native students.

She recalled that when she went to college at Dartmouth in New Hampshire, she realized that there are people who have lots of money while she had very little. In her experiences in college, she encountered many people who had negative attitudes about American Indians. She discovered that some people attribute the poverty on reservations to the character of Native people. She was introduced to gender politics and the emerging Native renaissance politics.

In her classes and in other experiences, Crazy Bull learned a language to describe racism, sexism, and colonialism. As a business student, she took classes on the world economy. It was amazing to her that whites had so little comprehension of the impact of colonialism and colonization on Native Americans and people around the world. Upon graduating, she took her skills as a business major and moved back to the Rosebud Reservation with her young family. Her plan was to use her business degree to obtain a job in community development. But jobs were scarce, and she took a job teaching business management classes at what was then Sinte Gleska College (now University). The university was founded in 1973 to bring higher education to the Rosebud Reservation.

Being at Sinte Gleska University changed the direction of her life. Crazy Bull was surrounded by a staff and faculty working on issues of Native identity, the role of higher education in supporting Native culture, what curriculum was appropriate, and other questions of how to create a university to serve people on the Rosebud Reservation and in the surrounding rural communities. She sees her identity as a Native educator intertwined with her personal and professional identities. From this point on, education became her professional focus.

As well as education, parenting is important to Crazy Bull. She finds it rewarding that her daughter and two sons "have security as Native people." She points to the importance of parents helping their children find their identity and their own spiritual path. She hopes for a time when not just parents but schools will show all children that their traditions and identity are important. It is frustrating to her that today so much of the school curriculum is prescribed, so there is little time for students to learn their own stories. She would like to see the curriculum modified to include more than just the white story.

Crazy Bull noted that the experiences of Native students in higher education can be particularly challenging because students experience what she terms *the insidious racism of numbers*. There are often so few indigenous students that little investment is made by institutions in their success. She calls on institutions to identify and support their indigenous students so that tribal people can achieve parity in college completion with the rest of the population. U.S. Census data shows that only about 13 percent of American Indian and Alaska Natives have a college degree compared to 26 percent of the general population.

Crazy Bull spent 17 years at Sinte Gleska University. Then she had a new opportunity. Many years before, the Jesuits had turned St. Francis Mission School over to the Rosebud Sioux Tribe to operate as a tribally controlled school. Crazy Bull became the chief educational officer, serving for over four years. Eventually Crazy Bull went back to her first path as a tribal college educator, becoming the president of Northwest Indian College in Bellingham, Washington, and then president of the American Indian College Fund in Denver, Colorado.

The College Fund raises money from corporations, foundations, and individuals to provide college scholarships and support toward college success for Native American students as well as building the capacity of tribal colleges and universities. Every year, the College Fund supports about 4,000 students. In this position, Crazy Bull is asked to explain the desire that Native people have to protect their cultural heritage and frequently has to consider the racist and stereotypic basis of images and belief systems. Some situations are very straightforward, such as sport teams' use of Indian mascots, which is a clear case of an application of a stereotype. She supports Natives selling their art but has problems with non-Natives profiting from art that copies

Native designs. She also points out that there are certain sacred objects, such as headdresses, that in Indian culture are either earned or given as a gift. She would like to see these traditions respected by others. Mostly, she proposes that cultural objects and practices should only be used with the permission of Natives. This goes for Native Americans or any other culture.

Crazy Bull's profession in education has been focused on helping her students develop as Native people, for themselves, for their people, and for all people. She points out that Native people have an understanding of the earth and our connection to it as human beings, and she would like to have this and other values recognized by the larger culture so that everyone can benefit.

DENNIS BENSON[5]

Dennis Benson grew up in a white environment in Michigan. He considered himself white. Only when his mother died after Benson retired and moved back to Michigan did he learn that he has a black grandfather he never met. By this time in his life, he had developed a self-identity that was based on the common humanity of everyone. I have been friends with Benson since we were both on the faculty of United Theological Seminary in the 1980s. Part of our bonding was a shared struggle as white men to make sense of working in an institution with its own struggles involving racism, sexism, and gender identities. Today he jokes with me that he is no longer my white brother. But knowing about a black grandfather has not changed what he learned and had become by living most of his life as a white man. It does, however, make him appreciate all the more those who take on the civil rights struggle, because they are not only doing it with him, they are doing it for him.

Benson grew up in an all-white environment. All his friends and teachers were white. The first time he had an experience outside of white culture was in high school when his school recruited volunteers to attend an event in Detroit. Benson had never heard of the organization, but it was an opportunity to get out of school for a day. It turned out to be a "rumor clinic." The student-run program was designed by the National Conference of Christians and Jews (now the National Conference for Community and Justice) to train students in interracial relations. The event was an eye-opener for him. One exercise made such an impression that he later used it in his professional career: Students were broken into small groups, and one group was taken to a separate room and shown a picture of a white man and a black man talking in a bar. The white man held a razor in his hand. After viewing the picture, the students rejoined the larger group and were asked to describe the picture. Benson said, "You can imagine what students from different backgrounds remembered seeing. The razor ended up in the black man's hand. The white man was threatening not talking." It was the beginning of a lifetime of trying to understand things from other people's perspective.

Benson went to the University of Michigan for undergraduate school. There he had African American friends and also got to know people from around the world. One of his friends was an African. To Benson's amazement, his friend met him one day during his junior year and said he was going home because his father had just become prime minister and needed his son to be secretary of education. Benson was just trying to get through college and this friend was dropping out to be a secretary of education. It was one of many experiences of seeing that people are very different.

After college, Benson moved to Chicago, where he attended theological school. He says, "I am so thankful for the friends who shared their lives with me." He had a roommate from Taiwan and made more African American friends. Benson remembers when a friend who had been drinking came to his house and told him and his wife, Marilyn, that he was gay. They stayed up most of the night talking with him. There were others who shared their experience of being black in America.

Benson wasn't just making friends; he became an activist. When he heard that a professor was recruiting students to go to Selma, Alabama, to join a civil rights march to Montgomery, he joined up, and this time it wasn't just to get out of class. He and his wife, Marilyn, knew that sacrifices were necessary. The round-trip ticket to Alabama was $350—about as much as Marilyn made at her job in a month. There had been publicity about a group traveling from Chicago to Selma, and as they waited on the plane at O'Hare Airport, police did a cursory examination of the plane in response to a bomb threat clearly intended to frighten the group. The group decided not to be deterred and flew to Selma.

In Alabama, Benson experienced the hatred of whites as the marchers walked toward Montgomery led by Martin Luther King Jr. and other civil rights leaders. He describes it as an experience of being on the other side. He was a white person marching for civil rights, and there were whites standing on the side of the road or on their porches yelling hateful words, throwing things, and spitting on them. As he walked, he linked arms with a young black woman as if he could comfort her, but as they walked together her strength and commitment inspired him. He says, "She did more for me than I could have possibly done for her."

He later took a job at a small Presbyterian college in Pennsylvania that was under pressure from the accrediting agency because it didn't have "intellectual and spiritual ferment." To rectify this situation, the school obtained a grant from the Danforth Foundation to hire a chaplain, which made it possible for them to hire Benson. There were about 1,000 students, and 30 of them were black. Benson started meeting with the black students and discovered that they had difficulty finding housing that the college approved.

A group of black and white students decided to conduct an experiment. First, a black student went to one of the houses on the approved list, where she was told that nothing was available. Half an hour later, a white student went to the same house and was shown a room to rent. After carefully documenting this, Benson worked with the students and held a press conference to expose the racism.

The next day he was summoned to the president's office. Now he says, "I was so naive. I thought the president was calling me in to congratulate me and give me a raise." He was fired on the spot. Many of the trustees were townspeople, and they were irate. This was an example of northern white rage and of another facet of racism. It was a lesson that stayed with him. He says, "It helped me realize the costs of standing with others. Because of my actions, my livelihood was taken away from me." He looked for support in the Presbyterian Church, but there he experienced another rejection.

Benson was rejected but not deterred. He continued to support civil rights actions in various cities. For example, he supported the civil rights marches organized by a white Catholic priest, Father James Groppi, in Milwaukee, Wisconsin. In this northern city, police helicopters flew overhead and the police harassed marchers.

In 1969, Benson published his first book. It set him on the path for the rest of his unconventional career as a Presbyterian minister. The book, *The Now Generation*, celebrated youth and their music and recognized the power of popular culture. The book brought him national attention, and he spoke at conferences and was invited to lead workshops. He was good at communicating with large groups, but he also enjoyed connecting with people one on one.

One of the sources of his ability to connect with individuals grew out of spending eight weeks in a Chicago hospital when he contracted polio during seminary. Even though the hospital chaplains didn't always connect with him or his needs, he recognized the importance of this work. He was motivated to go through chaplain training and become a hospital chaplain. This training increased his skills in listening to people and helping them tell their own stories.

His ability to see things from the other side as he had in Alabama, his appreciation for each person's story, and his ability to pick up on people's emotions made him an excellent interviewer. Benson combined his public speaking skills with his ability to connect with individuals by producing radio programs called *Passages*. Over the years, he interviewed thousands of people to help them tell their stories. He produced programs that featured rock stars, gang members, famous people, and not-so-famous people. The radio programs were carefully produced to capture each person's story, share struggles, and offer hope to listeners. The programs were broadcast on hundreds of radio stations across the country and over the Armed Forces Radio Network.

Today Benson lives in Michigan, where he is again in a mostly white environment. He is troubled by the insensitivity and blatant racism of some of his neighbors and is often disappointed in the church. He described going to a service that was completely irrelevant. Not only did it ignore what is going on in the world with militarism and racism, it avoided any engagement with the lives of the people attending. He is no longer surprised when white people show hatred not only toward nonwhites but also when he suggests any change. While he has some friends who amaze him with their sensitivity, the Internet provides most of his connections with people who inspire him. Benson has over 1,000 friends on Facebook and is particularly encouraged by people who identify as LGBTQ and African American women. He says, "They won't let go." Then he adds that African American women are "unbelievable. They're courageous. They have kept the race together. They are not backing off. They are committed. It blows my mind."

The Internet also connects him with people like Jim Rigby, the minister at St. Andrews Presbyterian Church in Austin, Texas. Rigby comments on current events with honesty and depth. Benson does the same thing on Facebook, sharing stories from his own experiences and celebrating what others have done and are doing.

BRENDA GIRTON-MITCHELL[6]

Today Brenda Girton-Mitchell's greatest desire is to help people of different racial backgrounds develop respect for one another and engage in transformational relationship building. Most recently she has done this as the director of the Faith-Based and Neighborhood Partnerships Center at the U.S. Department of Education. She says, "The older I get, the more I realize how much I was shaped by my childhood experiences. Many of my deeply held beliefs related to race and relationships between blacks and whites have been perpetuated by things I was taught as a child." As a young adult, she realized that she needed to challenge herself to explore some of the things she was taught about whites.

Girton-Mitchell lived with her grandmother, Mama, until Mama passed when Girton-Mitchell was 11 years old. Since her mother worked multiple jobs to help support the family, Mama was the one who was at home to get Girton-Mitchell and her siblings off to school and to greet them when they returned home. Mama did not have a high school education, but she was a wise woman. She taught Girton-Mitchell to love reading and learning new things. Girton-Mitchell preferred spending time with Mama more than with other children.

There was a recurring incident every Friday night. The landlord came to the door to collect the rent and Mama would tell the children to quiet down before she opened the door. She would clear her throat and immediately begin speaking in broken English. We would call it Ebonics today. The words were almost always the same: "Come on in, Mista. Good to see ya, suh." The tone was distinctly deferential. Mama shifted her eyes to the floor as she handed him the envelope with the rent money neatly folded inside. He would open it, count the money, put it back in the envelope, pat Mama on the shoulder or hand and say, "Thank you, Katie." On one of these occasions, Girton-Mitchell asked Mama why she acted like that whenever the landlord came. Her response was, "White people do not like colored people to be smart. We need him to like us so we have a place to live." Girton-Mitchell recalls that at that point in her life, the landlord was the only white person she knew, and she did not like the way his presence made her and her family feel.

The family moved from that neighborhood when a highway was constructed there. Her new school was integrated, and she had almost daily contact with white teachers and students. The kids and teachers were nice enough, and she even called some of them her friends, but Mama would always caution her to study hard and be nice. "God wants you to try to love everybody," she would say, "but be careful of white folks." Over the years, Mama shared stories about her life and how she prayed life would get better for her family. Mama died in 1959. As Girton-Mitchell looks back today, she recognizes how much Mama's words impacted her beliefs and behaviors.

Another impact on Girton-Mitchell's attitudes about people and racial differences was the childhood experience of listening to Rev. Jesse Jackson on the radio on Saturday mornings. He shared a message of hope. She remembers how encouraged she was as she "took his mantra into the depths of my spirit." Jackson proclaimed, "I am somebody. . . . I may be poor but I am somebody. . . . My face is different, my hair is different . . . but I am somebody. But I must be respected, protected, never rejected, I am God's child! I am somebody!"

By the time Girton-Mitchell graduated from Ball State University and was in her second year as an elementary school teacher in Indianapolis, she recognized that like everyone else she had a narrative, and much of it had come from Mama. Mama's legacy of love of education and respect for all people was important, but she also knew there were things that she needed to challenge. Then, through a series of events, she moved beyond Mama's advice that "white people do not like colored people to be smart." She not only found her voice to work for justice, but she also discovered that she could work with people, black and white, as a partner.

It started when she was approached to run against two white high school teachers to be the president of the Indianapolis Education Association. She claims that no one thought she could win, but the elementary teachers wanted to have a candidate who understood what happens in elementary schools since presidents in the recent past had been high school teachers. Once nominated, Girton-Mitchell started looking more carefully at the issues a president must deal with and the challenges of the position. She became convinced that the work was important because there were things in the teachers' contract that impacted the children's education. So she campaigned hard for the position. Girton-Mitchell was as surprised as others when she won the election.

For the first year, Girton-Mitchell was president-elect, so she had time to observe and learn about the process of negotiating a contract. She discovered that people were afraid to speak up and tell the truth about what was happening in their school building because of the possibility of losing their job. The result was that the kids were the losers. She worked with the union executive director, who tutored her in the negotiating process. The second year, when she sat down to represent the teachers at the negotiating table, she was the only person of color and the only woman in the room.

Today Girton-Mitchell still laughs when she tells about chastising the men when they cursed. In the end, she negotiated a contract that was designed to help the students. This was accomplished without a teachers' strike, which had been the recent pattern every year. Equally important, she discovered that she could work across racial lines as a full participant. She points out that "we are learning to live together in a nation that lifts up but does not always honor, the principle that we are all created equal. Embracing that principle requires me to try to be empathetic to the racialized context of the people around me even as I engage in intentional acts to build bridges of understanding founded upon mutual trust and respect of our shared humanity."

With the noteworthy exception of Dr. Dorothy Irene Height, president of the National Council of Negro Women, Girton-Mitchell was hired by white men throughout her professional life of working in education, for corporate America, for faith-based organizations, and in government. She says that "finding my voice was not always easy but I would remember Mama and Jackson and lots of folks in between."

She credits Mama with instilling in her a sense of obligation to prepare for educational and economic success. Others helped her develop the self-confidence that enabled her to work respectfully with people from different races. As Jackson says, "Everybody ought to be able to say, 'I am somebody!'"

RYAN CHUNG[7]

Ryan Chung is a first-generation Korean American. Shortly after he was born, his family moved from southern California to Marin County just outside San Francisco. Until he was four, Chung was completely immersed in Korean culture and only spoke Korean. He says that when he arrived at school, "everyone told me my culture is terrible. My classmates tried to make me American." Chung remembers trying to do everything he could to be a good American, including playing football and other sports. Chung has one sister, and together they started avoiding anything Korean. Their parents were active in a Korean Baptist church. After church services, when people stayed to share a meal, the two kids would get a plate of food and slip off to the attic or basement to avoid socializing. He went from a completely Korean environment to being mostly with whites. Sometime in elementary school, he lost the ability to communicate in Korean.

As he looks back, he is frustrated that the public school he attended pretended that race didn't exist, and that he experienced what he calls "insensitivity" to his Korean heritage on the part of students and staff. He remembers a case where a student called him Chinese. He responded, "No. Korean." The student said, "Where is that?" Now he realizes that the school didn't provide a language for dialogue about other cultures. White culture was always considered normal.

Chung's sister was very academic, but he was behind and labeled as low performing. Now Chung sees this as psychologically devastating. It shaped his view of himself. He began to think of himself as a "gap student." Rather than receiving more support and enrichment, he felt dismissed by his teachers.

In high school, Chung was selected to be a Next Generation Scholar. This program was created by Sally Matsuishi, a Marin County native who worked with students in South Central, East, and Koreatown, Los Angeles, before coming home in 2003 to create Next Generation Scholars. The program provides students with academic support and activities to prepare them to become successful college students. The College Access Center is open from 1:30 p.m. until late in the evening, Monday through Thursday. This gives students an opportunity to meet one on one with tutors and counselors. Wraparound social services are available for scholars' families also. Twice a week there are college-level lectures. Chung remembers how exciting it was to "read something that was not a textbook." The first book he read was Homer's *Odyssey*.

The program provided Chung with a supportive environment where he could both escape peer pressure to be a masculine white American student and experience academic success. With all the counseling, including mental health services, Chung says that he was able to avoid drugs and involvement with gangs. Their parents wanted his sister and him to be doctors. Chung laughs as he says, "Of course." Throughout high school, his parents were not very involved in his life, yet it was during this period that he reconnected with his Korean heritage and began to see himself as a Korean American.

The Next Generation Scholar program prepared him for success at a highly competitive college, but even more importantly, Matsuishi helped Chung find a direction in his life. She asked him, "If you could change one thing, what would it be?" He thought about the bullying and ill treatment that his sister experienced because she is bisexual. He wanted to see that changed. With the support of Matsuishi and others, he became an LGBTQ activist. As a high school senior, he made a presentation to the Marin County School Board to develop a policy regarding bullying of LGBTQ students. Today the school has a new policy.

This experience of being an activist showed him that he can make a difference in the world. Today, education is his passion. As a student at American University, he volunteers with Jumpstart, a program that works with preschool children in low-income neighborhoods to help them develop language and literacy skills. During the summers, he works with the program Matsuishi developed for junior high and high school students in Marin County. This has given him an opportunity to develop curriculum and provides opportunities to challenge racism in an education setting by working with high school students. He also has opportunities to work with communities to rewrite old policies.

Now he is studying to become a high school teacher and plans to go back home to Marin County and work in the public school. The difference he wants to make as an activist is to become an antiracist in that setting. There he will be able to work to address the racism that he experienced because he knows what it's like to grow up as a Korean American in Marin County, California. His main objective is to become a leader in education policy.

Chapter 13

Examples of Institutional Antiracism

Just as it is helpful to ask the question, "What skin are you in?" it is also helpful to ask, "What institutions are you in?" Each institution can be evaluated as a potential place for antiracist activity. Some institutions already have groups advancing an antiracist agenda. Advocating for full participation in the political process by protecting voting rights is an example of an antiracist activity where groups are already working. One might decide to initiate a voting rights effort, but in many cases working with an organization like the National Association for the Advancement of Colored People or Rainbow Push is a better idea.

Sometimes people in positions of power in institutions decide to face racism and bring antiracist leadership, and examples of this will be discussed in this chapter. This was the case with the Kellogg Foundation where the board of directors made a decision to become an antiracist organization. Virginia Organizing was founded to empower people for political action, but in creating the organization it was essential to build on a foundation of developing trust across racial lines. The All Stars Program was organized by people who wanted to address the problem of racism limiting opportunities for black children in New York City. Similarly, the Chavez School was created to provide students of color with skills to be full participants in the American political system. These were all institutions with leadership that is sensitive to racism. The examples in this chapter demonstrate that it is possible for us to have institutions that are not based on racism.

W. K. KELLOGG FOUNDATION[1]

In August 2016, Rev. Alvin Herring became the director of racial equity and community engagement for the W. K. Kellogg Foundation (WKKF). I spoke with him several months later about his work and that of WKKF. Herring told me that he was recruited by the foundation to leave California and move to Michigan. His decision to relocate was not surprising given his background and the foundation's commitment to community engagement and racial equity.

Most recently, Herring was the deputy director/senior leader for the PICO National Network, one of the largest faith-led community organizing networks in the United States. There he worked with community organizations in more than 150 cities and towns. Prior to working in California, he worked in programs to support community groups in Louisiana and Washington, D.C.

In seeking out Herring, WKKF was continuing to move in the direction initiated by its founder. Will Keith Kellogg was born in 1860 in Battle Creek, Michigan. In 1863, the Seventh-day Adventist Church was founded in Battle Creek, and Kellogg's parents raised their family in the new church. Kellogg's brother John became a doctor and returned to Battle Creek to head the Adventist Health Reform Institute, which was renamed the Battle Creek Sanitarium. John asked his brother to join him as business manager. The sanitarium was based on the prescriptions of the Seventh-day Adventists. One belief was in the benefits of eating grains. John and Will experimented with various ways to prepare grains and almost by accident discovered a way to make flakes from wheat. Later they figured out how to make flakes from corn and other grains.

The brothers started a business selling their flakes as a health food. Later the brothers separated and Will started his own food-processing company, Kellogg Company. The company was extremely successful, and in 1930 Will used his fortune to found the W. K. Kellogg Child Welfare Foundation, later named the W. K. Kellogg Foundation. His gifts to the foundation amounted to more than a billion dollars in today's currency.

Although one of the world's wealthiest men, Kellogg was not comfortable in that role and felt obligated to use his fortune to help others. In establishing the foundation, Kellogg said the funds were "for the promotion of the welfare, comfort, health, education, feeding, clothing, sheltering and safeguarding of children and youth, directly or indirectly, without regard to sex, race, creed or nationality." Today the foundation is one of the largest philanthropies in the United States and has become a leader in helping the philanthropic and other communities recognize the role of race in American inequity.

Into the 1980s, the foundation staff, which was primarily white, honored Kellogg's legacy by supporting organizations focused on children's well-being "without regard to sex, race, creed or nationality." In 1987, La June Montgomery Tabron was hired as controller, and in 2014, she became the first woman and person of color to become president and CEO of the foundation. Tabron represents the foundation and its commitment to racial equity. In a defining moment, in September 2007, WKKF declared itself an antiracist organization that promotes racial equity. The board of trustees directed the staff to develop a comprehensive programmatic approach to address racism, and today 60 percent of the members of the board of trustees are people of color. Additionally, 55 percent of the staff leadership team and 45 percent of the staff are people of color. Hiring a diverse staff is just the starting point. WKKF's goal is to create an environment and culture where everyone is valued and accepted. They actively facilitate staff awareness and growth around diversity and racial equity. For example, staff members have attended White Men as Full Diversity Partners training.

Ramon Murguia, who joined the foundation in 2007, was elected chair of the board in December 2015. He is the foundation's first Hispanic chair in its 86-year history and the first among the 30 largest foundations. The California Endowment is the only other large foundation with a Hispanic chair, that being Jane Garcia. Murguia is a lawyer in Kansas City, Missouri, and was previously the chairman of the board of the National Council of La Raza, the largest Latino civil rights organization in the country.

The antiracist approach of WKKF includes (1) developing an analysis of community that includes the role of race, (2) directing funding to support antiracist community action and organizations that work with children and families of color, (3) developing a program to support racial healing, (4) considering race in all decisions related to the foundation, (5) hiring a diverse staff and leadership team to run the foundation, and (6) intentionally making learning about diversity, inclusion, and racial equity part of the culture of the foundation.

Herring explained that the focus of the foundation's work is to ensure vulnerable children thrive, but this also requires supporting their families. So, for example, the foundation makes grants for things like job training because unless parents have living-wage jobs with opportunities for upward mobility, their children will not thrive. This is part of a comprehensive approach to supporting the environment that surrounds children. WKKF supports programs to ensure children are healthy, educated, and living in economically secure families. Their model recognizes that these programs are surrounded and supported by a commitment to community involvement and racial equity. Herring makes a distinction between equity and equality. The work of the foundation is directed toward an equity goal of breaking down barriers such as poverty and segregation that hold children back; thus the foundation addresses structural racism and its consequences.

The foundation intentionally works with community organizations that share a commitment to addressing equity. While traditionally WKKF supported organizations serving people of color with about 20 percent of their grantees falling into this category, by 2011, the percentage of grantees that served people of color increased to 88 percent.

This approach to grant making has also resulted in developing a strategy of identifying priority communities. Herring explained that WKKF supports work internationally, but priority places for their investments domestically are Michigan, Mississippi, New Mexico, and New Orleans, and internationally the Yucatan Peninsula and Chiapas in Mexico and the Southwest Corridor and Central Area in Haiti. A place-based approach enables the foundation to develop relationships with communities over a period of time.

In 2010, the foundation launched an antiracism initiative. America Healing is a strategy for racial healing toward racial equity designed to raise awareness of unconscious biases and inequities and to help communities heal from the legacies of racism. The goal is to support and empower communities in their efforts to dismantle the structures that limit opportunities for vulnerable children. Four conferences were held between 2010 and 2015 with the goal of framing national conversations on race so that the journey toward racial equity comes with a collective understanding among participants. The initiative worked to create open spaces for the community to come together and engage in meaningful dialogues so that true healing can begin. America Healing also helped organize and support civil rights organizations representing various races and ethnicities to strategize how to dismantle structural racism in America. The foundation calls these groups their anchor organizations.

In 2016, WKKF launched Truth, Racial Healing & Transformation, which strives to assist communities in embracing racial healing and uprooting the conscious and unconscious beliefs in racial hierarchy. This multiyear effort is designed to engage local, regional, and national organizations (in both the public and private sectors) to "explore historic patterns and structural racism, to identify both short-term and long-term strategies for meaningful change across the country. It is an adaptation of some of the most recognized Truth and Reconciliation Commission (TRC) models." Five design teams have made recommendations on how to implement truth and reconciliation programs in communities. The teams focus on narrative change, racial healing, separation, law, and the economy. Each team discusses and wrestles with how to transform our country by answering the following questions:

• What would the country look and feel like if we jettisoned the belief in a hierarchy of human value and the narratives that reinforce that belief?

• Where are we now, and how did we get here?

• What are the key leverage points for transforming the narrative to jettison a belief in a hierarchy of human value?

- Who must be involved in order to make the deep and lasting changes we need to make?
- What are the key initial activities that need to happen in order to heal from and transform the narrative?

WKKF leadership recognizes the role of race in all of society, so attention is being paid to all aspects of the foundation's activities. This goes beyond just making grants. Today the implications of structures of racism are part of all decisions, even which contractors and vendors they use to support the work.

WKKF provides leadership to the philanthropic sector by first recognizing that racism is at the center of preventing children from succeeding and then finding ways to use grants to bring change.

CESAR CHAVEZ PUBLIC CHARTER SCHOOL FOR PUBLIC POLICY[2]

I first heard of the Cesar Chavez Public Charter School for Public Policy when the executive director of the White House Initiative on Educational Excellence for African Americans, David Johns, invited students from the school to meet employees at the U.S. Department of Education. Several students showcased their senior thesis, which examines a public policy issue and proposes a solution. The students were well prepared, articulate, and convincing. They not only made very professional presentations; they also demonstrated depth of understanding during question-and-answer time.

Starting in the sixth grade, students at Chavez School begin to learn about policy. By the time they reach their senior year, they have visited public meetings, met with policy makers, and developed the ability to analyze, discuss, and promote policy positions. The promotional material for the school says, "Through a Public Policy Framework of developing understanding, taking action, and reflecting on attitudes and growth, our students build the character traits most conducive to our democracy and believe themselves to have the capacity to affect change." This structured program includes special projects each year. Students participate in summits and roundtables and visit the city council and Capitol Hill.

At the end of 9th and 10th grades, the students participate in a full-time two-week course where they analyze a problem, propose solutions, and advocate for change. The problem can be a local or international public problem. At the end of 11th grade, students participate in a full-time three-week internship where they gain firsthand experience in a public policy setting. All of this leads up to the senior year, when they prepare their senior thesis. Each student writes a 15–20-page policy paper and prepares a PowerPoint presentation on a public policy issue of his or her choice. They research the issue, identify policy proposals, determine what they recommend as a solution to the problem, and prepare arguments to support their opinions.

I was intrigued by the process and a little suspicious that chief executive officer Joan Massey had brought only the very best students to the Department of Education. Was it possible that every student goes off to college with the skills of an expert policy advisor? A short time later, I received an email saying that the school needed volunteers to help judge seniors' theses. I volunteered. It turned out that the judging had two purposes. The first was to ensure that every student met a very high minimum standard for graduation. The second was to identify three outstanding students who would be honored and given an opportunity to present their projects at a public policy symposium at Georgetown University.

I was assigned to a room with two other judges. A teacher served as host and moderator. Four students were scheduled to make presentations. After each presentation, we made comments and discussed the topic with the presenter and then filled out a judging sheet. By the end of the evening, I was convinced that my suspicions were unfounded. The students I judged were all well prepared and convincing. They were just like the students I had met at the Department of Education.

Cesar Chavez Public Charter School for Public Policy was founded in 1998 in Washington, D.C., by Irasema Salcido. The first classes met in a grocery store basement. Sixty ninth-grade students were in the first class. Today more than 1,400 students in grades 6 to 12 attend classes at three sites.

Salcido, who has now retired from administering the schools, grew up in Mexico. Her parents were migrant farm workers. When she was 14 years old, she came to the United States. Like children in many migrant families, she sometimes helped out in the fields, but she was determined to get an education. She didn't speak English when she arrived. Now she has a master's degree in education from Harvard University.

Salcido's degree landed her a job as an administrator in the District of Columbia school district. Soon she was frustrated that many students were graduating without knowing how to read, write, or multiply. In 1997, she was the mother of four children and pregnant with her fifth child when she decided to start her own school. She chose the name Cesar Chavez to remind students and the community that people of humble beginnings can make a difference in other peoples' lives. And she called it a school for public policy because that was what made the school stand out.

When Oprah Winfrey honored her with a $100,000 Angel Network prize, Salcido told Winfrey, "It's important for the schools to offer [students] a place that is a safe haven . . . where [students] can be and develop and try hard and see that they can achieve, that they have potential, that they have skills, that they have people that believe in them."[3] High expectations are built into the Chavez School. At the end of the first year of operation,

Salcido wasn't satisfied with the progress students had made, so she had them all repeat the sixth grade. Now students expect that to succeed takes a lot of work. They have to go to school six days a week, stay in the evenings for tutoring, and attend summer school.

Salcido also told Winfrey, "I honestly believe when they leave us, they will remember they can change what is going on in their community. The results are priceless because their lives are changed forever." From the beginning, Salcido saw community development as essential. The Parkside campus in the Kenilworth-Parkside community in northeast Washington, D.C., is home to about 5,800 residents, including 1,800 children and teenagers. Ninety-eight percent of residents are black, about half live below the federal poverty line, and nearly 90 percent of families with children are headed by single women.

Salcido was inspired by the work of Geoffrey Canada in New York City, which was made popular by Paul Tough's book, *Whatever It Takes: Geoffrey Canada's Quest to Change Harlem and America*. Tough describes the ups and downs of Canada's work to find a way to fix education in an environment where few students were succeeding. Canada had two strategies. One is the conveyer belt approach, and the second is the support of every aspect of a student's life. The conveyer belt approach is supported by a great deal of academic research on education. It claims that for children to successfully grow up to escape the poverty of their families, it is necessary to start them on that track even before they are born.[4] Then they need an educational environment that supports them moving toward college admission and graduation.

Second, Canada believed that this work demanded a commitment to developing the whole community. For Salcido, this required that she initiate a community organizing effort which included working with community based organizations to address issues in the school's neighborhood.

Before President Obama established his Promise Neighborhoods initiative, Salcido started working with the principals of nearby public schools. They partnered with other organizations and individuals to organize D.C. Promise Neighborhood Initiative (DCPNI). The primary goal was to encourage family participation in school and community activities. They also had an agenda to advocate for improved services to the community. DCPNI called for a network of services that would expand quality programs for infants and toddlers, improve college readiness, reduce teenage pregnancy, help families with financial literacy, and support workforce development.[5] Not surprisingly, when the Obama administration made funding available in a program that was largely inspired by the work of Canada in Harlem, DCPNI was one of the first recipients.

To learn more about the school, I met with Marla Dean, the senior director of school accountability. Dean explained that the philosophy of the school is to help students understand the role of social structures. With a public policy lens, she explained, students can address structures that will reduce individualism. The primary strategy is to use the public policy courses, but there is also an emphasis on preparing for college. Here the school plays an active role in helping each student identify possible colleges. The director of college success develops profiles of colleges where students can continue to expand on what they learned at Chavez School.

The school is designed with an antiracist agenda of not only preparing students to go on to college and succeed but also to participate fully in community and political arenas. I asked Dean about how the school specifically addresses issues of racism. She said that one of the things they are learning is that just because teachers and other staff are committed to the goals of Chavez School, they are not necessarily sensitive to how deeply racism is embedded in our society. When I talked to her, they were just starting a program with an outside consultant to bring a discussion of racism out into the open. Their strategy is to begin working with the home office and then expand the program into each campus.

THE ALL STARS PROGRAM[6]

I learned about the All Stars Program (ASP) from Henry Louis Gates's book *America behind the Color Line: Dialogues with African Americans.* Gates doesn't really have dialogues in his book; rather, he reports what African Americans are thinking and doing. Dr. Lenora Fulani is one of the people he reports on. I was fascinated by the way she uses performance to help black, Hispanic, and immigrant kids and their families, so I made an appointment to speak with her. On a very hot August morning, I met her at the midtown Manhattan center where young people come from all over New York City to participate in programs.

I was eager to ask her about the rational for what she does and why she thinks it is helping young people and the community. We got to that, but first she wanted to tell the story of what ASP does, how it got started, her own moments of insight that made it possible, and her personal story of growing up in poverty. It turned out that by the time she had finished her story, I had a good idea of why she believes the program is effective.

Fulani, an African American woman, and her white Jewish therapist and friend, Dr. Fred Newman, founded ASP in 1981. Today All Stars works with more than 10,000 students in poor communities every year. Almost all of their work is with black, Hispanic, and immigrant kids. There are programs in six cities: New York, Newark, Chicago, San Francisco, Dallas, and Bridgeport, Connecticut.

Fulani grew up in Chester, Pennsylvania, a poor neighborhood in a poor suburb of Philadelphia. It was the 1960s and there were increasing opportunities for African Americans, but her family did not have particularly high expectations for her. Today she has a PhD in psychology, but she thinks her family would have been satisfied as long as she graduated from high school. She is the youngest of five children. Since her closest sister is eight years older than she, it was almost like being an only child.

She remembers receiving special attention, but mostly she remembers the suffering that surrounded her. When Fulani was 9 or 10, her aunt went out to buy food for her favorite uncle, Ned. She never returned, but the story Fulani heard was that she was raped and murdered by white men who then tied her to a railroad track to be decapitated by the next train. When she was 12 years old, her father died when his trip to the hospital was postponed for hours because the ambulance driver refused to come into her neighborhood. When she was 15, one of her sisters died. Fulani watched what happened to her sisters, nieces, nephews, and others around her. "They drank, they did drugs, they fought and they had emotional crises that led to stays in psychiatric institutions." Despite all the trauma and suffering around her, she realized that the adults didn't talk about their pain. It was as if the suffering was just part of their lives. They couldn't do anything about it. So she decided that she would go to college and become a psychologist. Then she would come back and help everyone.

Fulani did become a psychologist, but on the way she had a life-changing realization. She shared with her friend, Newman, that she felt inadequate because her mother had taught her how important it is to save, but she'd been unable to do so. She had opened a savings account and put money in it from each paycheck, but by the end of each month she needed to take all the money out to pay her expenses. She remembers Newman saying to her, "You know you are poor, don't you?" In fact, she hadn't known she was poor. The realization provided insight that made sense of her life and put her experiences growing up into perspective. It was not that she and her siblings and nephews and nieces had something wrong with them. Poverty was a condition imposed on them by American society. In her case, and for the people in her hometown, poverty is a social problem, not an individual failing. She did not choose to be poor.

This recognition of her own poverty made it possible for her to apply her academic study to real lived situations. W. E. B. Du Bois described a parallel situation where blacks coming out of slavery did not have the resources to move directly into full participation as free citizens. The writings of Lev Semenovich Vygotsky were particularly formative. Vygotsky was a Russian psychologist and an academic in the early years of the Union of Soviet Socialist Republic. At that time, all academic work was conducted under the watchful eye of the Communist Party to ensure that Marxist ideology was supported. Vygotsky was a man of uncompromising academic integrity who took seriously the question of a Marxist psychology. Like Du Bois, he recognized the role of society in determining individual development. Vygotsky used the example of Marx's analysis of the development of capital to show how human capital is also developed.

At the time that Vygotsky was working, other psychologists, such as Jean Piaget, pointed out that there is a distinction between human development and education. Piaget was interested in education. He thought that children develop outside of school. Children are ready to advance their learning only to the extent that their development is sufficiently advanced. Vygotsky pointed out that development is a social process; it doesn't just happen. Fulani took all of this and applied it to her lived experience. She wrote, "How radical and liberating from the stagist theories of Piaget and others! And what possibilities it created for the poor—possibilities for continuous development attainable by what they and others do in the world together!" She now saw that poverty arrests development and imposes limits on human growth. Children do not ask to be born into poverty, but because they are poor they are isolated from the social and economic mainstream.

"Middle-class, mainly white, children are by and large provided with experiences of and contact with the larger world that develop them and help them to become learners. Poor kids, largely of color, are not."[7] Citing Martin Luther King Jr., Fulani says that he clearly understood the importance of moving African Americans into the mainstream of American life. "Although Dr. King is a celebrated hero in our nation, his insistence on the importance of connecting the African American population to mainstream America seems to have been grossly overlooked. In *Where Do We Go from Here: Chaos or Community?* King writes, 'What is needed is a strategy for change, a tactical program that will bring the Negro into the mainstream of American life as quickly as possible.'"[8]

Newman and Fulani were not satisfied to just have a theory that connected poverty to development. It wasn't enough to tell people they are poor, which Fulani still does regularly. They needed a strategy that would help poor people living in poverty to develop. So they started organizing in poor communities. Their goal was to help adults develop and become part of the political process. Soon leadership was coming from the Unemployed and Welfare Council they organized. Fulani says that the parents asked to have a talent show for their children. The result was another turning point. Fulani and Newman learned that talent shows have tremendous potential for providing an environment where young people can experience taking risks, being appreciated, and developing.

Newman and Fulani took the word *performance* and turned it upside down. The media and schools tell kids that they perform poorly on standardized tests and that they are stupid. They are told that their performance is not as good as it should be. The All Stars Program uses performance to help kids develop by showing them that they can learn how to be part of different environments. It is a matter of learning how to act in those settings. Young people and others are taught how to perform on a stage and then shown how they can use these same strategies when they visit a museum, attend a concert, or work in an office.

One place ASP puts the development strategy into practice is in the Development School for Youth program. This program recruits and trains business leaders across the country who invite students into their workplace as summer interns. The students learn about putting on the business costume. They experience that acting in a business environment is no different from acting on a stage in front of an audience. They develop in the Du Bois and Vygotsky sense.

Fulani's story was very impressive, but I still had a question. Isn't it necessary for young people to develop a positive self-identity to overcome the impact of racial stereotyping and the blatant racism they encounter? What did she mean when she told Gates, "I'm trying to get the kids in our programs to de-racialize?"[9] She was very patient in answering my question in several ways, and finally I think I understood. If racism is understood as one group of people defining another group, then she is working to end racism by challenging the assumption that people need to be defined. I had trouble understanding because I was focusing on who is defining. I wanted the kids of color, their families, and their community to do the defining, not whites and racist institutions. She didn't want to put kids into any boxes—no limiting definitions. She pointed out that white kids and kids of privilege are constantly given opportunities to be in new situations. They are encouraged to develop their skills and interests. "They have very active after-school lives—from ballet to gymnastics to sports. These experiences are key to their development. In contrast, many inner-city kids rarely step outside of the twenty-block radius in which they live." Her goal is to give poor kids the freedom to escape from limits defined by anyone, including themselves. This completely undercuts racism and makes it powerless.

But ASP doesn't just help individuals develop; it also addresses the structures that create and preserve poverty. One example is Operation Conversation: Cops & Kids. Fulani created it in 2006 in response to the shooting of Sean Bell in Queens, New York. In 2011, the New York City Police Department officially incorporated Operation Conversation: Cops & Kids into the training of its police officers and new recruits. Since its inception, Operation Conversation has facilitated better understanding between tens of thousands of cops and kids.

The program uses performance, improvisation, and conversation to help inner-city teenagers and police officers develop together. As Fulani explains, "They use performance to break through barriers to make cops and kids comfortable with each other." She pointed out that often cops and kids come from the same neighborhoods, and she believes that although they may be "on opposite sides of the barricades, they each have some insights into what is going on with the other."[10]

Once I understood Fulani's approach to development, I could see why she said that through the program both the cops and the kids develop. The goal of most cops is to get home safely each night. Their development is limited because they don't see ways that they can act except to be tough, directive, and violent when threatened. The kids' development is limited so that they do not have alternative ways to act except to see cops as adversaries. The program is successful when both cops and kids develop so that they don't let others or themselves set limits on how they can act. And more importantly, they develop together so that they can find ways to engage cooperatively rather than as adversaries. Operation Conversation moves beyond stereotyping of any kind. Both kids and cops are learning that they can perform in ways that support each other.

VIRGINIA ORGANIZING

Motivated by a desire to raise their family in a diverse setting, Joe and Kristin Layng Szakos moved to Charlottesville, Virginia, in the mid-1990s. Kristin was a writer and editor, and Joe had experience founding progressive organizations, including Kentuckians for the Commonwealth and the Southern Empowerment Project. He was also one of the founders of the Hungarian Environmental Partnership. They spent a year in Budapest helping the training program of the Hungarian Environmental Partnership get started before moving to Charlottesville.

For Joe Szakos, community organizing is different from being a campaign organizer. A campaign organizer has an issue with a goal and might work on voter registration or protecting an area from an environmental threat. They look for people who will support the goal. In small towns like Charlottesville, campaign organizers usually move on after a brief stay. In urban areas, campaign organizers may move to a new issue. However, a community organizer starts with the people rather than the issue. Szakos is a community organizer. He moved to Virginia to stay.

Shortly after moving to Charlottesville, Szakos was encouraged to contact Denise Smith. Smith had heard about Szakos from a professor she had when she was in college. She experienced firsthand being ignored by state elected officials and others in the government who would not take her seriously. She knew about the injustices that poor Virginians experience because she had experienced homelessness, lack of responsiveness to her needs as a person with disabilities, and more. She was frustrated because it seemed that legislators pretended "Virginia ends at Roanoke"—far from the state capital.

As Szakos and Smith talked at their first meeting at the McDonald's in Wytheville, Smith caught a glimpse of what might be possible. She knew about organizations that were doing good work to support people and the community, but no one was "organizing people to build power and create long term change."[11]

Between July 1994 and August 1995, Szakos drove more than 40,000 miles back and forth across Virginia. He had more than 250 conversations with people like Smith about what they would like to see changed. He confirmed that there were no grassroots, multi-issue, social change–oriented organizations in Virginia. He also learned about rampant racism, discrimination experienced by LGBTQ people, and special challenges that people with disabilities face. It became clear that many of the issues he heard about were no longer being addressed at the national level. Because of Ronald Reagan's "devolution," there was a shift at the policy level from the federal to the state level. This made the absence of a statewide grassroots organization particularly problematic.

Szakos wrote a report on his findings. One conclusion was, "One of the most important questions of all is: How can different races work together in Virginia on a pro-active agenda? Instead of always being against something, the organization must develop a platform of things to be for."[12]

Ten people emerged as leaders from the 250-plus conversations—none of whom had been part of a statewide organization before. This organizing committee met on August 19, 1995, and decided to build a grassroots organization that would be a political force in Virginia. It would be made up of low- to moderate-income people, people of color, people who identified as LGBTQ, and others who were excluded from Virginia political life. They recognized that the established patterns of racism made it impossible to ignore race. Because race had been submerged for so long, there were many community leaders around the state who were eager to talk about it.

Everything was in place. A need had been identified. Szakos was a professional community organizer with an academic degree, an international reputation as an organizer, and many years of experience. There was a strong and committed organizing committee. Under the white paradigm, the white man would have taken the next step and started applying for funding from foundations. But Szakos had an antiracist idea that rejected the role of a white professional with all the answers. So the committee members left the first meeting with a commitment to talk with others in their community and to raise the money they needed from the grassroots. Today, only 20 percent of Virginia Organizing's budget comes from foundations.

Organizing committee members started reading books and materials about community organizing. They visited groups across the country to learn what they were doing. They analyzed the structures and strategies that they could use to build bridges across racial and other lines that divide people. They came up with an organization plan that has guided the organization since 1995:

- Build strategic organizing capacity.
- Do a power analysis.
- Develop strategic communications.
- Work in coalitions and alliances.

- Participate in issue campaigns that make sense.
- Increase grassroots fundraising.
- Strengthen leadership development and political education.[13]

From the very beginning, meetings included people from across Virginia as well as people of all races, genders, ages, sexual orientations, faiths, political parties, and experiences. The first task was to break down the barriers that exist between people. Smith says that Szakos had everyone attend a Dismantling Racism workshop. The first meetings were more about building trust than setting an agenda for change.

Because racism had come up so often in the one-on-one meetings that Szakos conducted, they knew that racism had been a major factor in the failure of past attempts in Virginia to develop broad grassroots organizations. So a substantial amount of the early resources of time and money were devoted to developing Dismantling Racism workshops. Organizing committee members attended a four-day workshop sponsored by the Peace Development Fund. They sought out all the resources they could, but they knew that the workshops they developed needed to make sense to people in rural Virginia.

Developing sensitivity to differences and skills in communicating across lines brought the leadership to a decision to focus on three interrelated systemic issues: racist institutions, discrimination based on sexual orientation, and unfair wages. Affirming the worth of every person brought a diversity of new ideas and perspectives to problems facing Virginia. The systemic issues were addressed out of a rich set of experiences.

The organizing committee addressed the basic questions, Who are we? and What do we stand for? in the early years. They developed a list of shared beliefs, finally agreeing on 11 items. They started with, "We believe that all people should be treated fairly and with dignity in all aspects of life, regardless of race, class, gender, religion, sexual orientation, age, ability or country of origin."[14]

The first five years were spent establishing chapters and affiliates across the state, building relationships, and conducting racism workshops and local campaigns. The first local campaign success came in 1998 when the Lee County chapter forced changes in the jury selection process. Previously, five white men decided who would be in the jury pool. They chose their friends, which eliminated both low-income people and people of color. Because of the chapter's efforts, a random process was implemented. The result was that for the first time an African American served on a jury.

Local campaigns included organizing for living wages in more than a dozen communities and six college campuses. In Charlottesville, they convinced the school board to add sexual orientation to the nondiscrimination policy for students and employees. Because the choice of campaigns came from the grassroots, and because race and class had been submerged in Virginia, many of the campaigns focused on equity and racial issues. There were, however, local environmental campaigns, such as a cooperative effort with Montebello Clean Mountain Coalition to get Central Virginia Electric Cooperative to honor landowners' requests to refrain from spraying under power lines and to maintain vegetation manually.

In 2001, Virginia Organizing launched its first statewide campaign. Thirty-four percent of renters in Virginia could not afford a two-bedroom apartment at the time. It would take a minimum wage earner 94 hours a week to pay for an average two-bedroom apartment. As people investigated the Virginia Housing and Development Authority (VHDA), they discovered a "major fund balance surplus"[15] that could be used to alleviate some of the problems. Part of the campaign included a goal of modifying loan policies so that same-sex couples and domestic partners could obtain loans. They also wanted to eliminate questions about immigrant status on loan applications.

A careful examination of the 10-member VHDA showed that some of the members had financial interests in for-profit housing. Others were contributors to the governor's political campaigns or family members of high-level politicians. The Virginia Organizing board members knew the value of diversity on their board and wanted the same for VHDA. The years of building relationships across lines of difference and developing experience in grassroots action paid off. The first victory was that VHDA made loans available to documented immigrants. Other victories followed, and unlike issue campaigns, the community organizers stayed on top of the housing issue and continued to push for greater equity.

Dismantling Racism workshops played an important role in developing sensitivity, relationships, and strategies. Nonpartisan civil engagement was a focus of many chapters, and the statewide organization worked with others to register voters, provide nonpartisan voter education, and promote voting. After the 2008 general election and the 2009 statewide elections, the state leadership decided that putting a lot of effort into these elections was not consistent with the goal of more fully engaging people in civic life. The political process goes on every month, so a grassroots organization needs to focus on engaging people in holding elected officials accountable after Election Day.

One of the characteristics of Virginia Organizing is that it is constantly learning and adapting. In 2014, as the political climate in both the Virginia legislature and the national Congress made it difficult to affect policy changes, Virginia Organizing shifted its efforts to local or nonlegislative issues. Here victories were possible. Organizing around race issues was possible because people who had never been involved before could work on local issues, allowing organizers and community leaders to help people learn important leadership skills and "connect the dots" between issues.

This shift was possible because the organization existed to empower people rather than to focus on particular issues and also because the organization did not develop an institutional culture that needed to be preserved.

Another important characteristic of Virginia Organizing is that the leadership and staff focus on relationship building rather than short-term accomplishments. The staff is recruited with the understanding that they are committing to a community rather than to a career.

The four organizations described in this chapter illustrate serious antiracism efforts with organized effort. The following chapter identifies strategies that can be part of our cooperative efforts to address racism.

Chapter 14

Working Together

The most important lesson that the social scientists have to teach us is that overcoming racism and realizing the civil rights dream is extremely difficult but not impossible. Chapter 11 described the critical role that we as individuals need to play. Because racism is embedded in our institutions, it is essential, but not sufficient, for us to change as individuals. We must also work together to change social practices and policies that support racism through institutions. Because of the advances in social science since the 1960s, we can approach this task with strategies that are based on social theory. To briefly review, the theoretical tools include a better understanding of stereotypes, stigmas, and stereotype threats; new theories of structuration and habitus; and the description of disciplinary institutions. All of this helps us understand why racism is so persistent.

Social scientists have also shown the power of paradigms and the process by which we move from one paradigm to another. The social construction of reality is important in both preserving paradigms and helping with paradigm shifts, and sociologists have pointed to the role that charisma plays in breaking the power of institutions. Changing the direction of history was the intent of the civil rights movement in the 1960s. In part, the failure of that movement was that it did not have sufficient tools to analyze racism. Therefore, current attempts to address institutional racism need to begin with two foundational ideas. First, racism is recursive. The people in an organization benefit from racism, and the established practices support racism. Second, rooting out institutional racism requires sensitivity to the complex web that is based on the white paradigm. We can expect some whites to respond to antiracist initiatives by attempting to preserve white privilege. There can be great risks to everyone, but mostly to people of color, who address racism head on. Losing a promotion or a job is just one of the risks. For these and other reasons, forming support groups and working together is not only helpful but essential when addressing institutional racist practice.

Because collective action depends on a shared perception of reality, institutional antiracist activity depends on the definition of the civil rights dream. Even our most sincere attempts to end racism will fail if they are based on a desire for equality when equality is defined as "everyone is like the whites." A civil rights dream that is expressed as a hope that people of all races will have the opportunity to participate in all white institutions only perpetuates the idea of the superiority of white institutions. Another false expression of the civil rights dream that supports white superiority proposes that the dream is realized if tolerance is practiced toward every racial group. Tolerance can be practiced while still holding on to a belief in the superiority of whites. The dream needs to be stated and discussed in every institutional setting. We cannot assume that because others say they support antiracist strategizing, they will abandon the white paradigm and adopt a patchwork quilt paradigm.

Section 1 proposes a wording for the civil rights dream for the 21st century. Other wording may be more useful in a particular institutional setting. In many institutional contexts, defining the civil rights dream needs to involve consideration of policies and practices that go beyond skin-color racism. Gender, religion, age, ethnicity, and other identities are important considerations when dreaming about changing institutions. The common thread is that dreaming about any institution needs to begin with consideration of full participation and supporting individual aspirations.

Creative new nonracist institutions are important, but if we are going to have a paradigm shift to the patchwork paradigm it will be necessary for some existing institutions to be transformed. Institutions are resistant to change, but they are also constantly adjusting their policies and practices. Our challenge is to be supportive of institutional change that is not just an adaptation to the challenges of racism that preserve white supremacy. Four topics discussed below are areas where our intentionality can assist in making meaningful interventions: (1) the sense of institutional racism, (2) the role of charisma, (3) the concept of beloved community, and (4) the necessity of restitution.

These four topics need to be discussed as we approach developing specific antiracist strategies. However, when a patient arrives in an emergency room with a cut that is streaming blood, the first task is to stop the bleeding. In the early years of the 21st century, there are two institutions that create an emergency: education and criminal justice. As long as they continue to provide a foundation for American racism, it will be impossible to realize the civil rights dream. These two institutions are also important places to focus civil rights attention because they are dependent on government support. As Max Weber's theories help us understand, government plays a unique role in mediating the power of institutions in modern society. This means there is a source of power to support civil rights that is external to the logic of institutions. Therefore, following the discussion of the four topics, education and criminal justice are considered. Finally, this chapter concludes that it is time to give civil rights our full attention.

SENSE OF INSTITUTIONAL RACISM

A sense of racism was described in chapter 11. There it was pointed out that we can work intentionally on recognizing stereotypes and noticing when we or others support racism with our everyday conversation and actions. In the same way, we can increase our sensitivity to the racism in institutions. Chapter 9 described Neil Postman and Charles Weingartner's proposals for empowering schools, which are based on what they thought schools should produce. They wanted schools to train students to become "crap detectors." Detecting racism in institutions is the essential first step.[1] Identifying racism in institutions is a form of crap detecting. Michelle Molitor identified three areas where we can focus our attention to discern institutional racism: racial composition, climate, and opportunities.[2]

Racial composition is usually, but not always, visible. Looking around the room to see who is present is a first step. This quickly leads to questions about what barriers there are to getting into the room. Every institutional setting has barriers. Selections are made of who is invited, who is not invited, who is hired, who is fired, and who is promoted. There are policies and practices that create barriers so that the people in the room are there and others are not. Our sense of racism is enhanced as we talk with others and examine the barriers to discover if there are greater barriers for some people because of their race.

When an organization does not include both whites and people of color, then a place to start is with the question "why?" Does the culture of the organization preclude diverse participation? The white paradigm carries with it not only the claim of white superiority but also the claim that white privileges are deserved. This can make it particularly difficult for whites in institutions to imagine what it would look like if the institution were to adopt patchwork paradigm approaches to policies and practices.

There are also cases where the racial composition is not immediately visible. Molitor gives the example of school administrators. She says, "According to the American Association of School Administrators just 6% of superintendents are of color." If the superintendent of the school your children attend is a person of color, you may not be aware that she represents a small minority of superintendents. This is a good example of where observing racial composition can lead to questions about barriers. Being a superintendent is a prestigious if complex and challenging job. There are many barriers if an individual aspires to be a superintendent. A serious study of all the barriers and an examination of whether people of color experience additional barriers would consider many factors. The very last barrier to becoming a superintendent is that no matter how much one wants the job, the final decision in most cases is made by a vote of a local school board. Here the racial composition gives one reason to pause. "The National School Boards Association states that just 11% of school board members are of color."[3]

Institutional climate is the experience that people have of the social environment. Does everyone experience the same sense of support from the institution? Do people share the same level of belonging? Climate can be difficult to identify, but there are certain clear examples of an unfriendly climate. There are climate problems where bullying and sexual harassment are tolerated. Lack of attention to microaggressions also creates a toxic climate. An institutional climate based on the white paradigm can also be subtler. For example, if a business has Hindu employees, is there an attempt to make vegetarian options available in the cafeteria?

Bullying in schools and workplaces is often based on stereotypes. When identity is imposed, there is a tendency to focus on the oppression that results. This is important. Students who are bullied because they are Hispanic need to bring this to other people's attention. Teachers need to address the bullying, but identity groups also have gifts to bring to a school. It is important, even as steps are taken to address oppression, to be open to the gifts that identity groups provide.

Finally, Molitor talks about opportunity. Paying attention to who has opportunities in an institution provides a window into racism and can help us develop our sense of institutional racism. Opportunity is not limited to who is promoted. There can be a difference in opportunity to talk to the institution's leadership. If the president of an organization plays golf on weekends or only socializes with whites in the institution, then there is less opportunity for nonwhites to contribute to the institution. Opportunity is sometimes limited even when people of color are at meetings. They may not have the same opportunity to speak, or their ideas may not be taken seriously. Opportunity is indicated by the participation of all groups.

The three areas that Molitor suggests we use to heighten our sensitivity to institutional racism are situations where institutions themselves fall short. Another way to increase our sense of institutional racism is to consider what institutions are losing because they ignore the gifts that can come from groups that are not white. One example comes from Latino communities that have traditions of family values that can contribute to a school setting. There are patterns of sibling and parental support that could help a school develop stronger cooperation between what happens at home and what happens at school. This would benefit all children, not just Latino students. Or in this case, Latino parents might help teachers and administrators gain a better understanding of how home and school are connected so that the school could apply this understanding to a variety of identity groups.

ROLE OF CHARISMA

The role of charisma was described in chapter 8. Charisma was defined as "the authority that is based on a special personal Spiritual gift, and which is reflected in a personal dedication to, and a personal trust in revelation, heroism, or other traits characteristic of a Leader."[4] Charisma has the potential to stand against the racism that exists in institutions. Charismatic leadership proclaims truth because it is true; it "transforms all values and breaks all traditional and rational norms."[5]

Charisma is something that is inside every human being. It is what we all experience when we know something is not fair because we know it in our heart. Like a sense of racism, charisma can be developed and encouraged.

Weber started by observing that in some societies there are practices designed to provide charismatic education for shamans or priests. He uses examples where the education involves, among other things, isolating an individual from his community, physical and mental exercises to awaken the capacity for ecstasy, asceticism, and more. Weber says that charismatic education "is the radical opposite of specialized professional training." The purpose of charismatic education is the "regeneration of the whole personality."[6] Then Weber observes that there can be overlap between charismatic and professional education. An example of this is a workshop on racism where participants are exposed to the injustice of racism and are also given information about how to comply with civil rights laws. The first part is charismatic education to change their attitude about race. The second part is developing skills they can use even if they are committed to white superiority. This example illustrates why some attempts at cultural competency and diversity education have not been effective; they have not included the goal of charismatic regeneration.

As we look toward realizing the civil rights dream, a charismatic regeneration might be when an individual changes from someone who believes America should be a patchwork nation to someone who believes it is possible for America to become a patchwork nation. Or the regeneration might be from someone who believes in white supremacy to someone who believes that America should and can become a patchwork nation.

There is no single path to becoming committed to civil rights, but there is one commonality that everyone experiences: The conversion comes from the inside as a solution to the conflicts that exist in our habitus. The stories in chapter 12 are all examples of ways that individuals discover that racism is wrong. One person might reflect on the Golden Rule, "Do for others what you would like them to do for you." This can lead to the realization that no one wants to be treated the way nonwhites are in America. Another person may reflect on her religious tradition and decide to either reject its teachings or work to support the common humanity of all people. Another person may have experiences with people who are different and recognize that stereotypes make no sense, prompting him to promote civil rights. Another person may know that a stereotype applied to himself is not an accurate description of who he is. This motivates him to work for civil rights for himself and others. Or the process can be slow and involve small intentional attempts to expand one's experiences across racial lines. Sometimes there is a guide to help us discover the contradictions that lead to a conversion. Sometimes we make discoveries ourselves as we develop our understanding of who we are. Often there are many steps until we know in our hearts that we cannot ignore racism and we must do something. When that happens, we have charisma. We are ready to take a stand against racism.

The insights that come with charisma are an important resource for others. Charismatic leadership is an essential component in the transformation of institutions. Since charisma is available to each of us, we can all become charismatic leaders in the institutions we are part of.

BELOVED COMMUNITY

Dr. Martin Luther King Jr. introduced the concept of a beloved community. It was his image for what America will look like without racism. He proposed the phrase after visiting India and seeing for himself the results of the Indian struggle for independence against Great Britain. Clayborne Carson captured King's understanding of the beloved community: "The aftermath of hatred and bitterness that usually follows a violent campaign was found nowhere in India. The way of acquiescence leads to moral and spiritual suicide. The way of violence leads to bitterness in the survivors and brutality in the destroyers. But the way of nonviolence leads to redemption and the creation of the beloved community."[7]

King proposed seeking justice without violence. The problem that he saw with violence is that it seeks to defeat or humiliate. Nonviolence is directed toward friendship and understanding. He proposed economic boycotts and demonstrations as a way to raise consciousness across the society about injustice, but the end he hoped for was reconciliation. "Beloved community" is a good description of the final goal of the civil rights dream. It depends on the pluralistic vision of each person being accepted without judgment. The beloved community is also a place where the needs of every person are taken into consideration. And it is a place where the gifts of everyone and every identity group are celebrated.

In a beloved community, identifying gifts is not the sole responsibility of the identity group. Sometimes a person who does not identify with a group can see things that are hard for an insider to recognize. In beloved community, the role of politicians is not to put together a coalition that addresses a sufficient number of interest groups to win an election. Rather, a politician seeks out the gifts that come from various identity groups and looks for ways to articulate proposed policies and actions that benefit from these gifts. Under the white paradigm, the only gift politicians desire from racial groups is the gift of their vote. This is essential to preserve the privileged position of whites in politics. Immediately, aspiring political leaders can ask people of color for their ideas, not just their votes. This would undercut the idea that white is better.

The vision of a beloved community is a useful concept as we address institutional racism. It is a way to think about what America would look like without racism. The vision also helps us keep in mind that we can only accomplish the goal of building a beloved community through nonviolent means built on respect and seeking friendship and understanding. Even more importantly, the beloved community does not need to wait. Immediately, every American can begin to develop skills of living in a beloved community. We can work on building respect and seeking friendship and understanding.

RESTITUTION

Chapter 11 points to the importance of sharing stories. Racism, however, will not disappear just because we accept its reality and understand how it is embedded in our lives and social systems. The story of racism includes the fact that for more than two centuries, white Americans have benefited from a system of oppressing nonwhites. This gives whites an inheritance of ill-gotten wealth and undeserved advantages. The average wealth of white families is six to eight times that of Hispanic and black families.[8] Such a huge disparity can only be explained because whites have benefitted from racism. Robert Putnam, a Harvard professor who has studied inequity in America, paints a grim picture of the future of America unless we address the effect of poverty on all children. The "class-based opportunity gap among young people" that Putnam documents "has widened in recent decades," is serious, and needs to be addressed. The legacy of racism is part of this story. As Putnam points out, "Black parents in America remain disproportionately concentrated among the poor and less educated, so black children continue to be handicapped from the start."[9]

Reconciliation that King dreamed about is possible only if whites will admit their complicity in racism and accept accountability for the white paradigm. With accountability comes the need to confess in the sense that Christian theologians use the word. This is not the way *confession* is used in the criminal justice system. When a person confesses to breaking the law, he claims he is guilty. Sometimes a person charged with a crime will negotiate to confess to a crime he is not guilty of in order to avoid going to jail or some other penalty. As we have seen with the criminal justice system, this kind of false admission of guilt is used to perpetuate racism. James Steele has observed that white guilt has also been a contributor to preserving racism.

Steele writes that white guilt "has given America a new social morality in which white racism is seen as disgraceful. . . . It defines propriety in American life so that even those who harbor racist views must conform to a code of decency that defines those views as shameful."[10] Steele points out that white guilt has the same power as racial stigmas have over nonwhites. Whites are assumed to be racist until proven otherwise. As with all guilt, white guilt can either be denied or confessed. Whites chose public denial and internal recognition of guilt. Steele believes that blacks went along with it "and embraced racism as power itself." Because white guilt resulted in an obligation to blacks, Steele argues that it "had inadvertently opened up racism as the single greatest opportunity available to blacks from the mid-sixties on—this for a people with no other ready source of capital with which to launch itself into greater freedom."[11] The result for both whites and nonwhites is that racism was taken off the table. Everyone knows that whites are responsible for the consequences of racism, but the guilt is like a family secret that results in dysfunction.

Christian theologians have proposed another way forward. James Wallis is an evangelical Christian and the editor of *Sojourners* magazine. He has promoted racial and economic issues since the 1970s. Wallis points out that confession of guilt will not end racism. It is the first step toward repentance. In his book *America's Original Sin: Racism, White Privilege, and the Bridge to a New America*, he writes, "Repentance, clearly, is more than just saying you're sorry, or even just feeling guilty—which are popular misconceptions of the word. . . . Repentance means literally to stop, make a radical turnaround, and take an entirely new path. It means a change of mind and heart and is demonstrated by nothing less than transformed behavior."[12] Wallis writes from a Christian perspective, but his recommendations are supported by the sociologists who describe paradigm shifts. Racism will only be defeated if there is a radical turnaround.

American Christian communities' struggles with racism illustrate both the difficulty and the possibilities for moving forward. As we saw in chapter 5, Robert Jones studied what he calls "White Christian America." Jones claims that reconciliation has failed White Christian America largely because it moves to quickly find fellowship without acknowledging the history of white hostility, injustice, and violence that have been perpetrated by whites against people of color. Jones says this "may help explain why white evangelical Protestants' recent efforts aimed at racial reconciliation have been unsuccessful. The move from sincere apology to forgiveness seems logical, because evangelicals' theological individualism tends to obscure the enduring structural injustices that require ongoing, concrete efforts to dismantle." The white mainline Protestants who have a tradition of supporting civil rights have a similar problem. These groups endorse and even experiment with programs of racial reconciliation while still easing the guilt of whites because they propose reconciliation while not addressing racial history. As Jones says, "The effect of this framing is to prematurely push reconciliation to center stage, while reparation waits in the wings."[13]

From a military perspective, reparations are money paid to a nation that is victorious by a nation that is defeated in war. Reparations are the spoils collected for humiliating an enemy. This is not the kind of reparations that Jennifer Harvey envisions. In her 2014 book *Dear White Christians: For Those Still Longing for Racial Reconciliation*, she explains that the vision of a beloved community requires that "we bring our whole, authentic racial selves to the table."[14] She goes on to explain to her intended audience of whites that "without having responded to the acute moral crisis that resides in white racial identity, white Christians are simply not prepared to do this." Harvey challenges her readers to become "repairers of the breach." She uses a biblical image to call her white readers to "figure out how to begin paying back, several-fold when possible, what has been taken. We must do so even while cognizant that the atrocities that constitute our racial history can never be fully repaired."[15]

Participating in discovering history and considering ways to repair the damage that was and is being done does not require a large national project. Harvey describes the experiences of Episcopal Church congregations that have largely white membership. They approach conversations in their community from the perspective of reparations. They created a "forum conducive to significant and necessary transformation in white understanding, generated strong bonds among those engaged in this interracial work, and led to clarity among group members that a commitment to reparations rather than reconciliation is critical."[16] This sounds like taking meaningful steps toward a beloved community.

Harvey uses the imagery of repairing. This book uses a healing metaphor. Whether we are repairing or healing, there are two areas that demand immediate attention. We can think of them the same way we would if the roof blew off our house or if we were bleeding profusely from a wound. These areas are education and criminal justice. In both cases, history is filled with moral failures of whites. With education, whites have failed to address the educational needs of nonwhites or limited the availability of education for nonwhites. White privilege has been used to create a criminal justice system that limits the opportunities for nonwhites. In both cases, these systems are particularly critical to address immediately because they impact youth.

The schools and the criminal justice system are two places where we can begin to change the direction of racial history in America.

SCHOOL INTEGRATION

King's dream that descendants of former slaves and former masters will sit down at the table of fellowship together requires that we establish environments where this can happen. In 2005, Jonathan Kozol wrote a report on how America is doing on the signature achievement of the civil rights movement: school integration. The title of his book tells the story: *The Shame of the Nation: The Restoration of Apartheid Schooling in America*. He reported that "schools that were already deeply segregated 25 or 30 years ago ... are no less segregated now, while thousands of other schools that had been integrated either voluntarily or by force of law have since been rapidly resegregating both in northern districts and in broad expanses of the South."[17] This failure to accomplish the integration of schools was made possible with the support of the Supreme Court and the Justice Department of the federal government. In the 1977 *Milliken v. Bradley* Supreme Court case, the court opened the door for school districts to avoid integration if they provided a reason for not integrating. The result was that court-ordered integration became very rare. Particularly under the administrations of Richard Nixon and Ronald Reagan, the Department of Justice did not pursue the integration of schools.

Charles T. Clotfelter in *After Brown: The Rise and Retreat of School Desegregation*, described the reaction to the *Brown* decision. It was ferocity. He says the response of whites made it clear "that the states of the former Confederacy, at least, would not stand idly by while an imperial federal government sought to destroy a central pillar of its social order." This opposition was not only in the South. "Many whites outside the South had enjoyed privileged treatment in their public school systems as well. . . . More significantly, public schools in much of the urban North were characterized by pronounced de facto segregation, owing to the highly fragmented jurisdictional landscape in most metropolitan areas."

Clotfelter went on to explain, "White flight in the form of whites moving to suburban areas with largely white populations and white families moving their children into private schools also contributed to the resegregation of schools. The desegregation of school was a social experiment that impacted American children into the 1990s. The impact was impressive. Nonwhite student graduation rates increased sharply. The test score gaps between whites and others narrowed. And school achievement for students of all races improved."[18]

Kozol interviewed Gary Orfield, who now teaches at UCLA but at the time was on the faculty of the Harvard Graduate School of Education. Orfield has studied the desegregation experiment extensively and would like to see nonwhites who benefited during integration join with likeminded whites to build a popular movement for integration. He also suggested that the place to start the reintegration of schools is not Chicago or New York City; Des Moines is a more promising place to begin because its size makes it more manageable. At the time the book was written, Orfield had little hope that the courts or government would recognize the benefits and work to integrate schools. This prediction proved to be accurate by the time Barack Obama was elected the next president three years later.[19]

Despite the success of the desegregation experiment, by the time Obama became president in 2008, the push for school integration had disappeared. Busing children from one place to another was the only way to create integrated classrooms, but public opposition to busing was unrelenting. The Obama administration chose to completely ignore integration as a strategy for reforming education and instead focused on the lowest performing schools. So about 10,000 schools, mostly districts with largely students of color, were offered incentives to improve their quality. While hundreds of thousands of students benefited from these programs, the approach was based on the assumption that white education is the norm and the goal. The white paradigm was not questioned.

Linda Darling-Hammond, a professor at Stanford University, describes an alternative approach in her book *The Flat World and Education: How America's Commitment to Equity Will Determine Our Future*. The use of the word *equality* in the title of her book shows how embedded the concept is in our language, but the content of her book challenges the usual way that *equality* is used. She recognizes that we cannot overcome what she calls the "opportunity gap" by simply doing more of the same. This shift away from talking about the achievement gap is important because *achievement* sounds like something that individuals are responsible for. Saying that the problem is achievement suggests that nonwhite students are responsible for the problem. Opportunity is something that the community either offers or denies. Opportunity is what empowering institutions provide.

Darling-Hammond calls for a major redesign of schools with a new mission: "Instead of merely 'covering the curriculum' or 'getting through the book,' the new mission requires that schools substantially enrich the intellectual opportunities they offer while meeting the diverse needs of students who bring with them varying talents, interests, learning styles, cultures, predispositions, language backgrounds, family situations, and beliefs about themselves and about what school means for them."[20] Schools that take into account cultures, language backgrounds, and family situations as well as the beliefs students have about themselves could not avoid addressing the context of oppression of nonwhite students. Yet Darling-Hammond is an exception in school reform discussions.

Across the country, schools that previously served only students who speak English at home are now faced with the need to educate students with many different languages spoken at home. The 21st century is not the first time that schools in the United States have faced the challenge of a large immigrant group. Between 1881 and 1920, 4.5 million Italians came to the United States. As Richard J. Altenbaugh points out, there are many similarities between the Italians and the recent immigrants from Spanish-speaking countries. In both cases, many are escaping poverty, their faith tradition is largely Roman Catholic, and many are suspicious of American institutions, including the schools. In the case of Italians, the teaching profession made every effort to destroy Italian values that one researcher described as "family solidarity, male superiority, and the economic oneness of the family."[21] Into the 1950s and beyond, Anglo teachers ridiculed Hispanic students, ignored Mexican and other Hispanic cultures, obliterated the Spanish language, and used other strategies in an attempt to force students to conform to Anglo expectations.[22] The most difficult cultural characteristic to break was the strong commitment to family and community.

Today the federal government provides about 10 percent of the dollars that support primary and secondary education. The other 90 percent comes from state and local sources. Local communities can look at their own history and develop strategies to provide education for a new generation of children based on experience and commitment to a pluralistic nation.

CRIMINAL JUSTICE SYSTEM

The criminal justice system plays such a large role in preserving the white paradigm at the beginning of the 21st century that it demands our attention. As Michelle Alexander has documented, the growth of the prison population is not caused by an increase in crime. It is completely caused by the war on drugs and eagerness on the part of white politicians to gain white votes. There was an increase in crime in the 1960s, but since then crime itself has varied but has not increased greatly. In 1972, there were fewer than 350,000 people incarcerated in prisons and jails across the nation. Today, the war on drugs has resulted in that number increasing to over 2 million. There are more than twice that many people on probation or parole. The United States incarcerates its citizens at a rate that is 6 to 10 times that of any other industrialized nation.[23]

There is little evidence that incarcerating people makes them better citizens. As recently as the 1970s, experts discussed shutting down the prison system because it served little purpose. The National Advisory Commission on Criminal Justice Standards and Goals issued a report in 1973 that recommended "no new institutions for adults should be built and existing institutions for juveniles should be closed." They made 140 specific recommendations, including the repeal of legislation that deprives exoffenders of civil rights and opportunities for employment; decriminalizing activities such as public drunkenness and vagrancy; and developing treatment programs for alcoholics, drug addicts, prostitutes, and the mentally disturbed.[24] The proposals did not have a chance. The backlash against the civil rights gains of the 1960s was the first step. Richard Nixon was president in 1973. He noted increases in reported crime and claimed that the source was a civil rights movement that promoted lawlessness. Civil disobedience was called a criminal act rather than the political act that it was. Nixon had billed himself as a law-and-order candidate, so decriminalizing some activity and developing alternatives to prison was not on his agenda.

The criminal justice system in its current form is a disciplinary institution that supports and promotes racism. We need to look at how to reduce its impact on people of color. This is an important first step and the perspective of people who want to reform the system. From the perspective of the patchwork quilt nation, we need to look at how our police respond to threats to safety and how a justice system protects people from the selfish interest of others. These were the two concerns of the founders, and they remain critical roles for the government. Providing safety from physical danger and safety from the harmful self-interest of others is complicated, but from a patchwork quilt paradigm perspective, we can look for ways that government can be used to support participation in the beloved community.

IT'S THE RIGHT THING TO DO

It should be evident from the description of how racism works that we will not end racism just because there are a few people who dedicate themselves to solving this problem. Racism is not like going to the moon, where a small number of experts do all the work and the rest of us watch and celebrate. Racism will not end when those who take it up as a hobby or a specialization are finally successful. It will take all of us addressing everyday language and actions, taking responsibility for institutions and communities, and sharing political action.

Why should we do it? Because realizing the civil rights dream is making history. Humans make history. It is not only what we do—it is what makes us human. As one man who made history, Rev. Dr. Martin Luther King Jr. said, "The time is always right to do what's right."[25]

Chapter 15

Afterword 2016

Every book has a context. This book was written in 2016. The outline was written in January of that year and submitted to Praeger on the birthday of Rev. Dr. Martin Luther King Jr. The proposal was accepted quickly, and I immediately began researching and writing about the topics I had proposed in the outline.

As I began my research at the Georgetown University library and the Library of Congress, it was impossible not to notice daily news reports on a very contentious presidential election. Despite the issues related to race relations surfacing in the news, my editor at Praeger, Kim Kennedy-White, and I decided that I would finish the book as planned and then reflect on the events of 2016 at the end of the year. This book was written in 2016, but it was not written to specifically address the 2016 election.

Nevertheless, the content of this book is more relevant today than ever before. The message of the book is that if we will look beyond the daily headlines of racism in American society, we can see historical patterns and social structures that explain why racism is so persistent. More importantly, taking a broad and historical view makes it possible for us to address racism so that the civil rights dream can be realized.

The presidential campaign brought into focus the relationship between racism and the white paradigm. The point of this book and the lessons of the campaign are the same. The previous chapters make three proposals: (1) We need to be able to state our civil rights goal, our dream. Unless we can say what kind of a country we want, we can never achieve it. (2) We need to understand the processes and structures that preserve the existing social relations. The white paradigm provides the structure and is supported by three vehicles: stereotypes, institutional racism, and disciplinary institutions.

(3) Realizing the civil rights dream requires replacing the white paradigm with a new paradigm. Paradigms are socially constructed understandings of reality that depend on our everyday activity.

There were many examples in the presidential campaign that illustrate how pervasive the white paradigm is and the underlying processes that support it. The 2016 campaign felt more contentious, more driven by racism, and uglier than recent campaigns. That ugliness makes it all the more important for us to use the framework described in chapter 10 to address the white paradigm.

Three observations about the campaign illustrate the usefulness of the framework: (1) Trump capitalized on white racist anxiety; (2) Clinton attempted to label Trump a racist; and (3) references to stereotypes impacted the targets.

APPEALING TO WHITE RACIAL ANXIETY

In recent years, all winning presidential candidates have appealed to white anxiety regarding race as part of their strategy. Donald Trump did not invent using references to stereotypes and coded racist language. Every winning candidate in recent memory has promoted the white paradigm.

In Trump's acceptance speech at the Republican Convention, he said, "I only want to admit individuals into our country who will support our values and love our people." He did not specify who "our" includes, but he only used nonwhites as examples of people who are failing. At the end of the speech, he repeated the theme of his campaign, "Make America Great Again."[1] Since at all points in our history, the foundation of American society was the white paradigm, he signaled support for a white vision for America.

Ronald Reagan used two specific strategies to make sure white voters knew that he would not promote advances in civil rights. First, he invented the war on drugs. When Richard Nixon ran as a law-and-order candidate, his target was the danger of civil rights activists who participated in civil disobedience. By 1980, street activism had dissipated and Reagan needed a new target. He invented a drug problem in black communities and created the war on drugs. This provided a focus for white racial anxiety and a reason to support Reagan's law-and-order stance. Just to make sure that no one would suspect him of supporting civil rights, secondly, he said that the federal government should not be involved in civil rights enforcement because that impinged on states' rights.

In 1988, George H. W. Bush took a much more direct approach to gain the White House by exploiting white racism. In speeches and television ads, Bush made a connection between Michael Dukakis, his opponent, and a convicted murderer named William Horton. Dukakis was governor of Massachusetts when Horton was released on furlough under Massachusetts law.

Horton escaped to Maryland, where he committed several crimes, including raping a woman twice. Bush claimed that as president he could keep white people safe.

Bill Clinton was elected in 1992. He counted on the votes of nonwhites who were moving away from the Republican Party. He reached out to white voters with a strong anticrime message, and he also followed George H. W. Bush's example. In May of 1992, Clinton made his move to become the protector of whites against blacks. He identified a black threat, misrepresented it, and signaled that whites should vote for him because he understood racism and would protect them. Invited by Jesse Jackson to speak at the national convention of the Rainbow Coalition, he chose that moment to criticize the Rainbow Coalition for having Sister Souljah, a hip-hop artist, as part of the program the night before. Souljah's comment about killing white people had been taken out of context and quoted in the *Washington Post*.[2] It was a brilliant move, using the setting of Jackson's convention to convey the message to white voters that he understood white racial angst.

The politics of race were played out differently in the 2000 election of George W. Bush. Al Gore won the official popular vote and was the clear choice of nonwhites. The election came down to the 25 contested electoral college votes in Florida. In a five-to-four decision, the Supreme Court gave the election to Bush. Manning Marable explains, "Chief Justice William Rehnquist's refusal to acknowledge evidence of blatant voter fraud against African Americans was no surprise. Back in 1962 . . . Rehnquist successfully disfranchised hundreds of black and brown voters in Phoenix's poor and working-class precincts. In 2000, Rehnquist supervised the disfranchisement, in effect of the majority of American voters."[3] Bush was elected because whites used their power to ensure that the candidate favored by whites became president.

Obama's campaign for the presidency could, for obvious reasons, not avoid race. Obama adopted three strategies that proved to be successful in putting together the necessary coalition to win the presidency. First, he used questions that were raised about his membership in Trinity United Church of Christ to disassociate himself from the white image of radical black leadership. When statements by Rev. Jeremiah Wright Jr. were taken out of context and used by Obama's opponents to connect Obama with an antiwhite agenda, Obama at first defended his mentor and the church that had nurtured him. Then he resigned from the church and clarified his rejection of beliefs that were attributed to Wright.[4] Second, Obama addressed racism directly. In a speech on March 18, 2008, in Philadelphia, he said, "Throughout the first year of this campaign, against all predictions to the contrary, we saw how hungry the American people were for this message of unity. Despite the temptation to view my candidacy through a purely racial lens, we won commanding victories in states with some of the whitest populations in the country."[5] Third, Obama assured whites that he understood them through frequent references to his evangelical Christian beliefs and practices. Brian Kaylor analyzed the speeches and public statements of both Obama and his Republican rival. He concludes, "Obama linked several of his public policy positions to his religious beliefs. In citing scripture and testifying about his religious belief, Obama interjected religious rhetoric into the campaign much more often and comfortably than John McCain."[6]

Since the civil rights movement in the 1960s, no political party has nominated a candidate with a civil rights agenda. Jackson's vision for a patchwork nation in 1988 has not been picked up by any major candidate. Up to this point in our history, and 2016 was no different, presidential candidates have planned their campaigns under the assumptions of the white paradigm.

CALLING PEOPLE RACISTS

Clinton made Trump's character an issue. In her convention acceptance speech, she said, "So enough with the bigotry and bombast. Donald Trump's not offering real change."[7] Trump responded to the racist charge by telling *Washington Post* reporter Marc Fisher, "I am the least-racist person that you've ever encountered."[8] Clinton wasn't convinced. She used surrogate Senator Elizabeth Warren to attack Trump. Warren called Trump a "nasty, loud, thin-skinned fraud" and a "racist."[9]

"Racist" is not a category of people. Actions, comments, and even speeches can be racist, but not people. Yet the rush to describe Trump as a racist was a reflex reaction born out of years of perfecting a system of racism for the 21st century. Clinton used stereotyping when she described Trump supporters as a "basket of deplorables."[10] Labeling other people is the basis of stereotyping and one of the vehicles of the white paradigm. By attempting to claim the higher moral ground, Clinton used one of the strategies of 21st-century racism that has been extremely effective. Labeling other people as racist and denying being a racist avoids dealing with racism that hides in stereotypes, institutions, and disciplinary institutions.

THE "TRUMP EFFECT"

Between November 9 and December 12, 2016, the Southern Poverty Law Center collected evidence of just over 1,000 incidents of bias-related harassment and intimidation around the country.[11] This is clearly just the tip of the iceberg. Earlier in 2016, the Southern Poverty Law Center conducted an informal survey of teachers, who reported increases of bullying and of students of color expressing anxiety. They named it the "Trump effect" and said, "It's producing an alarming level of fear and anxiety among children of color and inflaming racial and ethnic tensions in the classroom. Many

students worry about being deported. Other students have been embold-
ened by the divisive, often juvenile rhetoric in the campaign. Teachers have
noted an increase in bullying, harassment and intimidation of students
whose races, religions or nationalities have been the verbal targets of candidates on the campaign trail."[12]

While the Trump effect increased fear and bullying, fear is not a new strategy to preserve the white paradigm. Ta-Nehisi Coates explained to his son,
"And I am afraid. I feel the fear most acutely whenever you leave me. But I
was afraid long before you, and in this I was unoriginal. When I was your
age the only people I knew were black, and all of them were powerfully,
adamantly, dangerously afraid. I had seen this fear all my young life, though
I had not always recognized it as such."[13]

It seems very unlikely that candidate Trump thought to himself that it
was a good idea to frighten children. He was involved in an election campaign. Yet, his words illustrate the stereotype threat described in chapter 7.
The constant reminder of racial stereotypes has an impact on the target. In
future presidential campaigns, the candidates can use the insights of social
psychologists and replace the use of stereotypes with demonstrations of full
participation of all racial groups. Candidates can also point to the gifts that
racial and other identity groups bring. We have an opportunity every four
years to discuss the future of our country. Finding an alternative to the white
paradigm should be at the center of that discussion.

LOOKING BEYOND 2016

If we take seriously what the social scientists have learned since the 1960s,
it is impossible to avoid our responsibility for the continued failure to realize the civil rights dream. As Michelle Obama expressed clearly, in an emotional speech in New Hampshire, "This is not normal. This is not politics as
usual."[14] The campaign exposed the white paradigm vividly. But what we
know now that we didn't know 50 years ago is that our everyday conversations construct our reality and the paradigms that organize our society. So
each one of us can give more attention to exposing stereotypes and standing
up to institutional racism. In our everyday life, we can claim the civil rights
dream that *America will be a nation where every race, ethnicity, and identity
group has full participation in the political, economic, and cultural life of the
nation so that the barriers to fulfilling individual aspirations are no greater
for one person than another.*

Acknowledgments

My family not only keeps me grounded, they also encourage me. My wife of 46 years, Kathie Hale Bedell, made it possible for me to write this book. Through the years our daughter, Charity Pelletier, kept saying things like, "Dad you have to do that." Her younger sister, Sarah Cook, helped me with the manuscript and encouraged me when I needed it most.

I have attempted to share in the text itself stories of many of the people who have talked with me both formally and informally during my life journey, the result of which is this book. Their names can be found in the index. I will not repeat all of them here. They have my gratitude and my hope that I have not embarrassed them by not understanding what they tried to teach me.

I particularly want to thank Rev. Jesse L. Jackson, Sr., his family, especially Jonathan and Yusef, and staff, specifically Frank Watkins, for the foreword for this volume. Rev. Jackson has been an inspiration to me over the years, so I am honored that he has contributed to this book.

Others who supported me, shared their stories, or listened to me are not in the index. Some of them are listed below. There were many more and some whose names I don't even know. All those named and unnamed have my gratitude.

Rev. Brenda Girton-Mitchell, my supervisor for the past six years, encouraged me with my first idea. I wanted to facilitate a book project at the Department of Education to clarify what Secretary Arne Duncan meant when he said, "Education is the civil rights issue of our time." After it became clear that the laws and other factors made it impossible for a book about civil rights to come from the Department of Education, Brenda said to me, "Ken, you should write your own book."

I send out special thanks to Kathie Engelken, Brenda Girton-Mitchell, Greyson Mann, Eddie Martin, Curtis Carr, Melody Fox Ahmed, Murali Balaji, Edward Adutwum, Hope Phillips, Richard Clemons, Grant Abbott, Ben Sanders, Don Struchen, Russella L. Davis-Rogers, Shirley Struchen, Paul Monteiro, David Rabin, Jackye Zimmerman, Terri LaVelle, Russella L. Davis-Rogers, Sherrill McMillan, Lela Harris, Peter Key, Erin Hatton, Daviree Velazquez, Elizabeth Naftalin, David Naftalin, Gail Naftalin, Jerry Sachs, Jason Cook, Abdel Elsiddig, David Myers, Jonathan Jackson, Frank Watkins, Alexander Levering Kern, Mark Siljander, Hal Hartley, Usra Ghazi, Bud Heckman, Ronn Noze, Charles Haynes, Marcus Coleman, Barbara Thompson, and Chad Frey.

This book is based on the social theory that we do things like write books as individuals, but we do it supported by a society that surrounds us. I am very thankful for the individuals and society that support me.

Glossary

Charisma

A charismatic person brings wisdom, understanding, or dedication that is based on a spiritual or personal revelation. Charisma results in the person becoming a leader when other people recognize that the wisdom is true. Charisma is not limited to leaders of large movements; everyone possesses charisma when they identify an injustice or just know that something is not fair. Charisma can be a counterforce to the logic of institutional organizations. Communities are founded by charismatic leaders.

Community

A community is a group of people who share beliefs, practices, and customs. It is held together because members choose to associate. An ethnic group is an example of a community. A community differs from an institution because it does not strive to be efficient. Rather, communities strive to be true to the shared beliefs, practices, and customs of the group.

Disciplinary Institutions

A disciplinary institution claims its purpose is to make people better, but it plays a role in supporting and sustaining racism and other forms of oppression. Schools and jails are sometimes disciplinary institutions. The opposite of disciplinary institutions are institutions that support the humanity of children and others.

Diversity	Diversity is the presence of different identity groups in an institution. It is an essential component of a patchwork institution or society. Being present does not guarantee that the represented identity groups have full participation. Therefore, diversity is not sufficient when attempting to realize the civil rights dream.
Double Consciousness	A concept introduced by African American sociologist W. E. B. Du Bois, double consciousness describes the experience an individual has of participating in two or more cultures. He explained how oppressed people have a consciousness of full humanity and a second consciousness of the denial of their humanity by the oppressing group.
Habitus	All of the resources that an individual has in all levels of consciousness to decide what to say and how to act is known as habitus. This includes knowledge about what others expect in social interactions as well as a sense of justice, humor, morality, and more.
Institution	An institution is an organization that is governed by policies and practices driven by efficiency and competition in the economy. Institutions are sometimes called bureaucratic organizations. They are distinct from communities in that they have a social reality that is independent of the commitment of individuals.
Institutional Racism	Practices and policies of institutions that result in privileges for whites or limit opportunities for nonwhites are collectively known as institutional racism.
Intolerance	Intolerance is a belief that one's culture is the only truly human culture and that people who are different are less human.
Microaggressions	Microaggressions intentionally or unintentionally target a person because of perceived or real membership in a stigmatized group with a verbal or nonverbal slight, snub, rejection, rudeness, or insult.
Paradigm	A paradigm is a theoretical framework that organizes reality and is a basis for society.
Patchwork Quilt Paradigm	Organizations or societies in which identity and other groups have full participation without one race or identity group claiming superiority over any other are following a patchwork quilt paradigm.

Pluralistic	Organizations that have full participation of all participants are described as pluralistic. A pluralistic organization differs from a diverse organization in that in addition to different groups being present, the groups all have equal participation. Pluralists believe that other people have beliefs that are as valid for them.
Society	A society is a group of people who share a collection of community organizations, institutions, and a government.
Stereotype	A widely held opinion of a characteristic that is ascribed to an identity group is called a stereotype.
Stereotype Threat	A stereotype that is internalized as a stigma is called a stereotype threat. The threat impacts the performance of individuals in the targeted group.
Stigma	A stigma is a negative stereotype that a society applies to an identity group. Stigmas are the result of one group (whites) claiming to be "normal" and defining a characteristic as not normal.
Structuration	Structuration is a way to describe the process where individual actions create and support social structures and paradigms. The social structures and paradigms then influence everyday actions, which in turn preserve the social structures.
Tolerance	Acceptance of others that can include a judgment about the relative value of different races or identity groups is called tolerance. Tolerant people do not believe that everyone should be exactly like they are, but they believe that they are better than others.
White Paradigm	A belief that white people are superior to all people who are not white is known as the white paradigm. It results in establishing barriers that make it more difficult for nonwhites to achieve their aspirations. The white paradigm is supported by stereotypes, institutional racism, and disciplinary institutions.

Notes

CHAPTER 1: INTRODUCTION

1. Bureau of Census, "Educational Attainment by Race and Hispanic Origin: 1970 to 2015 [Selected Years]," ProQuest Statistical Abstract of the U.S. 2016 Online Edition, ProQuest, 2016.

2. Michelle Alexander, *The New Jim Crow: Mass Incarceration in the Age of Colorblindness* (New York: New Press, 2010), 16.

3. Bureau of Census, "Median Income of People in Constant (2014) Dollars by Sex, Race, and Hispanic Origin: 2000 to 2014 [Selected Years]," ProQuest Statistical Abstract of the U.S. 2016 Online Edition, ProQuest, 2016.

4. John Howard Griffin, *Black Like Me: What Is It Like, to Be a Negro in the Deep South Today?* (New York: Signet Books, 1961), 29.

5. Andrew Hacker, *Two Nations: Black and White, Separate, Hostile, Unequal* (New York: Scribner, 2003), 77.

6. Shelby Steele, *White Guilt: How Blacks and Whites Together Destroyed the Promise of the Civil Rights Era* (New York: HarperCollins, 2006), 100.

7. Paul Kivel, *Uprooting Racism: How White People Can Work for Racial Justice*, 3rd rev. ed. (Gabriola, BC: New Society, 2011), 116.

8. Lynn Schofield Clark, *The Parent App: Understanding Families in the Digital Age* (Oxford, UK: Oxford University Press, 2013), xiv.

9. "On Views of Race and Inequity, Blacks and Whites Are Worlds Apart" (Pew Research Center, June 27, 2016), http://www.pewsocialtrends.org/2016/06/27 /on-views-of-race-and-inequality-blacks-and-whites-are-worlds-apart/.

CHAPTER 2: WHOSE IDEA WAS THIS?

1. Linwood Custalow and Angela L. Daniel, *The True Story of Pocahontas: The Other Side of History* (Golden, CO: Fulcrum, 2007), 35–37.

2. James D. Rice, *Tales from a Revolution: Bacon's Rebellion and the Transformation of Early America*, New Narratives in American History (New York: Oxford University Press, 2012), 220.

3. Benjamin Franklin, *The Autobiography of Benjamin Franklin* (New York: Open Road Integrated Media, 2014), 86.

4. Benjamin Franklin and Edmund S. Morgan, *Not Your Usual Founding Father: Selected Readings from Benjamin Franklin* (New Haven, CT: Yale University Press, 2006), 166.

5. Ibid., 163.

6. John Wesley, *John Wesley's Sermons: An Anthology* (Nashville, TN: Abingdon Press, 1991), 290.

7. Ibid.

8. Harriet Cornelia Cooper, *James Oglethorpe, the Founder of Georgia* (New York: D. Appleton, 1904), chap. 7.

9. Thomas Paine, *Common Sense: Addressed to the Inhabitants of America, on the Following Interesting Subjects* (Philadelphia: Author, 1776), 15.

10. Franklin and Morgan, *Not Your Usual Founding Father*, 221.

11. Christopher Cameron, *The Abolitionist Movement: Documents Decoded* (Santa Barbara, CA: ABC-CLIO, 2014), 25–26.

12. Benjamin Rush, *An Address to the Inhabitants of the British Settlements, on the Slavery of the Negroes in America. To Which Is Added, A Vindication of the Address, in Answer to a Pamphlet entitled, "Slavery Not Forbidden in Scripture; Or, A Defence of the West India Planters* (Philadelphia: John Dunlap, 1773), 26.

13. Joe R. Feagin and José A. Cobas, *Latinos Facing Racism: Discrimination, Resistance, and Endurance*, New Critical Viewpoints on Society Series (Boulder, CO: Paradigm, 2014), 17–18.

14. Spencer Tucker et al., eds., *The Encyclopedia of the Mexican-American War: A Political, Social, and Military History* (Santa Barbara, CA: ABC-CLIO, 2013), 278–80.

15. Charles Dickens, *American Notes: For General Circulation* (New York: Open Road Media, 2015), 28. First published 1842 by Chapman & Hull.

16. James Oliver Horton, "Slavery during Lincoln's Lifetime," in *Lincoln and Freedom: Slavery, Emancipation, and the Thirteenth Amendment*, ed. Harold Holzer and Sara Vaughn Gabbard (Carbondale: Southern Illinois University Press, 2007), 13.

17. Frederick Douglass, *Life and Times of Frederick Douglass* (New York: Pathway Press, 1941), 242–44. Originally published 1881.

18. Ibid.

19. Nell Irvin Painter, *Sojourner Truth: A Life, a Symbol* (New York: W.W. Norton, 1996), 170.

20. "Our Documents. Transcript of President Abraham Lincoln's Second Inaugural Address (1865)," https://www.ourdocuments.gov/doc.php.?doc=38&page=transcript.

21. Ibid.

22. Christian G. Samito, *Lincoln and the Thirteenth Amendment*, Concise Lincoln Library (Carbondale: Southern Illinois University Press, 2015), 29–31.

23. Ibid., 72.

24. C. Vann Woodward, *The Strange Career of Jim Crow*, 3rd rev. ed. (New York: Oxford University Press, 1974), 26.

25. Paul Teed and Melissa Teed, *Reconstruction: A Reference Guide* (Santa Barbara, CA: ABC-CLIO, 2015), 126.

26. Booker T. Washington, "Booker T. Washington Delivers the 1895 Atlanta Compromise Speech," accessed June 28, 2016, http://historymatters.gmu.edu/d/39/.

27. Aldon D. Morris, *The Scholar Denied: W. E. B. Du Bois and the Birth of Modern Sociology* (Oakland: University of California Press, 2015), 109–11.

28. Woodward, *The Strange Career of Jim Crow*, 65.

29. Ibid., 6.

30. James W. Loewen, "Sundown Towns," *Poverty & Race* 14, no. 6 (November–December 2005): 1.

31. Gunnar Myrdal, Richard Mauritz Edvard Sterner, and Arnold Marshall Rose, *An American Dilemma: The Negro Problem and Modern Democracy*, 20th anniv. ed. (New York: Harper & Row, 1962).

32. John F. Kennedy, "Report to the American People on Civil Rights, 11 June 1963," https://www.jfklibrary.org/Asset-Viewer/LH8F_0Mzv0e6Ro1yEm74Ng.aspx.

33. Civil Rights Act of 1964, Pub. L. No. 88-352, 78 Stat. 241 (1964).

CHAPTER 3: TEARING DOWN BARRIERS

1. Larry Ramey and Daniel Haley, *Tackling Giants: The Life Story of Berkley Bedell* (Loveland, CO: National Foundation for Alternative Medicine, 2005), vi.

2. Michael Harrington, *The Other America: Poverty in the United States* (New York: Macmillan, 1962), 9–10.

3. Ibid., 14.

4. Martin Luther King, "Martin Luther King I Have a Dream Speech—American Rhetoric," accessed November 3, 2015, http://www.americanrhetoric.com/speeches/mlkihaveadream.htm.

5. David J. Garrow, *Bearing the Cross: Martin Luther King, Jr., and the Southern Christian Leadership Conference* (New York: W. Morrow, 1986), 319.

6. Ayn Rand, *Atlas Shrugged* (New York: Random House, 1957).

7. Ayn Rand and Nathaniel Branden, *The Virtue of Selfishness: A New Concept of Egoism* (New York: New American Library, 1965), 131.

8. Ibid., 134.

9. Ibid., 33.

10. Milton Friedman, "What Every American Wants," *The Southeast Missourian*, January 16, 2003.

11. Ronald Reagan, "Ronald Reagan: Inaugural Address," accessed October 23, 2016, http://www.presidency.ucsb.edu/ws/?pid=43130.

12. Southern Poverty Law Center, "Active Antigovernment Groups in the United States," accessed October 24, 2016, https://www.splcenter.org/active-antigovernment-groups-united-states.

13. Morris Dees and James Corcoran, *Gathering Storm: America's Militia Threat* (New York: HarperCollins, 1996), 201.

14. Robert N. Bellah, ed., *Habits of the Heart: Individualism and Commitment in American Life: Updated Edition with a New Introduction* (Berkeley: University of California Press, 1996), 155.

15. Ralph Waldo Emerson, *Compensation, Self-Reliance, and Other Essays*, The Riverside Literature Series [No. 171], ed. Mary A. Jordan (Boston: Houghton Mifflin, 1907), 5–7.

16. Louisa May Alcott, *The Best of Louisa May Alcott*, ed. Claire Booss (New York: Gramercy Books, 2007), 117.

17. Henry David Thoreau, *Walden, Or, Life in the Woods; and Civil Disobedience* (New York: Vintage Books, 2014), 66.

18. Martin Luther King, "Martin Luther King I Have a Dream Speech—American Rhetoric."

19. Thomas Paine, *Common Sense: Addressed to the Inhabitants of America, on the Following Interesting Subjects* (Philadelphia: Author, 1776), 6.

20. Franklin and Morgan, *Not Your Usual Founding Father*, 257.

21. John Adams, *Thoughts on Government: Applicable to the Present State of the American Colonies: In a Letter from a Gentleman to His Friend* (Philadelphia: John Dunlap, 1776).

22. Alexander Hamilton, James Madison, and John Jay, *The Federalist: A Collection of Essays, Written in Favour of the New Constitution, as Agreed upon by the Federal Convention, September 17, 1787, no. 35* (New York: J. and A. M'Lean, 1788), 110.

23. Gerald McKnight, *Last Crusade* (Boulder, CO: Westview Press, 1998), 1–2, 42.

24. George W. Bush, "Inauguration of the President," accessed April 6, 2017, https://www.inaugural.senate.gov/about/past-inaugural-ceremonies/54th-inaugural-ceremonies/.

25. Ibid.

26. W. E. B. Du Bois, *The Souls of Black Folk* (Oxford, UK: Oxford University Press, 2007), 79.

27. Barack Obama, "Remarks by the President in State of Union Address (2011)," accessed October 24, 2016, https://www.whitehouse.gov/the-press-office/2011/01/25 /remarks-president-state-union-address.

28. Ibid.

29. Ibid.

30. Barack Obama, *The Audacity of Hope: Thoughts on Reclaiming the American Dream* (New York: Canongate, 2007), 25.

31. Barack Obama, "Remarks of President Barack Obama, State of the Union Address (2016)," accessed November 16, 2016, https://www.whitehouse.gov/the-press -office/2016/01/12/remarks-president-barack-obama-%E2%80%93-prepared-delivery -state-union-address.

32. George W. Bush, "Inaugural Address," 2005, https://www.inaugural.senate .gov/about/past-inaugural-ceremonies/55th-inaugural-ceremonies/

CHAPTER 4: THE DREAM OF FULL PARTICIPATION

1. Democratic National Convention, *The Official Proceedings of the 1988 Democratic National Convention, Omni Coliseum, Atlanta, Georgia, July 18–21*, ed. Dorothy Vredenburgh Bush et al. (Washington, DC: Democratic National Committee, 1988), 337.

2. Ibid., 338.

3. Ibid., 335.

4. Robert G. Parkinson, "A Declaration of Fear," *New York Times*, July 4, 2016, sec. A.

5. Ibid., 24.

6. *Rhode Island, Rhode-Island Charter, granted by King Charles II. in the fourteenth year of his reign. . . .* , London, 1653, Gale *Eighteenth Century Collections Online* (1766), http://www.gale.com/primary-sources/eighteenth-century-collections -online/.

7. "George Washington Letter," accessed October 24, 2016, http://www.touro synagogue.org/history-learning/gw-letter.

8. Theodore Crackel, "The Papers of George Washington," accessed October 24, 2016, http://rotunda.upress.virginia.edu/founders/GEWN.html.

9. Ibid.

10. George Washington, "Washington's Farewell Address to the People of the United States" (Washington, DC: U.S. Government Printing Office, 2000), 6, 16–17, https://www.govinfo.gov/content/pkg/.../pdf/GPO-CDOC-106sdoc21.pdf.

11. Quoted by Fawn Brodie, *Thomas Jefferson: An Intimate History* (New York: W.W. Norton & Company, 1974), 55.

12. Thomas Jefferson, *Notes on the State of Virginia* (New York: Furman & Loudon, 1801), 239.

13. Ibid., 235.

14. Jon Meacham, *Thomas Jefferson: The Art of Power* (New York: Random House, 2012), 470.

15. Ibid.

16. "The Fundamental Constitution of Carolina" (Boston, MA: Old South Meeting-house, 1669), 16.

17. John Locke, *A Letter Concerning Toleration*, ed. James Tully (Indianapolis: Hackett, 1983), 26.

18. V. C. Chappell, ed., *The Cambridge Companion to Locke* (Cambridge, UK: Cambridge University Press, 1994), 226–28.

19. Alexis de Tocqueville, *Democracy in America* (New York: Literary Classics of the United States, 2012), 119.

20. John Rawls, *A Theory of Justice* (Cambridge, MA: Belknap Press, 2005), 11.

21. Ibid., 15.

22. Kennan Ferguson, *William James: Politics in the Pluriverse*, Modernity and Political Thought (Lanham, MD: Rowman & Littlefield, 2007), 9.

23. Arthur M. Schlesinger, *The Disuniting of America* (New York: W. W. Norton, 1992), 13.

24. Ibid., 20.

25. Nathan Glazer and Daniel P. Moynihan, *Beyond the Melting Pot: The Negroes, Puerto Ricans, Jews, Italians, and Irish of New York City*, 2nd ed. (Cambridge, MA: MIT Press, 1970), 17.

26. Ibid., lxxxii–lxxxiv.

27. Ibid., xxiv.

28. Democratic National Convention, *The Official Proceedings of the 1988 Democratic National Convention, Omni Coliseum, Atlanta, Georgia, July 18–21*, 341.

29. Ferguson, *William James*, 1.

30. William James, *The Principles of Psychology*, ed. Robert Maynard Hutchins, vol. 53, Great Books of the Western World (Chicago: Encyclopedia Britannica, 1952), 645.

31. Robert Wuthnow, *America and the Challenges of Religious Diversity* (Princeton, NJ: Princeton University Press, 2005), 35.

32. "Pope Francis Welcomes American Jewish Committee Members to the Vatican, Urges a More 'Just and Fraternal World,'" *Huffington Post*, February 13, 2014, http://www.huffingtonpost.com/2014/02/13/pope-francis-american-jewish-committee _n_4781294.html.

33. Stanley Eugene Fish, *Is There a Text in This Class?: The Authority of Interpretive Communities* (Cambridge, MA: Harvard University Press, 1980).

34. R. W. Apple Jr., "The Democrats in Atlanta: Dukakis's Speech Offers His 'Vision of America,'" *New York Times*, July 22, 1988, http://go.galegroup.com/ps/i.do?id=GALE%7CA175899768&v=2.1&u=loc_main&it=r&p=AONE&sw=w&asid=5566e0f99b53fa0afa4bc8e143123101.

35. Democratic National Convention, *The Official Proceedings of the 1988 Democratic National Convention, Omni Coliseum, Atlanta, Georgia, July 18–21*, 391.

36. Pierre W. Orelus, ed., *Affirming Language Diversity in Schools and Society: Beyond Linguistic Apartheid* (New York: Routledge, 2014), 269.

37. Paulo Freire, *The Politics of Education: Culture, Power, and Liberation* (South Hadley, MA: Bergin & Garvey, 1985), 170.

38. Democratic National Convention, *The Official Proceedings of the 1988 Democratic National Convention, Omni Coliseum, Atlanta, Georgia, July 18–21*, 342.

CHAPTER 5: WHITE CULTURAL DOMINANCE IS NOT WORKING

1. Pew Research Center, "Public's Policy Priorities Reflect Changing Conditions at Home and Abroad," January 15, 2015, http://www.people-press.org/2015/01/15/publics-policy-priorities-reflect-changing-conditions-at-home-and-abroad/.

2. Derald Wing Sue, ed., *Microaggressions and Marginality: Manifestation, Dynamics, and Impact* (Hoboken, NJ: Wiley, 2010), 4.

3. Thomas McCarthy, *Race, Empire, and the Idea of Human Development* (Cambridge, UK: Cambridge University Press, 2009), 87.

4. Pew Research Center, "On Views of Race and Inequity, Blacks and Whites Are Worlds Apart," June 27, 2016, http://www.pewsocialtrends.org/2016/06/27/on-views-of-race-and-inequality-blacks-and-whites-are-worlds-apart/.

5. Algernon Austin, *America Is Not Post-Racial: Xenophobia, Islamophobia, Racism, and the 44th President* (Santa Barbara, CA: Praeger, 2015), 84.

6. Michelle Alexander, *The New Jim Crow: Mass Incarceration in the Age of Colorblindness* (New York: New Press, 2010), 6–7.

7. NAACP, "Criminal Justice Fact Sheet," accessed October 10, 2016, http://www.naacp.org/criminal-justice-fact-sheet/.

8. Lisa A. Bloom, *Suspicion Nation: The Inside Story of the Trayvon Martin Injustice and Why We Continue to Repeat It* (Berkeley, CA: Counterpoint Press, 2014), 32.

9. The Ferguson Commission, "Forward through Ferguson: A Path toward Racial Equality," accessed April 4, 2017, http://3680or2khmk3bzkp33juiea1.wpengine.netdna-cdn.com/wp-content/uploads/2015/09/101415_FergusonCommissionReport.pdf, 14.

10. Ibid., 38

11. National Urban League, "2016 Executive Summary," accessed November 9, 2016, http://soba.iamempowered.com/2016-executive-summary.

12. Jawanza Kunjufu, *An African Centered Response to Ruby Payne's Poverty Theory* (Chicago: African American Images, 2006), ix.

13. Ibid., 156.

14. The states were Connecticut, Arkansas, New Jersey, Florida, Idaho, New Hampshire, West Virginia, Iowa, South Dakota, Illinois, and Massachusetts.

15. National Center for Education Statistics, "Public School Graduates and Dropouts from the Common Core of Data: School Year 2009–10," January 22, 2013, http://nces.ed.gov/pubsearch/pubsinfo.asp?pubid=2013309rev.

16. U.S. Department of Education, "The New Spotlight on America's Opportunity Gaps," accessed July 7, 2014, http://www.ed.gov/news/speeches/new-spotlight-americas-opportunity-gaps.

17. NAACP, "Criminal Justice Fact Sheet."

18. Rakesh Kochhar and Richard Fry, "Wealth Inequality Has Widened along Racial, Ethnic Lines since End of Great Recession," accessed October 8, 2016, http://www.pewresearch.org/fact-tank/2014/12/12/racial-wealth-gaps-great-recession/.

19. Chuck Collins, "Racial Inequality," *Inequality.org*, accessed October 8, 2016, http://inequality.org/racial-inequality/.

20. Dedrick Asante-Muhammad, Josh Hoxie, and Emanuel Nieves, "The Ever-Growing Gap: Without Change, African-American and Latino Families Won't Match White Wealth for Centuries," Expanding Economic Opportunity, Racial Wealth Divide Initiative, Institute for Policy Studies, August 2016, http://www.ips-dc.org/wp-content/uploads/2016/08/The-Ever-Growing-Gap-CFED_IPS-Final-2.pdf, 5.

21. Ibid.,

22. Sam Pizzigati, *Greed and Good: Understanding and Overcoming the Inequality That Limits Our Lives* (New York: Apex Press, 2004), 4.

23. Chuck Collins, *99 to 1: How Wealth Inequality Is Wrecking the World and What We Can Do about It* (San Francisco: Berrett-Koehler, 2012).

24. Pizzigati, *Greed and Good*, 51.

25. Henry Blodget, "Walmart Employs 1% of America. Should It Be Forced to Pay Its Employees More?," *Business Insider*, September 20, 2010, accessed April 7, 2017, http://www.businessinsider.com/walmart-employees-pay.

26. "WMT Wal-Mart Stores Inc Executive Compensation," *Morningstar*, accessed October 6, 2016, http://insiders.morningstar.com/trading/executive-compensation.action?t=WMT&region=usa&culture=en-US.

27. James C. Collins, *Good to Great: Why Some Companies Make the Leap—and Others Don't* (New York: HarperBusiness, 2001), 21.

28. Ibid., 64.

29. Pizzigati, *Greed and Good*, 134.

30. Sam Pizzigati, *The Rich Don't Always Win: The Forgotten Triumph over Plutocracy That Created the American Middle Class, 1900/1970* (New York: Seven Stories Press, 2012), 256.

31. Sandra L. Colby and Jennifer M. Ortman, "Projections of the Size and Composition of the U.S. Population: 2014 to 2060, Current Population Reports, P25-1143" (Washington, DC: U.S. Census Bureau, 2015), 9.

32. Mark Hugo Lopez, "In 2014, Latinos Will Surpass Whites as Largest Racial/Ethnic Group in California," Pew Research Center, January 24, 2014, http://www.pewresearch.org/fact-tank/2014/01/24/in-2014-latinos-will-surpass-whites-as-largest-racialethnic-group-in-california/.

33. U.S. Department of Education, National Center for Education Statistics, Common Core of Data (CCD), "State Nonfiscal Survey of Public Elementary/Secondary Education," 1997–98 through 2011–12, accessed March 9, 2017, https://nces.ed.gov/ccd/stnfis.asp; and National Public Elementary and Secondary Enrollment by Race/Ethnicity Model, 1994–2011.

34. Robert P. Jones, *The End of White Christian America* (New York: Simon & Schuster, 2016), 51.

35. Ibid., 58–59.

CHAPTER 6: THE POWER OF PARADIGMS

1. Henry Louis Gates, *America behind the Color Line: Dialogues with African Americans* (New York: Warner Books, 2004), 282.

2. Andrew Hacker, *Two Nations: Black and White, Separate, Hostile, Unequal* (New York: Scribner, 2003), 77.

3. Ibid.

4. Thomas S. Kuhn, *The Copernican Revolution: Planetary Astronomy in the Development of Western Thought* (Cambridge: Harvard University Press, 1957), vi.

5. Thomas S. Kuhn, *The Structure of Scientific Revolutions*, 2nd ed. (Chicago: University of Chicago Press, 1970), 6.

6. Peter L. Berger and Thomas Luckmann, *The Social Construction of Reality: a Treatise in the Sociology of Knowledge* (Garden City, NY: Doubleday, 1966), 152.

7. Ibid., 51.

8. Ibid., 47–67.

9. Ibid., 150.

10. Ibid., 173.

11. Paula Ioanide, *The Emotional Politics of Racism: How Feelings Trump Facts in an Era of Colorblindness*, Stanford Studies in Comparative Race and Ethnicity (Stanford, CA: Stanford University Press, 2015), 2.

12. Ibid.

13. Herbert Spencer, *First Principles* (London: Williams & Norgate, 1863), 309.

14. Ibid., 236.

15. Ibid., 283.

16. Adolf Hitler, *Mein Kampf* (Boston: Houghton Mifflin, 2001), chap. 11.

17. Aldon D. Morris, *The Scholar Denied: W.E.B. Du Bois and the Birth of Modern Sociology* (Oakland: University of California Press, 2015), 115.

18. Robert Bonazzi, "Introduction: Beyond 'Black Like Me,'" in John Howard Griffin, *Prison of Culture* (San Antonio, TX: Wings Press, 2011), 115.

19. John J. Macionis, *Society: The Basics*, 7th ed. (Upper Saddle River, NJ: Pearson Prentice Hall, 1999), 348.

20. Karen D. Rudolph et al., "Adding Insult to Injury: Neural Sensitivity to Social Exclusion Is Associated with Internalizing Symptoms in Chronically Peer-Victimized Girls," *Social Cognitive and Affective Neuroscience* 11, no. 5 (May 1, 2016): 829–42.

21. Jennifer Kubota and Elizabeth Phelps, "Exploring the Brain Dynamics of Racial Stereotyping and Prejudice," *Social Cognitive Neuroscience, Cognitive Neuroscience, Clinical Brain Mapping* 3 (2015): 241.

22. Ibid., 244.

23. Fritjof Capra, *The Turning Point: Science, Society, and the Rising Culture* (New York: Simon & Schuster, 1982), 16.

24. Ibid., 297.

25. Thomas L. Friedman, *The World Is Flat: A Brief History of the Twenty-First Century*, updated and expanded ed. (New York: Farrar, Straus and Giroux, 2006), 387.

26. Margaret L. Andersen and Patricia Hill Collins, eds., *Race, Class, and Gender: An Anthology*, 9th ed. (Boston: Cengage, 2016), 1.

27. M. J. Matsuda, "Beside My Sister, Facing the Enemy: Legal Theory Out of Coalition," *Stanford Law Review* 43, no. 6 (1991): 1183.

CHAPTER 7: EVERYDAY RACISM

1. Nijole Benokraitis, *Introduction to Sociology* (Boston: Cengage Learning, 2015), 2.

2. Shelby Steele, *White Guilt: How Blacks and Whites Together Destroyed the Promise of the Civil Rights Era* (New York: HarperCollins, 2006), 172.

3. Erving Goffman, *Stigma: Notes on the Management of Spoiled Identity* (New York: J. Aronson, 1974), 2.

4. W. E. B. Du Bois, *The Souls of Black Folk* (Oxford, UK: Oxford University Press, 2007), 25.

5. Ibid., 3–4

6. Ibid.,

7. Claude Steele, *Whistling Vivaldi: And Other Clues to How Stereotypes Affect Us* (New York: W. W. Norton, 2010), 4–5.

8. Ibid., 11.

9. Claude Steele and Joshua Aronson, "Stereotype Threat and the Intellectual Test Performance of African Americans," *Journal of Personality and Social Psychology* 69, no. 5 (1995): 797–811.

10. Mary Murphy and Valerie Jones Taylor, "The Role of Situational Cues in Signaling and Maintaining Stereotype Threats," in Michael Inzlicht and Toni Schmader, eds., *Stereotype Threat: Theory, Process, and Application* (New York: Oxford University Press, 2012), 20.

11. Derald Wing Sue, ed., *Microaggressions and Marginality: Manifestation, Dynamics, and Impact* (Hoboken, NJ: Wiley, 2010), 3.

12. Ibid.

13. Ibid., 7–11.

14. Algernon Austin, *America Is Not Post-Racial: Xenophobia, Islamophobia, Racism, and the 44th President* (Santa Barbara, CA: Praeger, 2015), xi.

15. Morris Dees and James Corcoran, *Gathering Storm: America's Militia Threat* (New York: HarperCollins, 1996), 3.

16. Walter Laqueur, *New Terrorism: Fanaticism and the Arms of Mass Destruction* (Cary, NC: Oxford University Press, 2006), 110.

17. Ibid., 108.

18. Ian Haney-López, *Dog Whistle Politics: How Coded Racial Appeals Have Reinvented Racism and Wrecked the Middle Class* (Oxford, UK: Oxford University Press, 2014), 3–4.

19. Ibid., 4–5.

20. Kasie Hunt, "Gingrich: Bilingual Classes Teach 'Ghetto' Language," *Washington Post*, April 1, 2007.

21. Anthony Giddens, *Central Problems in Social Theory: Action, Structure and Contradiction in Social Analysis* (Berkeley: University of California Press, 1979), 2.

22. Ibid., 5.

23. Ibid., 6.

24. Anthony Giddens, *The Constitution of Society: Outline of the Theory of Structuration* (Berkeley: University of California, 1984), 41–45.

25. Steven D. Levitt and Stephen J. Dubner, *Think Like a Freak: The Authors of Freakonomics Offer to Retrain Your Brain* (New York: HarperCollins, 2014).

26. Giddens, *Central Problems in Social Theory*, 5.

27. Pierre Bourdieu, *Outline of a Theory of Practice* (Cambridge, UK: Cambridge University Press, 1977), 8–9.

28. Talcott Parsons, *Societies: Evolutionary and Comparative Perspectives*, Foundations of Modern Sociology Series (Englewood Cliffs, NJ: Prentice-Hall, 1966), 5.

29. Max Weber introduced the term, but Bourdieu expanded its meaning and application to understanding human behavior.

30. Bourdieu, *Outline of a Theory of Practice*, 124.

31. Peter L. Berger and Thomas Luckmann, *The Social Construction of Reality: a Treatise in the Sociology of Knowledge* (Garden City, NY: Doubleday, 1966).

32. Bourdieu, *Outline of a Theory of Practice*, 169.

CHAPTER 8: INSTITUTIONAL RACISM

1. Aldon D. Morris, *The Scholar Denied: W. E. B. Du Bois and the Birth of Modern Sociology* (Oakland: University of California Press, 2015), chap. 6.

2. Murali Balaji, *The Professor and the Pupil: The Politics of W. E. B. Du Bois and Paul Robeson* (New York: Nation Books, 2007), 384–85.

3. Tony Waters and Dagmar Waters, eds., *Weber's Rationalism and Modern Society: New Translations on Politics, Bureaucracy, and Social Stratification* (New York: Palgrave Macmillan, 2015), 71.

4. Max Weber, *The Protestant Ethic and the Spirit of Capitalism*, trans. Talcott Parsons (New York: Charles Scribner's Sons, 1958), 181.

5. Germain Gabriel Grisez and Russell B. Shaw, *Personal Vocation: God Calls Everyone by Name* (Huntington, IN: Our Sunday Visitor Pub. Division, 2003), 79.

6. Weber, *The Protestant Ethic and the Spirit of Capitalism*, 182.

7. James Stewart, "Looking for a Lesson in Google's Perks," *The New York Times*, March 15, 2013, sec. Business, http://www.nytimes.com/2013/03/16/business/at-google-a-place-to-work-and-play.html.

8. W. E. B. Du Bois, "The Talented Tenth," Teaching American History, accessed October 19, 2016, http://teachingamericanhistory.org/library/document/the-talented-tenth/.

9. Max Weber's "Politics as Vocation," found in Waters and Waters, *Weber's Rationalism and Modern Society*, 137.

10. From Weber's "Politics as Vocation" in ibid., 194.

11. Max Weber's "Discipline and Charisma" in ibid., 62.

12. Max Weber, *Economy and Society: An Outline of Interpretive Sociology* (New York: Bedminster Press, 1968), 1146.

13. Morris Dees and Steve Fiffer, *A Season for Justice: The Life and Times of Civil Rights Lawyer Morris Dees* (New York: Charles Scribner's Sons, 1991), 59–60.

14. Stephanie Strom, "Failed Dreams—The Collapse of a Harlem Bank: Freedom Bank's Demise: A Trail of Risky Loans and Fast Growth," *The New York Times*,

December 3, 1990, sec. N.Y./Region, http://www.nytimes.com/1990/12/03/nyregion/failed
-dreams-collapse-harlem-bank-freedom-bank-s-demise-trail-risky-loans-fast.html.

15. Richard Sennett and Jonathan Cobb, *The Hidden Injuries of Class* (New York: Knopf, 1972), 264.

CHAPTER 9: DISCIPLINARY INSTITUTIONS

1. David Wallace Adams, *Education for Extinction: American Indians and the Boarding School Experience, 1875–1928* (Lawrence, KS: University Press of Kansas, 1995), 6.

2. Mary Stout, *Native American Boarding Schools, Landmarks of the American Mosaic* (Santa Barbara, CA: Greenwood, 2012), 70.

3. Julie Davis, *Survival Schools* (Minneapolis, MN: University of Minnesota Press, 2013), 129.

4. Michelle Alexander, *The New Jim Crow: Mass Incarceration in the Age of Colorblindness* (New York: [Jackson, Tenn.]: New Press; Distributed by Perseus Distribution, 2010), 17.

5. Michel Foucault, *Discipline and Punish: The Birth of the Prison* (New York: Vintage Books, 1979), 242.

6. Ibid., 18.

7. Katherine Klippert Merseth, *Inside Urban Charter Schools: Promising Practices and Strategies in Five High-Performing Schools* (Cambridge, MA: Harvard Education Press, 2009), 118–119.

8. Ibid., 28–29.

9. Foucault, *Discipline and Punish*, 231.

10. Merseth, *Inside Urban Charter Schools*, 190.

11. Roxbury Prep, *Student & Family Handbook, 2016–2017*, n.d., 11, http://roxburyprep.uncommonschools.org/sites/default/files/downloads/studenthandbook201617final_0.pdf Accessed 6/18/2017.

12. Ibid., 11–15.

13. Merseth, *Inside Urban Charter Schools*, 191.

14. Ibid., 57.

15. Foucault, *Discipline and Punish*, 138.

16. Ibid., 152.

17. Ibid., 153–54.

18. Merseth, *Inside Urban Charter Schools*, 177.

19. MATCH, *Proactive Management Mentality*, n.d., https://www.matchminis.org/videos/for-teachers/16/proactive-management-mentality/, accessed 6/17/2017.

20. Ibid.

21. Ibid., 47–48.

22. Ibid., 178.

23. Foucault, *Discipline and Punish*, 249.

24. MATCH, *Match High School Student and Family Handbook 2016–2017*, n.d., 24, https://static1.squarespace.com/static/5408c2a1e4b00aec95aee0d4/t/5853 0733b3db2b542488195a/1481836343321/Eng_MHS+Handbook+16-17.pdf accessed 6/17/2016.

25. Merseth, *Inside Urban Charter Schools*, 45.

26. Foucault, *Discipline and Punish*, 304.

27. Merseth, *Inside Urban Charter Schools*, 150.

28. Ibid., 163.

29. Ibid., 135–136.

30. Foucault, *Discipline and Punish*, 200.

31. Jean Edward Smith, *Grant* (New York: Simon & Schuster, 2001), 569.

32. Theresa Perry, ed., *Quality Education as a Constitutional Right: Creating a Grassroots Movement to Transform Public Schools* (Boston: Beacon Press, 2010), ii.

33. Seymour Papert, *Mindstorms: Children, Computers, and Powerful Ideas* (New York: Basic Books, 1980).

34. M. Shannon Helfrich, *Montessori Learning in the 21st Century : A Guide for Parents and Teachers* (Troutdale, OR: NewSage Press, 2011), 195.

35. Ibid.

36. Paulo Freire, *Education for Critical Consciousness*, Continuum Impacts (London ; New York: Continuum, 1973), 3–4.

37. Ibid., 7–8.

38. This list is adapted from Neil Postman and Charles Weingartner, *Teaching as a Subversive Activity* (New York: Delacorte Press, 1969), 24–26.

39. Lisa A. Bloom, *Classroom Management: Creating Positive Outcomes for All Students* (Upper Saddle River, N.J: Merrill/Pearson, 2009), ii–iv.

40. Angeles Arrien, *The Four-Fold Way: Walking the Paths of the Warrior, Teacher, Healer, and Visionary*, 1st ed. (San Francisco, CA: HarperSanFrancisco, 1993), 7–8.

41. Paulo Freire, *The Politics of Education: Culture, Power, and Liberation* (South Hadley, MA: Bergin & Garvey, 1985), 2–3.

42. Ibid., 15.

43. Ibid., 51.

CHAPTER 10: A FRAMEWORK TO OVERCOME RACISM

1. "Obama Has Vastly Changed the Face of the Federal Bureaucracy," *Washington Post*, accessed September 28, 2016, https://www.washingtonpost.com /politics/obama-has-vastly-changed-the-face-of-the-federal-bureaucracy/2015/09/20 /73ef803a-5631-11e5-abe9-27d53f250b11_story.html.

2. Michelle Alexander, *The New Jim Crow: Mass Incarceration in the Age of Colorblindness* (New York: New Press, 2010), 185.

3. Karl Alexander, Doris Entwisle, and Linda Olson, "Schools, Achievement, and Inequality: A Seasonal Perspective," *Educational Evaluation and Policy Analysis* 23, no. 2 (Summer 2001): 171–91.

CHAPTER 11: BEING ANTIRACIST IN EVERYDAY LIFE

1. Eboo Patel, *Sacred Ground: Pluralism, Prejudice, and the Promise of America* (Boston: Beacon Press, 2012), xiii–xiv.

2. Jon O'Bergh, *Song of Fire* (self-published, 2011).

3. Michelle Molitor, "FREE, Fellowship for Race & Equity in Education" (workshops, U.S. Department of Education, winter 2015–16).

4. Barack Obama, *Dreams from My Father: A Story of Race and Inheritance* (New York: Crown, 2007).

5. Paulo Freire, *The Politics of Education: Culture, Power, and Liberation* (South Hadley, MA: Bergin & Garvey, 1985), 129.

6. Michelle Molitor, "FREE, Fellowship for Race & Equity in Education."

7. John McKnight, *The Abundant Community: Awakening the Power of Families and Neighborhoods* (San Francisco, CA: Berrett-Koehler, 2010), 55.

8. Martin Luther King, *Where Do We Go from Here: Chaos or Community?* (New York: Harper & Row, 1967), 67.

9. Margo Murray, *Beyond the Myths and Magic of Mentoring: How to Facilitate an Effective Mentoring Process*, rev. ed. (San Francisco, CA: Jossey-Bass, 2001), xiii.

CHAPTER 12: WE ALL HAVE STORIES

1. Ralph Singh (founder, Wisdom Thinkers), in discussions with the author, October 2016.

2. Naomi Cottoms (director, Tri-County Rural Health Network), in discussion with the author, November 2016.

3. Marco Davis (partner, New Profit, Inc.), in discussion with the author, November 2016.

4. Cheryl Crazy Bull (president and chief executive officer, American Indian College Fund), in discussion with the author, November 2016.

5. Dennis Benson (retired), in discussion with the author, December 2016.

6. Brenda Girton-Mitchell (founder and president, Race and Grace Ministries, Inc.), in discussion with the author, August 2016.

7. Ryan Chung (student, American University, in discussion with author, October 2016)

CHAPTER 13: EXAMPLES OF INSTITUTIONAL ANTIRACISM

1. Alvin Herring (director, racial equity and community engagement, W. K. Kellogg Foundation), in discussion with author, December 2016; W. K. Kellogg Foundation, "Truth, Racial Healing, and Transformation," http://wkkf.org/what-we-do /racial-equity/truth-racial-healing-transformation.

2. Marla Dean (senior director of school accountability, Cesar Chavez Public Charter School for Public Policy), in discussion with author, October 2016; and http://www.chavezschools.org/

3. "Featured Use Your Life Award," *Oprah.com*, February 5, 2001, http:// www.oprah.com/angelnetwork/cesar-chavez-public-charter-high-school-for-public -policy-us#ixzz4N0lqSVsi.

4. Paul Tough, *Whatever It Takes: Geoffrey Canada's Quest to Change Harlem and America* (Boston: Houghton Mifflin, 2009), 188–213.

5. Michael Alison Chandler, "School Choice Complicates Promise Neighborhood's Efforts to Help Kids," *Washington Post*, September 12, 2015, https:// www.washingtonpost.com/local/education/school-choice-complicates-fulfillment -of-promise-neighborhood/2015/09/12/79ffa702-4286-11e5-8e7d-9c033e6745d8 _story.html.

6. Lenora B. Fulani (co-founder, All Stars Programs, Inc.), in discussion with author, August 2016; and https://allstars.org/.

7. Ibid.

8. Lenora B. Fulani, "The Development Line: Helping the Poor to Grow: A Special Report on Solving the Poverty Crisis in America," April 2013, 2.

9. Henry Louis Gates, *America behind the Color Line: Dialogues with African Americans* (New York: Warner Books, 2004), 117.

10. Fulani, "The Development Line: Helping the Poor to Grow," 1.

11. Ruth Berta and Amanda Leonard Pohl, *Building Power Changing Lives: The Story of Virginia Organizing* (New Orleans: Social Policy Press, 2015), 14.

12. Ibid., 21.

13. Ibid., 23–24.

14. Ibid., 34.

15. Ibid., 128.

CHAPTER 14: WORKING TOGETHER

1. Neil Postman and Charles Weingartner, *Teaching as a Subversive Activity* (New York: Delacorte Press, 1969), 1–15.

2. Michelle Molitor, "FREE, Fellowship for Race & Equity in Education" (workshops, U.S. Department of Education, winter 2015–16).

3. Ibid.

4. Max Weber's "Politics as Vocation," found in Tony Waters and Dagmar Waters, eds., *Weber's Rationalism and Modern Society: New Translationson Politics, Bureaucracy, and Social Stratification* (New York: Palgrave Macmillan, 2015), 137.

5. Max Weber, *Economy and Society: An Outline of Interpretive Sociology* (New York: Bedminster Press, 1968), 1114.

6. Ibid., 1143–44.

7. Martin Luther King and Clayborne Carson, *The Autobiography of Martin Luther King, Jr* (New York: Warner Books, 1998), chap. 13, re: March 1959.

8. Dedrick Asante-Muhammad, Josh Hoxie, and Emanuel Nieves, "The Ever-Growing Gap: Without Change, African-American and Latino Families Won't Match White Wealth for Centuries," Expanding Economic Opportunity, Racial Wealth Divide Initiative, Institute for Policy Studies, August 2016, The-Ever-Growing-Gap-CFED_IPS-Final-2.pdf.

9. Robert D. Putnam, *Our Kids: The American Dream in Crisis* (New York: Simon & Schuster, 2015), 19.

10. Shelby Steele, *White Guilt: How Blacks and Whites Together Destroyed the Promise of the Civil Rights Era* (New York: HarperCollins, 2006), 27–28.

11. Ibid., 35.

12. Jim Wallis, *America's Original Sin: Racism, White Privilege, and the Bridge to a New America* (Grand Rapids, MI: Brazos Press, 2016), 57–58.

13. Robert P. Jones, *The End of White Christian America* (New York: Simon & Schuster, 2016), 190–91.

14. Jennifer Harvey, *Dear White Christians: For Those Still Longing for Racial Reconciliation*, Prophetic Christianity (Grand Rapids, MI: William B. Eerdmans, 2014), 65.

15. Ibid., 251–52.

16. Ibid., 232–33.

17. Jonathan Kozol, *The Shame of the Nation: The Restoration of Apartheid Schooling in America* (New York: Crown, 2005), 19.

18. Charles T. Clotfelter, *After Brown: The Rise and Retreat of School Desegregation* (Princeton, NJ: Princeton University Press, 2004), 9.

19. Kozol, *The Shame of the Nation*, 224–36.

20. Linda Darling-Hammond, *The Flat World and Education: How America's Commitment to Equity Will Determine Our Future*, The Multicultural Education Series (New York: Teachers College Press, 2010), 237.

21. Richard J. Altenbaugh, "Italian and Mexican Responses to Schooling: Assimilation or Resistance?," in Stanley William Rothstein, ed., *Class, Culture, and Race in American Schools* (Westport, CT: Greenwood Press, 1995), 93.

22. Ibid., 101.

23. Michelle Alexander, *The New Jim Crow: Mass Incarceration in the Age of Colorblindness* (New York: New Press, 2010), 7–9.

24. NCJRS, "Abstract: National Criminal Justice Reference Service," 1973, https://www.ncjrs.gov/App/Publications/abstract.aspx?ID=10865.

25. Martin Luther King, Jr., Oberlin College Commencement 1965, http://www.oberlin.edu/external/EOG/BlackHistoryMonth/MLK/CommAddress.html

CHAPTER 15: AFTERWORD 2016

1. "Transcript: Donald Trump at the G.O.P. Convention," *New York Times*, July 22, 2016, http://www.nytimes.com/2016/07/22/us/politics/trump-transcript-rnc-address.html.

2. Manning Marable, *The Great Wells of Democracy: The Meaning of Race in American Life* (New York: Basic Books, 2002), 79.

3. Ibid., 87.

4. Michael Powell, "Following Months of Criticism, Obama Quits His Church," *New York Times*, June 1, 2008, http://www.nytimes.com/2008/06/01/us/politics/01obama.html.

5. Barack Obama, "Transcript of Obama Speech," *Politico*, accessed November 28, 2016, http://www.politico.com/story/2008/03/transcript-of-obama-speech-009100.

6. Ibid.

7. Hillary Clinton, "2016 Acceptance Speech," Politico, accessed April 7, 20016, http://www.politico.com/story/2016/07/full-text-hillary-clintons-dnc-speech-226410

8. Marc Fisher, "Donald Trump: 'I Am the Least Racist Person,'" *Washington Post*, June 10, 2016, https://www.washingtonpost.com/politics/donald-trump-i-am-the-least-racist-person/2016/06/10/eac7874c-2f3a-11e6-9de3-6e6e7a14000c_story.html.

9. Philip Rucker, "Elizabeth Warren to Call Donald Trump a 'Nasty, Loud, Thin-Skinned Fraud,'" *Washington Post*, June 19, 2016, https://www.washingtonpost.com/news/post-politics/wp/2016/06/09/elizabeth-warren-to-call-donald-trump-a-nasty-loud-thin-skinned-fraud/?utm_term=.c626f3025576.

10. Aaron Blake, "Did Hillary Clinton Just Make Her Own '47 Percent' Gaffe?," *Washington Post*, September 10, 2016, https://www.washingtonpost.com/news/the-fix/wp/2016/09/10/republicans-think-hillary-clinton-just-made-her-own-47-percent-gaffe-did-she/?tid=a_inl&utm_term=.dacc5eb738b5.

11. "Update: 1,094 Bias-Related Incidents in the Month Following the Election," *Southern Poverty Law Center*, accessed December 22, 2016, https://www.splcenter.org/hatewatch/2016/12/16/update-1094-bias-related-incidents-month-following-election.

12. Maureen Costello, *Teaching the 2016 Election, The Trump Effect: The Impact of the Presidential Campaign on Our Nation's Schools* (Birmingham, AL: Southern Poverty Law Center, 2016), 4.

13. Ta-Nehisi Coates, *Between the World and Me* (New York: Spiegel & Grau, 2015), 14.

14. Julie Hirschfeld Davis, "Voice Shaking, Michelle Obama Calls Trump Comments on Women 'Intolerable,'" *New York Times*, October 13, 2016, http://www .nytimes.com/2016/10/14/us/politics/michelle-obama-donald-trump-women.html.

Index

About the Author

KENNETH B. BEDELL, PhD, is a longtime civil rights activist and was senior advisor of the Faith-Based and Neighborhood Partnerships Center at the U.S. Department of Education under the Obama administration. Dr. Bedell is an ordained minister and served as associate general secretary for the General Board of Higher Education and Ministry in the United Methodist Church. He is the author of *Different Ships—Same Boat* (2000) and numerous other books and popular and academic articles and reviews.